UNIVERSITY OF NORTH CAROLINA AT CHAPEL HILL
DEPARTMENT OF ROMANCE LANGUAGES

NORTH CAROLINA STUDIES
IN THE ROMANCE LANGUAGES AND LITERATURES

Founder: URBAN TIGNER HOLMES

Editor: FRANK A. DOMÍNGUEZ

Distributed by:

UNIVERSITY OF NORTH CAROLINA PRESS

CHAPEL HILL
North Carolina 27515-2288
U.S.A.

NORTH CAROLINA STUDIES IN THE
ROMANCE LANGUAGES AND LITERATURES
Number 280

SUBJECT TO CHANGE:
THE LESSONS OF LATIN AMERICAN
WOMEN'S *TESTIMONIO* FOR TRUTH,
FICTION, AND THEORY

SUBJECT TO CHANGE:

THE LESSONS OF LATIN AMERICAN WOMEN'S *TESTIMONIO* FOR TRUTH, FICTION, AND THEORY

BY

JOANNA R. BARTOW

CHAPEL HILL

NORTH CAROLINA STUDIES IN THE ROMANCE
LANGUAGES AND LITERATURES
U.N.C. DEPARTMENT OF ROMANCE LANGUAGES

2005

Library of Congress Cataloging-in-Publication Data

Bartow, Joanna R.
   Subject to change: the lessons of Latin American women's testimonio for truth, fiction, and theory / by Joanna R. Bartow.
     p. cm. – (North Carolina Studies in the Romance Languages and Literatures; no. 280).
     Includes bibliographical references.
     ISBN 0-8078-9284-X (pbk.)
     1. Latin American prose literature–Women authors–History and criticism. 2. Reportage literature, Latin American–History and criticism. 3. Latin American prose literature–20th century–History and criticism. 4. Self in literature. 5. Feminism and literature. I. Title. II. Series.

PQ7081.5.B37 2005
868'.608099287'098–dc22   2004061740

Cover design: Heidi Perov

ISBN 0-8078-9284-X

IMPRESO EN ESPAÑA

PRINTED IN SPAIN

DEPÓSITO LEGAL: V. 1.993 - 2005

ARTES GRÁFICAS SOLER, S. L. - LA OLIVERETA, 28 - 46018 VALENCIA

CONTENTS

		Page
ACKNOWLEDGMENTS		9
INTRODUCTION		11
CHAPTER 1: LEGITIMATION: MEDIATED *TESTIMONIOS*, AUTHORITY AND VICARIOUS IDENTITIES		31
CHAPTER 2: FICTIONS OF TESTIMONY: ESSENTIALIZED IDENTITIES AND THE OTHER IN ONESELF IN TWO WORKS BY CLARICE LISPECTOR		100
CHAPTER 3: READING *TESTIMONIO* WITH THEORY: VIOLENCE, SACRIFICE, DISPLACEMENT		144
CHAPTER 4: BEYOND *TESTIMONIO* IN TWO WORKS BY DIAMELA ELTIT		197
CONCLUSION		229
WORKS CITED		239
INDEX		249

ACKNOWLEDGMENTS

W HILE this book has undergone several additions and theoretical shifts, it evolved from my dissertation directed by Nicolas Shumway, whom I thank first and foremost. I remain grateful for his enthusiastic support and his knowledgeable guidance, as well as for those of James Fernández. My thanks go to Marta Peixoto for introducing me to Clarice Lispector's work and kindly providing feedback on early versions of my discussion of *A Hora da Estrela*. Also, even though she left Yale before I began work on my dissertation, Sylvia Molloy's generosity and superb scholarship were invaluable to my education and continue to inspire me, so I would like to thank her here. Needless to say, these mentors inspired all that is good in my work; I alone am responsible for any shortfalls.

Through the generosity of a Fulbright-García Robles grant, at an early stage of the project I carried out research at the Programa Interdisciplinario de Estudios de la Mujer at the Colegio de México, and would like to express my appreciation to both the Fulbright Program and to the faculty of the PIEM for opening their doors to me. I also wish to thank Elena Poniatowska for her warmth and generosity during an interview at her home and at subsequent meetings. In Mexico I also met two dear friends and invaluable intellectual interlocutors: Juan Carlos Segura and Alejandro de Oto. I am particularly grateful for Alejandro's knowledge of postcolonial theory and for his encouragement over the years.

Linda S. Maier, Deirdre Lashgari, Merry Pawlowski, Magdalena Maiz, and Becky Boling have read or listened to parts of this project and given crucial feedback and support: I cannot thank them enough.

Austin College in Texas also furnished important support during my years there, both through a Richardson grant and through engaging colleagues, especially in the Department of Classical and Modern Languages. My heartfelt thanks go to CML for the academic home they gave me.

My new home at St. Mary's College of Maryland has also provided generous faculty development funds for this book, in addition to collegiality and a stimulating scholarly environment. My friends and colleagues in the Department of International Languages and Cultures have all been supportive, yet I particularly appreciate Jorge Rogachevsky and Israel Ruiz's confidence in this project and their expertise that pushes my thinking to the next level.

Finally, I dedicate this book to my parents Judy and Arthur Bartow, who from the beginning have been inspirational in every sense, and to my husband and compañero Joe Orlando, whose creativity, word play, and love of books make every day a joy.

INTRODUCTION

> Sentí, en la última página, que mi narración era un
> símbolo del hombre que yo fui, mientras la escribía y
> que, para redactar esa narración, yo tuve que ser aquel
> hombre y que, para ser aquel hombre, yo tuve que
> redactar esa narración, y así hasta lo infinito. (En el
> instante en que yo dejo de creer en él, "Averroes" desa-
> parece.)
>
> Jorge Luis Borges, "La busca de Averroes"

> I sensed, on the last page, that my narrative was a sym-
> bol of the man I was while I wrote it, and that to write
> that story I had to be that man, and that to be that man
> I had to write that story, and so to infinity. (The instant
> I stop believing in him, "Averroës" disappears.)
>
> Jorge Luis Borges, "Averroës' Search"

U SING Borges as an epigraph to a book that employs *testimonio*
and feminist theories as its points of departure may strike the
reader as odd. [1] This book in fact takes an unorthodox approach to
testimonio by mixing it with fiction and theory to reduce its separation from other writing, to emphasize its medium rather than mini-
mizing the pitfalls its written process creates for *testimonio*'s political impetus. The medium's relationship with testimonial content,
which seeks to break repressive silence, holds a critical key to *testimonio*'s lessons for the current period of debate about the nature of
globalization and who participates in it. In other words, new perspectives on *testimonios* as non-idealized, subjective and still important tools for human rights–a purpose necessary to the crisis
moments of revolutions, genocides and dictatorships–allows more
room to approach testimonial texts as the mediations and translations of others' experiences that they are. There has been a shift to

---

[1] I have come across one other instance of Borges used in an analysis of *testimonio*: Antonio Vera León uses "Borges y yo" in his 1992 essay "Hacer hablar: la transcripción testimonial" (188-9).

this perspective on *testimonio* in the last decade, but the Rigoberta Menchú controversy shows the still heated conflict over these texts' transparent truth value. The dilemmas *testimonio* comes to represent bear interesting resemblance to those Borges's narrator faces, as does any narrator.

Although a central point of contention has been the definition of *testimonio* and its related *novela testimonial*, a question addressed further ahead in this introduction, one can safely say that *testimonio* is based on the previously untold, first-person story of a real individual or group of individuals, commonly referred to as informants, witnesses, testimonial subjects, speakers, or narrators. This first-person perspective, the "real thing," becomes crucial to the account's authority. The informant either writes his or her own narrative, or in mediated *testimonio* tells his or her story to a journalist, ethnographer, or other transcriber. Mediated testimonial writing forms the focus of this study, although my conclusions are relevant to other variations. *Testimonios* generally carry the collective import of a group experience–a principal distinction from autobiography–through a single witness or many witnesses, marginalized in some way. The texts therefore arise from a political urgency, ranging from abuse under dictatorship, to genocide of indigenous populations, to poverty, to insurgent guerrilla movements, to slavery. They thus rewrite or contribute to historical discourse about the particular nation involved, in order to question the status quo and attract national or international attention to the crisis at hand. While they often question dominant nationalist rhetoric, testimonial texts frequently work to construct alternative national identities or are used by others to do so. For example, in Elena Poniatowska's testimonial novel *Hasta no verte, Jesús mío* the protagonist Jesusa Palancares denies her Mexican identity because of her almost complete disenfranchisement, but she still comes to represent Mexican characteristics that Poniatowska admires. This identity then crosses into an international context as the story is published.

Understandably, the *testimonio*'s production increased during the growing social upheavals of the 1960s, and the Cuban Casa de las Américas prize institutionalized the term as a "genre" in 1970. Nevertheless, *testimonio*'s roots extend into the history of Latin American narrative's mixture of document, fiction and political engagement, and well-known *testimonios* predate the "boom," such as *Benita* (1940) from Mexico and *Quarto de Despejo* (1960) from

Brazil, the latter studied in this volume. *Testimonio* as a textual mode written by or narrated through privileged intellectual channels combines long-time literary concerns with the act of writing and the revolutionary movements of the twentieth century (the Mexican Revolution and especially movements beginning with the Cuban Revolution). The political power and subversive potential of ceding published space to the "authentic" voices of marginalized groups served to begin breaking down limits on concepts of authorship. The post-Cold-War moment now allows reflection on leftist strategies and *testimonio*, reflection that critiques the possibilities of *testimonio* as a tool for the disenfranchised–versus for concerned elites–in an international, Western context where, for example, the Zapatistas publish their own statements on the internet. Mediation's possibilities to empower the marginalized also constitutes an important preoccupation in much fiction and poststructuralist and feminist theories contemporary with the testimonial boom: fiction and theories that also strove to alter the traditional power relationships under attack in other contexts during the 1960s and 70s. The intertextual reading of *testimonio*, fiction, and theory therefore highlights several important parallels among these groups of texts and the ways in which they serve as commentaries for the others. Even more interesting for this book's focus on Latin American texts by women, however, is the fact that for European and US theorists the Third World, women, or Latin American women have been the marginalized groups they have aspired to empower through their ideas' mediation. Texts by Latin American women thus experience the very mediation problematized in their own work, without recognition of their contribution to these issues explored in European and US theories. Furthermore, like testimonial writing from other regions, Latin American mediated *testimonio* does incorporate the voices of actual people previously silenced and thus reveals the complications of really interacting with those the intellectual elite desires to empower, of *really* translating another's experience. Thus, while this book reads testimonial writing with emphasis on its textuality and its parallels in fiction and theory, the book does privilege testimonial writing's engagement and political and philosophical consequences. These are the lessons of *testimonio* for fiction and theory.

Returning to Borges, my epigraph catches his narrator at the moment when he senses the absurdity of representing, of "translating," a distant time and philosophical perspective into the present. The narrator describes Averroes's struggle to translate a commentary by Aristotle that includes the words "tragedy" and "comedy," whose meaning Averroes is unable to grasp with the resources at his disposal. Later that evening Averroes's conversation with erudite company at a Koran scholar's home indirectly visits and revisits questions of singular essence and transitions from one form or another of certain objects–fruit into birds, rose petals into words from the Koran, the Koran into human or animal form. The conversation then turns to the theater piece the traveler Abulcásim saw in China, a scene the listeners cannot comprehend since, what is the point of acting out a story when one person could tell it? Finally Averroes returns to his library and adds a note to his translation that Aristotle referred to "panegyric" when he used the word "tragedy," and "satire" when he wrote "comedy." Borges's story ends with the narrator reflecting on the equal absurdity of his own efforts at translation. The narrator considers that Averroes's imagining drama without suspecting the nature of theater is no less absurd than his own task of imagining Averroes with only nineteenth-century European texts as tools. As the narrator struggles with the same dilemma of representation across centuries and translations, Averroes's search eventually becomes the narrator's search for Averroes.

The narrator and the object of his search overlap in yet another form of translation in one of Borges's familiar circularities, and the story's narrator converts his words into actions in the telling. He not only writes about Averroes's search, but also *acts out that search*, leading to identification with Averroes and therefore with the text itself, which becomes a symbol of the narrator at the moment of narration when he repeats Averroes's act of interpretation. Through a chicken-egg conundrum, believing in Averroes involves mimicking Averroes's own act. The philosopher therefore only exists now when the narrator writes him. . . and the narrator as such only exists as he writes Averroes.

Shifting this universal experience of writing to a testimonial context, as the transcriber approaches the narrator through metonymic association with her, or valorization of her importance, and through reproduction of her language, the transcriber exhibits a desire to act out what is valuable about the narrator. I am certainly not referring to the informant's suffering, but rather to the moral and authoritative weight of the identity defined by that experience. Yet, like the narrator's reproduction of Averroes's search, the act of translation involved becomes questionable for various reasons elaborated in the chapters ahead. Moreover, while Borges's narrator must somehow mimic Averroes to conceptualize him, Averroes must be accessible to this representation. The testimonial subject's identity must also remain accessible to the transcriber—and reader—to make the text possible. As we shall see, the informant must construct an appropriately translatable identity that lends needed authenticity.

Even though these layers of representation evoke theater and performance, Averroes does not grasp theater's supplementary layer of meaning and commentary that disguise, gesture, comedy, and tragedy add to real events, nor the layer of interpretation underlying these acts. Averroes attempts to work in a space of contained meanings ("no hay otro dios que el Dios" 'there is no god but God'), of literal translations possible within his sphere of experience, near the comforting sound of a fountain in al-Andalus, far from the Arab desert. This is the idealized, literal translation and interpretation of another's life, more comforting than a story that resists our grasp. With the addition of theatrical layers of gesture and disguise, limits are broken, a desert with no boundaries opens like an arid, material, subversive atmosphere: "El temor de lo crasamente infinito, del mero espacio, de la mera materia, tocó por un instante a Averroes" ("Terror of the crassly infinite, of mere space, of mere matter, laid a hand on Averroës for a second"; 99, 106). [2] This is the desert we shall also see *testimonio*'s readers enter, Clarice Lispector's protagonist enter in *A Paixão Segundo G.H.,* and Deleuze and Guattari vicariously enter through their nomads. Those adventures, however, share Averroes's agoraphobia when faced with loss of discursive control, as the following chapters will explain.

Borges's story opens this book not because it relates a narrative process exactly analogous to the meeting of transcriber and narrator; indeed *testimonio*'s political urgency and anti-elitism are clearly distinct. Yet, although Borges easily represents an elitism and politics unpalatable to the authors and defenders of the testimonial

---

[2] Unless otherwise specified, all translations in the book are mine. The translations of Borges are by Anthony Kerrigan, including the epigraph.

project he squarely critiques a forced authenticity that ultimately
plagues the testimonial informant's options for self-expression.
Borges's point here is perhaps best known through his essay "El
escritor argentino y la tradición," but also articulated in Averroes's
and the narrator's frustrated translations, representations, and
attempts to limit meaning that highlight a certain desire for authenticity and truth, ostensibly more attainable through mimesis, that
lies at the heart of readers' expectations in testimonial writing.

Several aspects of Borges's story reflect the links between testimonial texts and works of fiction: translations of one reality into
another, self-legitimation through the text, acts of disguise and gesture, interpretive and creative power and destruction, and the
threat of uncontained signification. These issues examined together
and informed by feminist and other critical theories lead to my conclusions on the relationships among authority, legitimation and violence in selected texts by Latin American women, and also to the
need for a reevaluation of *testimonio*'s meaning now that the political situations motivating its production have changed. In 1996 John
Beverley stated, "the moment of *testimonio* is over," but its *importance* is not ("Real Thing" 280). One of this book's essential aims is
to contribute to the recent second wave of readings that critically
and self-reflectively examine testimonial writing in the context of its
confrontation with privileged readers. The less idealized view of *testimonio*'s success in lending agency to the previously silenced leads
to a broader discussion of all kinds of privileged representations of
the marginalized that attempt to forfeit elite authority, issues with
which feminist theory has struggled for some time. Thus, the present book inserts Latin American women's testimonial discourse
into a theoretical discussion not as raw material for US and European criticism, but as a complex critique on equal standing with
theories whose contradictions *testimonio* brings to light. Feminist
theories' relevance, in turn, sheds light on the relatively ignored
question of gender in *testimonio*. The book does not offer an all-
encompassing theory of Latin American women's writing, or of all
testimonial writing, but rather a specific reading of mediated *testimonios* with narratives and theoretical texts that reflect or should
see themselves reflected in testimonial narrators' negotiation of the
testimonial process and consequent critique of its efforts to cede
authority to the narrators.

The Latin American women's testimonial texts and fiction chosen for this project provide, among other things, a response to US and European feminist theories' history of homogenizing women's experience, a history more difficult to carry out when confronted with Latin America's poverty, racial politics, political instability, and many regions. Latin American feminism, moreover, has from early on been divided along class lines between grassroots *movimientos de mujeres* and middle and upper-class feminism. How do differences in privilege produce the need for legitimation by both sides? How do the differences at the heart of testimonial writing belie feminist projects to develop a narrator-transcriber relationship that challenges hierarchies, undoes violences and is based on shared experiences? Caren Kaplan ("Resisting" 124) and Julia Watson and Sidonie Smith (xv) have noted the tendency to homogenize the marginalized female subject once she has been recognized by post-colonial criticism, and earlier criticism on *testimonio* poses no exception. Doris Sommer's work reflects the changes in reading this relationship, for example. Quoted in 1993 by John Beverley, Sommer finds women's testimonies in particular work toward alliances across global divisions: "to read women's testimonials, curiously, is to mitigate the tension between First World self and Third World other. I do not mean this as a license to deny the differences, but as a suggestion that the testimonial subject may be a model for respectful, nontotalizing politics" ("Second Thoughts" 90). Yet, by Sommer's 1995 essay on Elena Poniatowska's *Hasta no verte, Jesús mío*, this relationship has become considerably more difficult, with greater emphasis on the testimonial narrator's autonomy in resisting the First World "self's" comfortable reading ("Taking a Life"). In her seminal essay "Can the Subaltern Speak?," Gayatri Spivak writes: "Belief in the plausibility of global alliance politics is prevalent among women of dominant social groups interested in 'international feminism' in the comprador countries." She continues: "On the other side of the international division of labor, the subject of exploitation cannot know and speak the text of female exploitation, even if the absurdity of the nonrepresenting intellectual making space for her to speak is achieved. The woman is doubly in shadow" (288). Like Spivak's negative answer to "can the subaltern speak?," Daphne Patai also replies negatively to the title of her own article, "U.S. Academics and Third World Women: is Ethical Research Possible?" While these critics focus on the relationship between First World and Third World, an external dynamic fundamental to *testi-*

monio's purposes, similar internal tensions exist between transcriber and informant from Latin America, but speaking across divisions of privilege and public authority. The international division of labor becomes a local division within Latin America. In this case, the identification between transcriber and informant incorporates a very personal concern with Latin American identity, especially evident in Elisabeth Burgos and Elena Poniatowska's comments on their transcription work, studied in Chapter 1.

Clearly, the testimonial process carried out in Latin America raises key questions for feminism, but we can also ask what questions feminist theory raises for *testimonio*. To some extent feminist ethnography and feminist theory on *testimonio* do in fact repeat theory in general on testimonial discourse. For instance, Caren Kaplan has asserted that *testimonio*, among other alternative autobiographical forms, belongs to a feminist sensibility through its subversion of rigid genre boundaries tied to the same structures that reinforce gender boundaries ("Resisting" *passim*). Yet, the same could be said for other marginalized sensibilities. Testimonial writing may serve as a useful feminist tool, yet many feminist analyses echo theoretical aspects of criticism on Latin American *testimonio* in general. The testimonial project in general challenges genre and intends to challenge traditional authorial and authoritarian relationships. What particular insights can feminist perspectives then bring to the examination of testimonial narrative? For one thing, and on the most obvious level, feminist analysis of testimonial genres becomes meaningful precisely in testimonial discourse's openness to participation by women and the possible effects of that participation. In other words, although several central arguments of feminist theory on *testimonio* coincide with theories unconcerned with feminist issues, the very challenges to authority on which all those theoretical frameworks agree constitute aspects of *testimonio* that welcome greater participation by women. Women have participated in Latin American testimonial writing, as informants and transcribers, since its early stages in this century. One of the most important and most cited examples is one mentioned earlier, *Benita* by Benita Galeana, a Mexican working-class woman who becomes active in the Communist Party. First published in 1940, her testimony exhibits a strong, independent tone similar to Jesusa Palancares's voice in *Hasta no verte, Jesús mío*. Later, with the acceleration of testimonial production after the Cuban Revolution, the first Casa de las Américas prize for the genre was awarded in 1970 to a woman: María Esther Gilio.

With a greater number of women participants a greater variety of female speaking subjects appear in testimonial texts–not only mothers or outstanding cultural figures, but also independent working-class women and *guerrillas*. Significantly, women's testimonies lend authority and agency to the female transcriber and reader since they portray women as protagonists of history: this vicarious fulfillment forms one of my main concerns in the next chapter and beyond. *Testimonio*'s collective, representative value thus potentially includes the transcriber herself within the collective, within a certain reading. While this inclusive interpretation of collective identity primarily legitimates the transcriber and suggests the tendency to homogenize women's experience, collective womanhood also occasionally appears acknowledged by the informants. Patai, outspokenly critical of a naive, utopian feminist ethnography, notes that most of the women she interviewed recognized "some sort of bond with other women," including potential readers, despite differences (*Brazilian Women* 4). The language of several women's testimonies indeed stresses the "we" over the "I," as Sommer discusses throughout "'Not Just a Personal Story.'" While the collective import of the informant's experience, whether female or male, reinforces his or her authority, as well as that of the transcriber, women's *testimonios* frequently, though not always, stress within the text itself the collective significance of the life story, be it as woman, Indian, or economically impoverished.

Emphasis on the collective, combined with some transcribers' tendencies to fulfill not only their political projects through the informants' testimonies, but also their personal identities, suggests the particular need to carefully examine potential textual violences where the narrator could all but disappear through appropriation. Here textual freedom and violence mesh with sexual freedom and violence, as theory on *testimonio* and the content of most testimonial texts carefully reinforce controls on female sexuality, even as the women who tell their stories depart from other aspects of traditional female roles. Theory on *testimonio* and the circumstances that testimonial subjects must negotiate do not necessarily make the leap from questioning genre boundaries to questioning some gender boundaries, nor do testimonial texts include in their alternative political agendas those gender issues that risk the reader's sympathy. Thus, the limits on the testimonial narrator's textual freedom within the parameters of the authentic identity she should represent extend to her sexual freedom, even when the *testimonio*'s content begs questions about how the narrator's unusual life changed her sexual roles and the narrator hints at such changes. The disguises, gestures, and interpretations–the theater–present in the transcriber and informant's roles also suggest the utility of theories of performativity and gender for studying *testimonio*. As we shall see in Chapters 2 and 4, the works of fiction that bear relevance to the intricacies of the testimonial process combine explicit violence with sexuality or sensuality, in some cases suggesting literal violation. In these fictional reflections, woman as desired object of attention, no matter what the intentions, becomes sexualized.

Resistance to a feminist analysis of testimonial writing may arise from concern with feminism's bourgeois and even imperialist connotations for some leftists in Latin America. More important things are at stake. This is often true, yet overlooks some key points: the growth of grassroots Latin American feminism from poor and working-class women's efforts to better their basic conditions; the identification, if problematic, between transcriber and narrator, which can include the factor of gender; and the way power relationships in general in Latin America are often expressed through gender. [3] Therefore, just as testimonial writing offers lessons for the indeed more elitist, homogenizing tendencies of many feminist theories, to ignore gender in *testimonio*'s efforts to break down traditional hierarchies is to incompletely investigate those hierarchies. It is also to miss a tool in understanding the informant's negotiation with the conditions of her self-expression, with the conditions under which she is allowed to tell her story, and with what she is allowed to be.

Similarly, the aesthetic concerns associated with fiction, with literature, have seemed inappropriate to mix with the urgency of authorizing the reality and truth of marginalized accounts denied by official history. Again, this forced separation between testimonial accounts and self-conscious discursive fashioning imposes precon-

---

[3] The volume of essays edited by Marit Melhuus and Kristi Anne Stølen, for example, offers many illustrations of power relations expressed through gender relations. (*Machos, Mistresses, Madonnas: Contesting the Power of Latin American Gender Imagery* [London, New York: Verso, 1996].)

ceived notions on the form the informant's truth takes, limiting her autonomy and ignoring the testimonial process itself that produces a written artefact. A study combining *testimonio, novela testimonial,* and fiction also allows us to pose the same questions to each text and to address questions arising from the testimonial process as they are reflected in other narrative modes concerned with lending voice to the voiceless. Although previous critical work attempts to clarify distinctions among terms or the difficulty of establishing those distinctions, few studies have integrated analyses of these different texts, however they may be defined. By bringing together texts from these categories I do not equate them, nor do I assert that my conclusions apply to all texts or texts by women authors. Nevertheless, the definitions of the terms *testimonio* and *novela testimonial* are subjective to begin with, and the nature of their differences have occupied much past critical attention to testimonial genres, further exposing the limits of separating analysis of testimonial writing from analysis of fiction. As Mary Louise Pratt observes, literary treatment of *testimonio* has been criticized but there is still confusion about its genre ("*I, Rigoberta Menchú*" 41).

One should add that traditional notions of literature also resist mixture of the two, protecting literature from contamination by inferior style, political propaganda, and temporary fads. For example, in the context of economic difficulties that lower book sales, Mempo Giardinelli perceives opportunism by *testimonio* authors who take advantage of the public's passing interests in order to sell books. For Giardinelli the *testimonio* is not art and aims to "speak" the truth, albeit subjective truth, while literature "alludes to" the truth through the lies that characterize fiction (30). John Beverley also rightly views the *testimonio* as threatening or questioning bourgeois literary discourse in a productive manner that creates both a representation of *and* a means to subaltern resistance and struggle ("Second Thoughts" 97, 90). According to Beverley, *testimonio's* importance lies in its alternative status, its separation from literature. In other words, to maintain its authority and authenticity, testimonial texts must not "allude to" the truth through lies, even when the creation of those lies in fact leads us to a more profound truth about marginalized narrators' necessary manipulation of their story to negotiate for a public who will listen to them. I will return to this important point in Chapter 1. René Jara, on the other hand, asserts that *testimonio* has infused literature with a subversive quality (4), thus valuing *testimonio*'s role in literature and influence on the novel, perhaps without considering historical truth's role in previous Latin American narrative. More importantly, Claudia Ferman notes testimonial discourse's value as a framework for literature: "reading and analyzing *testimonio* deconstructs the literary tradition as the canon knows it and exposes the social fabric on which its circulation and reproduction relies" (162).

Several terms and relationships must be clarified to respond to these assertions: literature and fiction; *testimonio* and fiction; *novela testimonial, testimonio* and fiction. Hugo Achugar distinguishes literature from fiction by loosely defining literature as an "elaboración ideológico-formal" ("formal-ideological elaboration"), which would certainly include the transcribed *testimonio* in its final, formalized manifestation (65). Achugar calls *testimonio* literature, as the *testimonio*'s documentary aspirations resist fiction, as the legal connotations of "testimony" indicate. From this perspective, in the relationship fiction versus literature, fiction carries the weight of the truth-lie dichotomy and thus better functions as a potential opposite to *testimonio*'s (albeit subjective, constructed) truth. The mediated *testimonio* and *novela testimonial* do stem from real oral interaction between two or more interlocutors, regardless of how the participants may manipulate the interview or its written result. Novelistic simulation of documents highlights this manipulation's proximity to literature as opposed to Achugar's concept of fiction, and Elzbieta Sklodowska recently characterized testimonial texts as a "peculiar mixture of experience, creation, manipulation and invention, more akin, perhaps, to a novel, than to a scientific document" ("Poetics" 256). Nevertheless, to develop his concepts of *testimonio* and novel, Héctor Mario Cavallari also focuses on the relationship to the "referent"–the informant or the fictional protagonist: in the case of *testimonio*, real interviews did take place. This focus, according to Cavallari, also allows an examination of interpretive practice in general (73), and, as I signaled earlier, the presence of a real human being does complicate the text's production, no matter who holds the pen. Furthermore, the testimonial dialogue almost always occurs across differences of one sort or another that entail differences in authority or privilege, although, as Sklodowska notes, the great variety of texts written as the voice of the marginalized discounts that gesture as an exclusive criterion of testimonial discourse (*Testimonio* 72). One crucial distinction between testimonial texts and novels (and literature and fiction) does lie in the fact that the former must prove themselves. Literature may incorporate concern with self-legitimation, but a novel does not have to legitimate its existence as such.

The *testimonio* and the novel place different emphasis on literary value; however, as Achugar states, "el testimonio no implica ausencia de 'literatura'" ("*testimonio* does not imply the absence of 'literature'"; 65). Ultimately, aesthetic qualifications such as literary or non-literary, artistic or non-artistic are as subjective as the *testimonio*'s truth can be and are less valuable as taxonomic labels applied by theorists than as clues to the processes of authorization and legitimation behind the texts. In other words, the question "is this literature?" can lead to irreconcilable disagreement on ideological grounds and does little to advance a definition of *testimonio* or an understanding of its importance, while the question "does this text present itself as literature and why or why not?" provokes a series of problems that productively investigate testimonial discourse's creation. Roberto González Echevarría has written that "literature is the equivalent of critical thought in Latin America, and critical thought most certainly includes politics" (*Voice* 3), and it is indeed as an artefact of Latin American critical theory that I use testimonial writing as a point of departure for readings of novels, short stories, and theory.

Although equally complicated, establishing distinctions between unmediated testimonies and fiction generally poses less controversy than determining differences between mediated testimonies and fiction because of the transcriber's explicit presence as author figure. Elzbieta Sklodowska's book-length study of testimonial writing's variations emphasizes mediation as a chief organizing factor, since that mediation constitutes a central source of contention over truth, fictional content, betrayal and the *testimonio*'s validity as a means toward political change. Sklodowska lays such emphasis on mediation that the unmediated *testimonio* in fact falls under her category of "pre-text." Yet, the subjective truth of any testimony and degree to which any testimony depends on a publisher or editor threaten to blur those distinctions between mediated and unmediated forms. For example, I will demonstrate how one unmediated testimony dependent on an editor, Carolina Maria de Jesus's diaries *Quarto de Despejo*, exhibits in one person the conflict between transcriber and informant. This tension emerges in part from Carolina Maria de

Jesus's dependence on an editor, of whose presence she is clearly conscious, to publish her diaries. The tension also arises from the necessary distancing from the community of which she is simultaneously part, in order to write.

The debate intensifies, however, with the *novela testimonial*'s ambiguous relationship to fiction and *testimonio*. Versions and variations of the *novela testimonial* have as many names as definitions: *novela-testimonio*, documentary fiction, documentary novel, nonfiction novel, *documento literario, investigación etnológica*. Needless to say, the difficulty in defining the *novela testimonial* lies in its simultaneous reference to an internal, controlled, imaginary world and the external world imposed upon it (or rather elicited by the author). *Novela testimonial* and novel, as one would assume, share explicit literary aspirations, but also greater irony, even when ironic contradictions are indeed evident in *testimonio*. Significantly, several critics do not distinguish well between *novela testimonial* and *testimonio*, referring to both with the term *testimonio*, and in so doing approximating *testimonio* to fiction, since some fictional content is therefore assumed for *testimonio*.

While one of this book's purposes is to blur some of the boundaries mentioned above, with the ultimate goal of in fact reinforcing the political impetus of testimonial writing, for organizational reasons the structure of the following chapters does divide my arguments into discussion of testimonial texts, fiction, and theory. Beginning with the second chapter, however, I return to texts from previous sections to build upon my points.

Chapter 1, on mediated testimonial texts, lays the ground work for the following chapters through examination of testimonial discourse's imperative to cede space to marginalized voices, a need that places great importance on the veracity of the text's content. Both the political motivation for testimonial discourse and the consequent effort to prove its truth value produce transcription processes that paradoxically undermine the original purposes of the text. Put simply, the text's authority has conventionally come to depend on three ideas: what we define as truthful, the collective representativity of the narrator, and the transcriber's disappearance by his or her transparent intervention. In fact, however, since the *testimonio* was produced to counteract official "truths," it fundamentally questions the concept of any singular truth, including the informant's, and sometimes works against concepts of truth in a society based on writing. In fact, the informant, through the process of recounting her story and leaving the community can no longer be truly representative of the collective identity provided for the reader. In fact, the mediated *testimonio*'s written production and commodification depend on the intervention of a transcriber whose presence cannot be without effect. Emphasis on the degree to which a testimonial text conforms to its idealized notion as transparently representational does not lead us to the heart of its significance, but in fact to its paradox that produces a series of discursive displacements skirting the issues the testimonial subject really confronts when speaking from a disadvantaged position. Such is the case of the recent controversy regarding inaccuracies in Rigoberta Menchú's life story. The "truth" her *testimonio* communicates about a marginalized experience involves as much negotiation of an authorized space for self-expression as biographical facts of a woman expected to be representative of an identity packaged for a privileged reader. Elena Poniatowska's testimonial novel *Hasta no verte, Jesús mío* and Elisabeth Burgos-Debray's transcription of Rigoberta Menchú's *testimonio Me llamo Rigoberta Menchú y así me nació la conciencia* reflect these issues, discussed through the terms "legitimation," "authority," and "truth," as do Poniatowska's and Burgos-Debray's gesture of self-legitimation by identifying with their informants, producing a "vicarious identity" that compensates some lack the authors perceive in themselves. Later in Chapter 1, Carolina Maria de Jesus's *Quarto de Despejo* demonstrates the narrator's division into two distinct roles: those of transcriber and informant. The division illustrates testimonial discourse's *dependence* on the tension between the two, a tension that produces many of its inner contradictions and makes evident testimonial discourse's display of the writer's dilemma in general upon transcribing another's life. Ultimately all these texts become most meaningful in their investigation of the possibilities of self-representation and subject construction in testimonial writing.

The ambiguity of veracity's uses in testimonial discourse and the discourse's clear exploration of the writer's task lead me to interweave discussion of the above mentioned texts with that of two novels by Clarice Lispector that also probe ethical issues: *A Paixão Segundo G.H.* and *A Hora da Estrela*. Lispector's novels covered here do not consciously respond to *testimonio*, but rather the dynamics of *testimonio* reflect broader narrative processes at work, placing *testimonio* as a genre of Latin American literature of resistance. *Testimonio* lays bare the struggles with authority, agency, and self-legitimation existing in all forms of narrative, but uncannily pertinent to the specific works of fiction in this section. At the same time, the fiction I study here exaggerates the tensions present in the transcriber-informant relationship to such an extent that these texts serve as commentaries on testimonial paradoxes glossed over in the past. The comparison does not trivialize the life stories seen in Chapter 1, but rather explores further their violence and the possibility of self-representation from a subaltern position.

Chapter 3 begins precisely with violence, linking it through René Girard's concept of sacrifice to the discursive disappearance with which the testimonial informant or her fictional counterpart is threatened. The disappearance of her voice, of her story, would commit the worst crime, considering the *testimonio*'s reason for being. Yet, paradoxes in the texts risk the "purity" of that voice. In order to search for the other person that allows one to understand the self, boundaries must be transgressed and limits violated even as they are created through struggles for authority and differences in privilege. At the same time, boundary crossings provoke apertures that threaten hegemonic structures, such as literary genre, gender hierarchies or official versions of history. The chapter then turns to Hélène Cixous, Jacques Derrida, and Gilles Deleuze and Felix Guattari, principally. While each of these authors' philosophy has enabled a critical reading of power structures that shut out marginalized voices, the same philosophy exhibits paradoxes similar to those in *testimonio*. *Testimonio* has opened a space for marginalized voices at the same time it has manifested its own limitations. Cixous misreads Lispector, ignoring the violence in her work so that Cixous can see in Lispector the embodiment of her own theories of women's writing. Derrida opens the rhetorical space of woman, liberating woman form regulated identity, yet depending on "woman" as a shifting position open to occupation by anyone, like the prostitute's identity. Deleuze and Guattari empower the "minor" literature that subversively questions "major" discourses, yet, as is the case for nomadic identities, the marginalized must remain outside the center as the margins become a space open to occupation by those seeking a rhetoric of subversion. Nomadic movement across boundaries still seems limited to those privileged enough to possess a passport. The multiple displacements–physical, discursive, violent—at the heart of the paradoxes inherent in testimonial texts, and reflected in works of fiction, are critical in two senses. They are critical since they mark decisive moments in testimonial discourse and since they are displacements reflected in critical theories.

Chapter 4 reads Diamela Eltit's *El Padre Mío* and particularly *Lumpérica* as texts that seem acutely aware of the issues confronting the narratives I examine until this point. Eltit's complex writing undermines as artifice the aperture to subaltern voices in representational *testimonio*. In Eltit the truly subaltern cannot speak, but the subaltern disturbs our expectations of the easily consumable story by communicating the violence against the "informants" in part by violating our comfort with graphic, unsettling images and difficult text. At the same time Eltit's vanguard work remains accessible to an elite few, *testimonio* is ultimately meant to shake an elite audience that otherwise sits isolated from the informant's experience. Both protagonists in these works are homeless. The schizophrenic in the *testimonio* (or anti-*testimonio*) *El Padre Mío* produces a monologue that defies comprehension, yet certain repetitions, his paranoia, and the frightening, confusing world he inhabits may better capture the truth of this experience of dictatorship and utter lack. *Lumpérica* does the same in a work of fiction where the protagonist utters no words about her condition but rather performs the obscene, violent gestures and groans that give testimony to dehumanization under dictatorship and under anaesthetizing capitalist consumption following the return to democracy. Chapter 4 therefore turns specifically to *Lumpérica* and *testimonio* as performance after examining both *El Padre Mío* and *Lumpérica*'s relevance to truth, violence, borders, and nomadism. The chapter's final section contrasts the explicit female sexuality in *Lumpérica* with its absence in *testimonio* and presence of a different sort in the narratives of Chapter 2, a contrast that highlights in gender terms the informant's possibilities for autonomous expression.

This book is a study of testimonial texts, fiction, and critical theory contemporary to the height of *testimonio*, with the purpose of rereading that idealism with which positions of otherness were adopted and adapted, with particular attention to feminist theory's part in idealist readings as well as its evolution into a framework for enabling us to read *testimonio*'s possibilities beyond its previously idealized interpretation. Gender has both accompanied struggles with issues of identity and has been ignored with relation to testimonial writing for ideological purity at the cost of overlooking important critiques that move our reading or use of *testimonio* beyond a tendency toward the stagnation of subaltern identity. Any intellectual discussion will abstract reality, but the point is that militant use of *testimonio* did not escape elite intellectualizing of the other, eventually limiting the informant's agency. The present critique does not keep the testimonial informant in a realm outside abstraction, but rather allows her participation in the process of representation, recognizing the shifting circumstances under which that representation is constructed.

Borges concludes his story of Averroes and initiates his thoughts on the futility of his project with these words: "[Q]uise narrar el proceso de una derrota" ("I have striven to narrate the process involved in a defeat"; 103, 110). The paradoxes and contradictions I describe in this study could lead one to view *testimonio* as a failed attempt to change authority relationships, and as textual form that winds up replicating relationships of exploitation. As Antonio Vera-León writes: "Si los criollos letrados del XIX hacían azúcar con el trabajo negro, el intelectual revolucionario en el XX se da a la tarea de hacer discurso con (y por) el 'otro' para legitimar el orden revolucionario" ("If the lettered creoles of the 19th century produced sugar with black labor, the intellectual revolutionary of the 20th century is devoted to the task of creating discourse with (and for) the 'other' to legitimate the revolutionary order"; quoted in Sklodowska, *Testimonio* 63). To ignore that traditional authority relationships continue to exist in the *testimonio* would be to lack an understanding of the nature of the writing process, as well as the fundamental paradox of the testimonial project. On the other hand, testimonial discourse does not simply replicate exploitative relationships; testimonial genres represent complex, self-reflective writings that expose their own disguises and limitations through critical dialogue. Testimonial discourse reflects an important will to lend authority to marginal voices and brings to light displacements and violences in its own texts, in certain theoretical constructions, and in concrete political realities. *Testimonio*'s broad appeal has indeed contributed to concrete change. Testimonial texts challenge borders, limits and duplicitous discourse. If, according to Giardinelli, literature alludes to the truth through lies, perhaps the *testimonio* and *novela testimonial* allude to lies through their truth: truth about negotiating a space of authority.

My title develops from these ideas by playing on two opposite meanings of "subject": agent of an action and someone who is under another's authority or control. The opposite meanings reflect testimonial writing's inherent contradictions as a discourse of solidarity that opens discourse to the previously silenced and delimits their self-representation. The testimonial speaking subject (agent) becomes the subject (object) of discursive practices and readings that require a negotiation of these two opposite "subjectivities"; therefore, rhetoric shifts or changes. In the process, the "subject" in its meaning as "topic" is liable to change: when we thought we were talking about the speaker's experience, we might find ourselves changing the subject to the readers, transcribers, academics, or intellectuals who cannot quite cede their agency in *testimonio*'s medium. (The irony of the scholarly book you have in your hand is not lost here.) Finally, the title also refers to changes in approaches to reading *testimonio* over the past few years, from a previously idealized, overly transparent and comfortable reading to one that pays greater attention to the testimonial speaker's complex self-representation as subject (agent) where she is still subject to (under the authority of) the social circumstances she denounces. This change in approach constitutes one of the underlying purposes of the present book.

CHAPTER 1

LEGITIMATION: MEDIATED *TESTIMONIOS*, AUTHORITY AND VICARIOUS IDENTITIES

> . . .paresción me no tomalle por el medio, sino del princi-
> pio, porque se tenga entera noticia de mi persona; y
> también porque consideren los que heredaron nobles
> estados cuán poco se les debe, pues Fortuna fue con
> ellos parcial, y cuánto más hicieron los que, siéndoles
> contraria, con fuerza y maña remando salieron a buen
> puerto.

> . . .it seemed best to start not in the middle, but at the
> beginning, so that you have some idea of my person;
> and also so that those who inherited their noble status
> consider how little is owed to them, because Fortune
> favored them, and how much more the others did,
> who without Fortune's favor, with skill and might came
> out ahead.
>
> *Lazarillo de Tormes*

> En mis largos años cruzando fronteras de un lado a
> otro, en un determinado momento tenía que trabajar en
> la ONU. Tenía que sacar quizá una docena de elegantes
> credenciales para poder explicar mi rostro indígena.

> In my long years crossing borders from one place to
> another, at a certain moment I had to work at the UN.
> I had to get perhaps a dozen elegant forms of identifi-
> cation to be able to explain my Indian face.
>
> Rigoberta Menchú, *Rigoberta: la nieta de los mayas*

THROUGH the testimonial process, does the testimonial subject achieve, "with skill and might," with *discursive* strength and skill, the agency and enunciative authority to make of the testimonial text, and the transcriber, a tool for reversing traditional power

31

relationships? Does, on the other hand, the *discursive* mechanism itself of mediated testimonial texts reinforce the narrator's appropriation and therefore location "inside" dominant political and cultural structures as the other, belying the advertised reversal of inside and outside, center and margin, being for oneself and being for others? True to *testimonio*'s resistance to black and white interpretations, the answer to either question is neither fully yes nor fully no, although either interpretation of the testimonial process carries ethical weight that discounts gray areas. Both interpretations incompletely satisfy criteria for veracity, as in such debates on truthfulness as the Rigoberta Menchú polemic. Moreover, either version by itself exhibits certain naiveté toward the possibilities afforded by mediated *testimonio* (at times overestimated) and the speaker as autonomous subject (at times underestimated).

The analysis in this chapter of Elena Poniatowska's *Hasta no verte, Jesús mío*, Elisabeth Burgos Debray and Rigoberta Menchú's *Me llamo Rigoberta Menchú*, and Carolina Maria de Jesus's *Quarto de Despejo* dedicates attention to the latter interpretation of absorption and appropriation because it runs counter to *testimonio*'s ideals, but the chapter ultimately demonstrates that neither characterization fully describes the results of the inherently paradoxical project of transcribed *testimonio*. More importantly, the paradoxical element, the innate contradictions that resist stable or thoroughly convincing conclusions in much previous criticism on *testimonio*, reveals crucial links with theoretical considerations and consequences for politically engaged writing in the future now that "the moment of *testimonio* is over," if we agree with Beverley ("Real" 280). Mary Louise Pratt also points out that because it is produced transculturally, "*testimonio* exists in a state of permanent, and often productive, contradiction." Specifically, the narrator relates personal experience that presupposes a subjectivity the testimonial speaker is understood not to possess ("*I, Rigoberta Menchú*" 44). Those considerations highlight *testimonio*'s significance beyond that frequently accorded: its significance as an inquiry into identity and solidarity, as a form of Latin American narrative where inner workings of the writerly task are brought to the surface, and as a text that concretely engages with the socio-political realities that concern so many Latin American writers. These links integrate testimonial discourse into broad theoretical debates in western and specifically Latin American cultures without lessening its urge for political activism. Mediated testimonial discourse, when studied critically, cannot be considered a tangential development in Latin American narrative because its rhetorical twists and conflicts expose those of fiction and theory, and indicate the need to carry its political project beyond the limitations of testimonial process.

LEGITIMATION

The contradictions I study critically in the present chapter stem in one way or another from the question of legitimation, leading in the end to what I describe as the "vicarious identities" that link the testimonial, fictional, and theoretical texts studied in this book. Legitimation entails: the transcriber and the testimonial subject's authority before each other; shifting and stable boundaries of discursive location; the text's authority before the consumer; veracity's legitimating role; and one of the reasons for concentrating on women's *testimonio*, as I will explain ahead.

This chapter focuses on three texts that illustrate different manifestations of the struggle for authority and legitimation in allowing to speak and speaking through a marginalized woman. Poniatowska's *novela testimonial Hasta no verte, Jesús mío* is based principally on the life of one woman whom Poniatowska sought out to interview, but includes voices from other women Poniatowska had met (Poniatowska, "Testimonios" 159-60). The text also declares Poniatowska's creative composition of the novel from the raw material. In her prologue Elisabeth Burgos Debray emphasizes her role as only conduit for Rigoberta Menchú's narration of her *testimonio*, although the Menchú controversy has brought greater attention to Burgos Debray's editing. Carolina Maria de Jesus pens her own *testimonio* but depends on a newspaper journalist to publish her diaries, who also cuts out a great deal of the original material.

Referring here in part to points made in the introduction, the mediated *testimonio* constitutes a form of speaking through the voice of another for legitimation. This process is not unidirectional: both transcriber and testimonial subject use each other's voice, legitimating one another. The ethnographer or journalist has access to publishers; the narrating individual offers a reason for which the transcriber's work should be published. Mutual legitimation encourages association at times to the point of identification with the other, but this identification becomes particularly complicated in the mediated *testimonio* by the multiple roles the participants assume and the effort inherent in this discourse of the privileged abdicating authority, of relinquishing control. Each occupies shifting discursive locations that separate or overlap (passive listener, active creator, narrator, authority, author, unusual individual, representative of a group) while the boundary between subject and transcriber remains intact as it must to in fact justify taking down the testimony of someone quite different. Yet, while both participants use each other's voice, the *testimonio*'s political location makes suspect any suggestion of the transcriber's ventriloquism through the subject. The transcriber's relinquishment constitutes the ideal that in reality is critiqued and undermined by the very texts produced by the discursive gesture of ceding authority. The author-transcriber-editor-listener-ethnographer seeks to legitimate herself and her project before the reading public as well as before the narrator-informant who in turn must legitimate her testimony before those who possess authority through buying power or potential political clout. The perceived reader/consumer's expectations do play an important role regarding legitimation and authority, but not in the self-celebrating role Doris Sommer describes in her essay "Taking a Life."[1] There Sommer describes the reader elevated from voyeur to "partner, collaborator, coauthor" (919). Recognizing the reading public's expectations as consumers of *testimonios* does not necessarily imply the indeed naive role Sommer associates with reader-response theory. Kimberly Nance's article, for example, dissects the various ways readers have approached and "disarmed" *testimonio*'s denunciatory nature, including ways akin to self-celebration. Yet she links this focus on the reader to reaffirmation of the testimonial speaker's agency in resisting readers' evasive strategies. The Menchú controversy, as we shall see later, certainly bears out the importance of examining testimonial texts as, indeed, dialogues.

Strict definitions of legitimation and testimony of course suggest legal discourse, hence my epigraph from the *Lazarillo de*

---

[1] Sommer has later versions of this essay that do not change her main point: "Taking a Life: Hot Pursuit and Cold Rewards in a Mexican Testimonial Novel," *The Seductions of Biography*, eds. Mary Rhiel and David Suchoff (New York: Routledge, 1996) 147-72; "Hot Pursuit and Cold Rewards of Mexicanness," *Proceed with Caution, When Engaged by Minority Writing in the Americas* (Cambridge, Mass. and London: Harvard UP, 1999) 138-59.

Tormes, and constitute one justification for my integrating discussion of testimonial and fictional texts in the next chapters. [2] The strict definitions include reference to the truth, presuming a stability for that notion that from the beginning, from these terms' roots, spawns the contradictions addressed here. The *testimonio*'s content is, in the very word, advertised as true, therefore legitimating the project; however, struggles to authenticate the text's truthful appearance according to an anticipated preconception of what the truth *should* sound like produce absences or contradictions that may be glossed over, or, if noted, can signal another sort of truth in the text's process in addition to the accuracy of its content.

"To legitimate" is to prove or justify the truth of something or the character of a person or thing in conformity to the law. [3] Whose law? Before whom does one legitimate oneself and with what authority? How do, or must, the disenfranchised legitimate themselves? How are boundaries of truth and identity shifted in order to legitimate? "Testimony" is an attestation or affirmation; a document authorized by a scribe or notary in which a fact is authenticated, a document entirely or partially copied or summarized by way of a report; proof, justification or verification of the truth. [4] "Testimony" both legitimates as verification of the truth and depends upon the "scribe or notary" for legitimation. Who authorizes the "scribe or notary"–the transcriber–to authenticate, copy or summarize? Why do the privileged need testimonies of the marginalized to legitimate their views or themselves? How do privileged women speak through other women's experiences?

Authority acts to lend legitimacy to the person or thing that then receives legitimate status. Leigh Gilmore notes in relation to women's autobiographical writing: "Some higher authority or recourse to its function is a fixture in scenes where truth is at issue, for it is necessary in this construction of truth telling to speak to someone" (121). Certain characteristics traditionally lend the power of authority: a sanctioned position in the hierarchy established by dominant groups and their discourses; possession of certain knowl-

---

[2] See such sources as Roberto González Echeverría's *Myth and Archive* on legal discourse in Latin American letters.

[3] Definition adapted from *Diccionario de la lengua española de la Real Academia Española* (twenty-first edition, 1992).

[4] Definition adapted from *Diccionario de la lengua española de la Real Academia Española* (twenty-first edition, 1992).

edge, of *the* truth; the power to make people listen, to create an audience. Thomas Docherty's reference to the connection between the Latin origins of "author" and "reader," and the authority to write a law that must be followed, again highlights underlying legal discourse as well as the question of collective versus individual subjectivity, significant to the *testimonio*'s legitimacy and political meaning. A proposed law had to be read and debated critically before the Roman Senate until Augustus, when this authority passed from the Senate to one person with the authority to determine the meaning of written law (Docherty 6), the authority to interpret a text's "truth." "Author" becomes singular. In the context of a court of law, the truth is then sought in an *individual's* testimony, then various individuals' interpretations considered collectively. In testimonial writing, the individual subject carries the moral weight of representing a collective experience, a position simultaneously empowering through sheer numbers and disempowering through the group's possible continuance at the margins as a monolithic entity. Moreover, should the group be revealed as not monolithic, should the individual's *testimonios* contradict each other, both potentially lose authority. The testimonial subject's collective status harkens to the word "author's" Latin roots and aims to redefine authority. John Beverley places this redefinition in *testimonio*'s historical context of solidarity with armed liberation struggle where *testimonio* "marked a new site of discursive authority, which challenged the authority of the 'great writer' to establish the reality principle of Latin American culture and development" ("Real" 281). The clash between *testimonio*'s act of challenging traditional authority and legitimation, and its simultaneous reliance on them for dissemination of the testimonial text points back to the clear correspondence between current discussions of identity in feminist theory, feminist ethnography, and testimonial discourse.

Neither as law makers nor as witnesses have women historically possessed legitimacy. The *testigo*, he who has *testiculi*,[5] has not

---

[5] *Testigo* and *testículo* are both derived from the Latin *testis*, witness. *Testigo* originates from the verb *testiguar*, which derives from *testificare* in Latin, a combination of *testis* (*testigo*) and *facere* (*hacer*). *Testículo* derives from *testis* by way of *testiculus*, "testigo de la virilidad." (See Joan Corominas and José A. Pascual, *Diccionario crítico etimológico castellano e hispánico*, vol. 5, Madrid: Gredos, 1983, 478).

been a woman, since women have been considered untruthful. [6] Therefore the issue of authority in women's *testimonios* and through women's *testimonios* becomes especially crucial, especially problematic. A lack of authority has certainly meant silence for men belonging to disenfranchised groups as well as for women. Women, however, have been doubly silenced within those groups and before more privileged women. Limited access to education has denied both men and women access to writing. Women, however, have been excluded from writing as unnecessary to their designated role. As I have explained, I concentrate on women's writing not just for these reasons but also for the ramifications that the transcriber-speaker relationship has for assumptions about female identity and the nature of female relationships. Also relevant here is legitimacy's usage in reference to legitimate offspring that guarantees continuity of patriarchal genealogy, maintaining the stability of the family, of the male surname, and thus of meaning. Legitimate meaning is singular, not open to other interpretations. Speaking idealistically, authority through an alternative female "genealogy" could arise from relationships among women and becomes one of the many motives for women writing-transcribing other women's testimonies. As Ruth Behar asserts, "The woman who is turning others into the object of her gaze is herself already an object of the gaze" ("Out of Exile" 2), lending a certain urgency, *theoretically* lessening the distance between transcriber and speaker. [7] The texts examined in this chapter and the next at the same time dispel temptations to believe an idealized sisterhood. As Doris Sommer points out in "Taking a Life," "feminist enthusiasm" underestimates differences among women and overestimates the "dissolution of difference," creating a monolithic universalism (921-2). Further ahead I will develop the idea that expecting a certain performance of truthfulness from *testimonio*, without legitimating a broader definition of truth to include contradictions resulting from necessary shifts and negotiations of a disadvantaged position, risks a similar silencing homogenization.

From the U.S. perspective the "feminist" in feminist ethnography is variously read as non-exploitative; sensitive to multiplicity of identity and partial identifications; with poststructuralist ethnogra-

---

[6] See Leigh Gilmore's introduction to her *Autobiographics*.
[7] Patai ("US" 143-4) and Stacey (111-3) cite examples of feminist ethnographies that engage in a naive sisterhood of sympathetic interaction.

phy, conscious and cautious of the power relationships inherent in ethnographic methodology; concerned with uniting writing with political action; engaged in an experimental ethnography that uses literary elements in response to failure of the positivist science of ethnography. Nevertheless, the reality of socio-economic differences between transcriber and testimonial subject, particularly in a Latin American context, belies the narrowing separation between the two that some (U.S.) feminist researchers have advocated and seen as particularly feminist.

In fact, Kamala Visweswaran views imposed silence as a tool of feminist ethnography when feminist ethnography theorizes "a kind of agency in which resistance can be framed by silence, a refusal to speak" (51). For Visweswaran, imposed silence transformed into instrument becomes a method of analyzing power among *women* in feminist ethnography (51). In other words, feminist ethnography should involve self-reflection on the obstacles to non-exploitative identification between female transcriber and narrator, contradicting the supposed potential of feminist ethnography: "locating the self in the experience of oppression in order to liberate it" (Visweswaran 19). The narrator's resistant silence, or detour around certain facts, makes impossible the location of the transcriber's self in the experience of silence since to enact that role would mean silencing the testimonial text's production, obviously counter to the urgency of disseminating the life story contained therein. A feminist ethnology based on "such traditionally feminine capacities as intuition, empathy, and relationship" thus undermines its liberational project through essentialist blindness to its own processes (Stacey 111-12 and *passim*). The dilemma silence poses for notions of feminist ethnography appears in and problematizes Poniatowska's and Burgos Debray's projects, since the two transcribers exhibit tendencies toward identification with the narrator and therefore, paradoxically, with resistant silence that comes to question the project's veracity and legitimacy on conventional terms. Silence begins to undermine authority's legitimacy, its right to invasively question. Thus, the text undermines the transcriber's identification with the narrator, for the reasons explained by Visweswaran and Stacey, and undermines her legitimation through the narrator. The silences in *Hasta no verte, Jesús mío* and *Me llamo Rigoberta Menchú* resist identification and perform the silencing that facile identification could impose.

JESUSA'S CONTRADICTORY SILENCE IN PONIATOWSKA'S *HASTA NO VERTE, JESÚS MÍO*

Silence in the testimonial texts studied in this chapter does not denote an absence as the opposite of language, but rather a problematic strategy, a circumstance imposed from outside, a silencing, or an absence of representative space: those voices without representation in written language that Tillie Olsen described in *Silences*. As resistance these silences have of course functioned as languages in themselves, like a will to say what is not permitted, as languages of double meanings to hide the truth (Castillo 40-41), as Sor Juana's negotiation of "saber" ("knowing") and "no decir" ("not saying"). In legal discourse silence is defense before representatives of the law's authority. Resistant silence appears in *Hasta no verte* as a demonstration of Jesusa Palancares's strong personality before authority and as a rhetorical device that draws out the many self-contradictions in this and other testimonial texts. Jesusa's stance certainly seems to support Doris Sommer's adamant assertion that Jesusa is not a poor marginalized woman who is easily appropriated or an object of pity for whom we must fight (Sommer "Taking"). Silence is a weapon of independence through knowledge of a truth withheld:

> Mi papá se enojó porque yo venía hablando la [*sic*] idioma zapoteca con los muchachos tehuanos de la corporación. Ellos me hablaban en la idioma yo les contestaba porque yo me enseñé de chica en Tehuantepec con la mamá de mi madrastra. Y mi papá me alcanzó y me regañó. Yo no le dije nada. (*Hasta no verte* 78-9)

> My father got angry because I got to talking Zapotec with the Tehuano guys in the company. They spoke to me in that language and I answered them because I taught myself Zapotec when I was little in Tehuantepec with my stepmother's mother. And my father caught up with me and scolded me. I didn't say anything to him. [8]

Jesusa's father scolds her for speaking a language unknown to him, in this case a language taught by a figure of feminine and maternal

---

[8] All translations are mine unless otherwise noted.

authority, and a language of inferior status in Spanish-speaking society. Although her father attempts to prohibit the unfamiliar language, Zapotec places communication and Jesusa outside paternal and moral control; outside the law of the father. She prefers silence to a language that would place her in an inferior position. Later, she does not respond to her father's calls while she hides from him: "se me trabaron las quijadas, se me hizo un graznido en la garganta y me quedé silencia" ("my jaws jammed shut, my throat croaked, and I kept silent"; 79). Jesusa resists through maintaining silence or through speaking a language silenced before the dominant language. Jesusa's description of her silence is also modified by a strong personal marker in the word "silencia," a word reminiscent of Sor Juana's "yo despierta" ("I awake"). "Silencia" departs from the noun "silencio" or the passive adjective "silenciada" to insert a gender marker that asserts Jesusa's active choice in remaining silent, not her being silenced. She *is* silence. "Silencia" serves not only as one of Jesusa's colloquial idiosyncracies preserved by Poniatowska for authenticity, but also as an emphatic statement of female identity that breaks from the dominant language one expects in written texts.

In this instance and throughout *Hasta no verte* Jesusa lives in silence, whether imposed by others, brought by solitude, or used as an act of resistance and self-defense. Paradoxically, the ostensible purpose of Poniatowska's text, and the purpose of the *testimonio* and the *novela testimonial*, is to translate silence into a dominant written language in order that silence might speak for itself, usually as a voice that challenges what that dominant language itself represents. Mediated testimonial discourse as a written medium works contrary to one of Jesusa's defiant tactics, *and* sets up an attack on its own methods. While in the long run resistant silence offers a limited political strategy since only through privileged means of communication does the testimony's impact increase,[9] the strategy is prevalent in the texts studied in this chapter. Silence becomes most powerful in fact through its representation or suggestion in the transcription process rather than in the powerless silence imposed on the narrators or the groups they are meant to represent.

Returning again to Sor Juana, in an oft-quoted passage she

---

[9] Debra Castillo points this out as well in her discussion of silence as resistance (40-41).

explains how her silence must be represented and interpreted: "casi me he determinado a dejarlo al silencio; pero como éste es cosa negativa, aunque explica mucho con el énfasis de no explicar, es necesario ponerle algún breve rótulo para que se entienda lo que se pretende que el silencio diga; y si no, dirá nada el silencio, porque ése es su propio oficio: decir nada" ("I have almost decided to leave it in silence; but since the latter is a negative thing, although it explains much by the emphasis on not explaining, it requires a brief note so that one understands what the silence is supposed to say; and if not, the silence will say nothing, because that is its job: to say nothing"; 828). Among other points in her well-known essay "Las tretas del débil" ("Tricks of the weak"), Josefina Ludmer investigates the relationship between "(no) decir" ("(not) saying") and "(no) saber" ("(not) knowing") in *La Respuesta*. Ludmer explains how Sor Juana's rhetorical devices disassociate "no decir" and "no saber," whereby the first does not denote the latter. Sor Juana does not say what she knows and knows what not to say. Silence's authority lies in what the testimonial subject chooses not to reveal. In the testimonial context this weakens the transcriber's legitimacy as conduit for "the whole truth and nothing but the truth" but seduces, as Doris Sommer has also shown, by indicating there is something we still have not discovered. We, unlike the narrator, cannot speak authentically about her experience. Silence is a tactic on the part of the silenced that exposes the processes of the text's transcription, a barrier to be overcome, and a means to reinforce authenticity. Silence is one of the factors of legitimation that expose the inherent paradoxes of testimonial discourse and link Jesusa's feisty silence and her solitude to uncertain veracity that destabilizes the text's authority, although not necessarily its authenticity. Significantly, most examples of Jesusa's silence incorporate oblique references to the interlocutor and the process of transcription, reinforcing my point about silence needing explanation. For instance, while describing her situation caring for the grandchildren of her *madrina*, Jesusa says: "Fuera de los chiquillos no tenía con quién hablar, porque mi único amigo era el metate. De eso me viene lo callado. Hasta ahora de vieja me he puesto a hablar un poquito" ("Aside from the little kids I didn't have anyone to talk to, because my only friend was the metate [for grinding corn]. That's why I don't talk much. Only now as an old woman have I begun to talk a little"; 56). Poniatowska's intervention also appears in Jesusa's

recounting the episode when she and other women are captured by
Zapata's troops, an episode she was sworn to keep secret at the
time: "Yo hasta ahorita se lo estoy platicando" ("I haven't talked
about it until right now"; 77). Jesusa may refer to the fact that in
Poniatowska she has an interlocutor to whom she has begun to
speak, and yet suggests that she has been silent until now, contradicting her own narration in which she tends to emphasize her ability to defend herself verbally as well as physically.

Nevertheless, giving testimony to one's life story does function
as self-defense, a central point in my later discussion of *Quarto de
Despejo*. Jesusa's silence linked to her solitude is sometimes portrayed as a conscious choice, at other times as a consequence of
abandonment. At one point Jesusa denies that she is alone because
of circumstance but rather "porque no me gusta que me gobierne
nadie" ("because I don't like anyone to tell me what to do"; 153).
In another moment where the rhythm of the narration accelerates
with polysyndeton and particularly evokes the spoken language of
testimonio, Jesusa's almost wistful sensation of solitude and abandonment becomes keen:

> Y yo siempre sola, y el muchacho que recogí de chiquito y que se
> fue y me dejó más sola y me saludas a nunca vuelvas y no es por
> ai María voltéate y yo como lazarina, encerrada en mi cazuela, y
> en la calle cada vez menos brava y menos peleonera porque me
> hice vieja y ya no se me calienta la sangre y se me acabaron las
> fuerzas y se me cayó el pelo y nomás me quedaron unas clavijas
> de dientes, rascándome con mis uñas, pero ya ni uñas tengo de
> tantos uñeros que me salieron en la lavadera. (147-148)

> And me always alone, and the boy I took in when he was little
> went off and left me even lonelier, say goodbye and never come
> back, and it isn't that way, María, turn around, and me like a lep-
> er, closed up in my pots and pans, and less and less fierce in the
> street and less and less wanting to fight because I got old and my
> blood doesn't boil like before and I've lost my energy and my
> hair's fallen out and I only have a few pegs for teeth, I'd scratch
> myself but I don't even have fingernails because so many got
> ingrown and came out in the laundry sink. [10]

---

[10] Translation here adapted from *Here's To You, Jesusa!*, trans. Deanna Heikkinen (New York: Farrar, Straus and Giroux, 2001).

Deborah Shaw and Beth E. Jörgensen illuminate contradictions such as this one in their insightful essays on Jesusa Palancares where they utilize Paul Smith's concept of "individual subject," a term usefully describing the dialectic between Jesusa's agency as individual and her subjection (Shaw 194), and her alternating resistance and conformity (Jörgensen 33). Shaw connects Jesusa's postmodern, shifting identity and her contradictory self-representation to the reality of the situation where she relates her story to a literate writer. "Her realities are constantly being interrupted," forcing movement between conflicting positions for survival in certain circumstances (193-4). The above passage supports Shaw's observation of Jesusa's shifting between agent and subject, between denying the capacity for emotion and revealing emotion (Shaw 200), and, in this particular case, shifting between the desire for solitude and being abandoned. Rigoberta Menchú speaks of similar shifts in identity when she had to disguise herself, her Mayan identity, her Quiché identity, or her name, in order to protect herself in exile (Menchú 141, 159, 246).

In addition to illustrating Jesusa's silence that arises from solitude and produces contradictions, this passage questions indirectly the relationship between transcriber and testimonial subject as one characterized by sympathy: ". . . y me saludas a nunca vuelvas y no es por ai María voltéate . . . ." '. . . say goodbye and never come back, and it isn't that way, María, turn around . . . .' These words told to the interlocutor underscore their separate worlds through the possibility of the transcriber's abandoning the narrator upon the transcription's completion. As the epigraph to *Hasta no verte* suggests, nobody will pay much attention the day she no longer exists and they will be lying if the say they will feel her loss: "Si ya no le sirvo para nada, ¿qué carajos va a extrañar? Y en el taller tampoco. ¿Quién quiere usted que me extrañe si ni adioses voy a mandar?" ("If I'm already useless, what the hell is anyone going to miss? And not at the workshop either. Who do you think will miss me if I'm not even going to send goodbyes?"; 8). This hint of doubt in the interlocutor's commitment fosters the sense that communicating one's experience, breaking the silence, creating the *testimonio*, connotes weakness or frivolousness: "Ninguno dice nada. Nadie tiene que andar diciendo nada. A mí cuando me pasó algo, no fui a decirle a mi madrastra" ("No one says anything. No one has to go around saying anything. When something happened to me I didn't run and tell my stepmother"; 49). "Yo ya no daba pie con bola, si decirles que sí o que no. Soy muy desconfiada" ("I couldn't do anything right anymore, if I say yes or no. I don't trust anyone"; 217). More directly: "No con que les cuente yo mi vida, se me van a quitar las dolencias" ("It's not as if when I tell you my life story, my pain will go away"; 98). Why bother? Jesusa suggests that breaking silence does not necessarily mean just that. What, then, is the legitimate purpose of an engaged intellectual writing down a life if nothing will change? Considering Shaw's arguments and the exaggerated tone of Jesusa's dismissals, the surreptitious challenges to Poniatowska's project construct a pose that like silence produces contradictory results that prohibit grasping the text based on singular veracity. Yet, even if Jesusa were speaking completely forthrightly here, the content alone of these assertions questions the project. If we do read these words as a pose, Jesusa's narration at that moment becomes what it should not appear to be, in order to satisfy a reader's desire for a straightforward glimpse into this other's life: a creative manipulation. Creative manipulation is not commonly accepted testimonial truth, a point that will gain even more importance when we turn to *Me llamo Rigoberta Menchú*.

Along with questioning the purpose of exposing herself to the transcriber, Jesusa therefore adopts a pose questioning the *value* of what she has to say. Nevertheless, this gesture, reminiscent of Ludmer's reading of Sor Juana, results in highlighting what she indeed has to say. Jesusa denies having anything to say and thus having any reason to break her silence, yet the entire book that follows contradicts this, just as Sor Juana's letter belies the ignorance she confesses. Jesusa asserts: "No puedo decir que he sido buena. Nada puedo decir" ("I can't say I've been good. I can't say anything"; 13). This phrase's placement immediately before a pause in the text serves as emphasis and similarly gives the reader a pause in which to consider its accuracy. Just as Sor Juana utilized a self-effacing stance as a "treta del débil," Jesusa uses solitude and silence as a resistance tactic, as a diversion that must be contradicted by testimonial speech, which in turn disguises the silences its discursive requirements produce. Sommer views the flood of information following Jesusa's protestations as another strategy: to withhold information by burying it amidst endless detail ("Taking a Life" 935). By downplaying the content of what she testifies Jesusa also disguises the passages where she delivers criticisms to the author and disguises her authority behind silence.

TRUTH, IDENTITY, AND THE *NOVELA TESTIMONIAL*

Since Jesusa retains information from others in her narrative, she clearly alludes to her withholding or altering information. Silence therefore returns us to questions of verisimilitude and authenticity around which much of the struggle for legitimacy revolves. As charged as the term *testimonio* may be with promises of truth and "the real thing," veracity or verisimilitude should not constitute the sole basis for value judgment or conclusions about the text's content or the definition of *testimonio*. Excellent essays have explained various sides of the truth issue for testimonial discourse, yet often they exhibit contradictions that reliance on a singular representation of truth produces. [11] This is not to facilely restore the narrator's authority on the basis of a completely relativized notion of truth where anything goes. Thus do some opponents of post-structuralist theory oversimplify arguments like mine that consider the discursive representation of experience and truth, which does produce contradictions because of very real situations, not academic fashion. Those contradictions include discrepancies in Jesusa's testimony, untrustworthy appearances, readers' expectations, ambivalent agency, and the tension between a crisis of hegemonic truth and the essentializing effect of alternate truths. Shaw's essay coincides with some of my points here, as do aspects of Moreiras's and Colás's 1996 essays on *testimonio*. Though invalid as a stable rhetoric, the question of veracity must be addressed here since its very instability supports this chapter's main points about *testimonio*'s inherent contradictions, and because truth's compelling attraction has created a considerable quantity of critical attention. The veracity of the testimonial text and the consequent public interest in the narrator's testimony contribute to the project's legitimacy, supplying the transcriber with the authority to record the story. Truth's importance has emerged from the need to publicize very real, silenced experience; however, the rigid demands on that truth work against the genre's aims of authorizing those experiences. Faith in the ability to step outside structures that silence the marginalized in order to transmit a marginalized, essential, and pure

---

[11] Deborah Shaw and George Yúdice have explicitly addressed the futility of sorting out one consistent truth in testimonial writing.

truth simplifies the speaker and testimonial discourse. In a broader context, the truth's actual multiplicity naturally lies at the heart of debates on representativity and identity, and at the heart of textual violence and the potential weaknesses of theories that attempt to speak from the margins, all issues addressed further ahead.

The link between truth and identity makes it understandable that Jesusa's inconsistent self-representation constitutes one of the principal contradictions produced by reliance on the truth as criterion of *testimonio*'s value. According to traditional rules of authority linked to stable truth, her inconsistencies will inevitably delegitimize her testimony. Since authorial intervention is more explicit in the *novela testimonial* than in the *testimonio* one naturally thinks that verisimilitude rather than truth becomes the issue in *Hasta no verte*. Separating verisimilitude from *testimonio*, however, begins the vicious circle of deciding whose truth is definitive. We rightly fear that to deny that real story could reproduce the silencing used to deny the pasts and identities of victims of disappearance and oppression. Shoshana Felman writes, "To testify is thus not merely to narrate but to commit oneself . . . to *take responsibility* –in speech–for history or for the truth of an occurrence" (39-40). Nevertheless, the rhetorical paradigm of stable truths lends itself, paradoxically, to essentialization of the testimonial subject as a perpetually marginalized identity, limiting his or her choices for self-representation.

For these reasons, when considering, for instance, the difference between *testimonio* and *novela testimonial*, of greater significance than truth content is that both variations of testimonial discourse arise from a historically marginalized experience and exist in order to raise a privileged audience's consciousness of official truth's deceptions, to denounce abuses obscured by official rhetoric. George Yúdice has asserted that the dichotomy truth-fiction lacks meaning in trying to understand the *testimonio*, but rather that the *testimonio*'s *modus operandi* "es la construcción comunicativa de una praxis solidaria y emancipatoria" ("is the communicative construction of a praxis of solidarity and emancipation"; 216). Both Yúdice and Shaw indicate how departure from stable truths in testimonial discourse can be reconciled with the social realities from which the discourse originates. The present study addresses how departure from notions of stable truth *in tension with* a persistent dependence on notions of stable truth in fact outlines a key to testimonial writing's denouncement of oppressive and appropriative mechanisms, in addition to its denunciatory content. Both *testimonio* and *novela testimonial* disabuse the reader of a singular concept of truth, the truth therefore constituting a manipulable notion in these two forms of text also concerned with and dependent upon communicating an unquestionably concrete experience of deprivation or oppression. Both the *novela testimonial* and the *testimonio* are expected to shoulder a responsibility to the truth and history at the same time they investigate the validity of those concepts. Although the *novela testimonial* is indeed a novel, the testimonial element still lends authenticity to the text and leads a reader like Cynthia Steele to analyze Jesusa's life as portrayed by Poniatowska along sociological lines. [12] Although *testimonio* is not a novel it manifests fictions or elaborations of memory. Elzbieta Sklodowska sees testimonial texts as a "peculiar mixture of experience, creation, manipulation and invention, more akin, perhaps, to a novel, than to a scientific document" ("Poetics" 256). Testimonial texts stand at various points on the ambiguous territory between document and fiction just as they negotiate a space between important, fixed truths and the dissolution of preconceived truths imposed on the testimonial speaker. The fictional or elaborated side of the testimony is, however, relatively greater and may *announce itself more self-reflexively* in the *novela testimonial*, producing an explicit display of the conflicts present in all mediated testimonial discourse.

ORAL AND WRITTEN TRUTH

The oral quality of both *novela testimonial* and *testimonio*, resulting from translation of spoken to written words, also has an impact on the issue of veracity that cannot be ignored. The transcription from oral to written language leaves remnants of another concept of truthfulness that guarantees tension within the written format of testimonial discourse. Compensating for silence is carried out by transforming the voiced word into the silent, written word while retaining the illusion of orality. The need for consistency in

---

[12] See Steele's discussion of *Hasta no verte* in *Politics and Gender in the Mexican Novel 1968-1988: Beyond the Pyramid* (Austin, TX: U Texas P, 1992).

the testimony in order that it *appear* true, the need for lack of contradictions, and the singular speaking voice are preconceptions in
written culture that negate much of the oral nature of the interview
process. In the final written form different criteria are imposed
upon the testimony. Thus, the transcriber must alter the original
material to maintain written criteria for accuracy or must leave the
inconsistencies and make the text's accuracy questionable in some
eyes, bringing to mind the cliché that sometimes a lie is more credi-
ble than truth. For instance, Jesusa's contradictory statements about
silence might not only refer to the multiple implications of silence
discussed earlier, but also to a transcription process which forms a
collage of different moods recorded at each dispersed interview and
of the different informants who together created the figure of
Jesusa Palancares.

Indeed, as Walter Ong has pointed out, objectivity itself, the
idea of a truth without subjective intervention, is a concept made
possible by writing. Writing stabilizes the words and style of the
narrative, if not necessarily the narrative's possible meanings and
interpretations, thereby eliminating participatory variations by the
teller. Recounting the past in oral cultures brings with it expected
variations within formulaic expressions; in fact this is the source of
the teller's creativity rather than the creation of innovative material
we expect in writing (Ong 46). The teller may be an individual; the
words, however, are collective, the result of contributions, set
phrases and variations through time. With reference to collective
identity in *Me llamo Rigoberta Menchú*, Sommer quotes Georges
Gusdorf as stating that the fact that a history is told by one person
is "un síntoma de penetración occidental" ("a symptom of western
penetration"; Sommer, "Sin secretos" 142 and "Not Just" 111)–and
it is a symptom of *written* penetration. The characteristics that Ong
describes refer, however, to primary oral cultures: those that have
had little or no contact with writing. Orality in primary oral cultures is characterized by acceptable subjective variations and at the
same time little experimentation outside traditional patterns (Ong
41, 45). In the written culture of document and the courtroom, on
the other hand, oral testimony carries the expectations of written
truth. Although sanctioned to bring new elements to a case or story,
oral testimony is not allowed to vary from telling to telling by one
person, who is not allowed to represent others, or it will lose its
credibility. The audience no longer listens unless departure from

these norms is announced by the designation "literature" or "fiction." For all its instability oral testimony is subordinate to written testimony in written culture. Testimonial texts are not products of oral culture, but of written culture; yet to maintain authenticity they display some characteristics of oral origins. Ironically the subjective variations that would be most "authentic" and "true" exceed the limits of literate authenticity, thus only disguising testimonial texts as oral in a sense.

On the other hand, only by denying the complexity of the testimonial narrators' situations can we fit them into the role of authentic representatives of primary oral culture. The narrators of most published Latin American *testimonios* and *novelas testimoniales* live in a world structured by writing even if they are illiterate. These books' narrators acknowledge writing's authority, thus recognizing its authority in the person of the transcriber. After all, if they did not consider writing's power to reach elites or otherwise transcend their communities, their interest in the testimonial process would probably be limited.[13] For example, as Jesusa speaks from old age she regrets not being able to read: "Lo que yo quería era que me enseñaran a leer pero no se preocuparon [las monjas]. Ahora ¿ya para qué? Ya voy para el camposanto" ("What I wanted was for them to teach me to read but [the nuns] didn't bother. Now, why bother? I'm on my way to the graveyard"; 52). She and other testimonial subjects embed literacy in their relationship to others who have power over them. Her stepmother, whom she described as "una persona estudiosa, instruida y sabía [*sic*]" ("a studious person, educated and wise"; 13), wanted her to go to a government school,

---

[13] Other examples of this respect before the influence and power of the written word appear in comments by Cristina Pacheco and in the *testimonios* of Domitila Barrios de Chungara and Benita Galeana. In a talk given at the Universidad de las Americas in Mexico City, in November 1992, Cristina Pacheco mentioned how various people from the poorest areas of Mexico City had asked her to write their stories that without appearing in print would never be heard. Domitila overcame many difficulties to be able to attend school for some years, and Benita learns the value of literacy in society when two suitors abandon her after she cannot read their letters. When it is convenient for them the men in Benita's life want her to read, and she criticizes the subordinate role allocated to women in the Communist Party regarding literacy. The Party leaves her in ignorance, not helping her to develop her potential, in part by not teaching her to read: "Veía que camaradas muy capaces e inteligentes, eran los que más mal trataban a sus compañeras, con desprecio, sin ocuparse de educarlas, engañándolas con otras mujeres como cualquier pequeño burgués y, en cambio, los primeros en decir: '¡Son unas putas!', cuando la mujer anda con otro" (Galeana 146-7).

but her father sent her to a convent. Jesusa's husband Pedro dominates her by reading to her without teaching her to read for herself. In fact, when he asks her what she understood from what he read aloud to her, he disagrees with her interpretation: "–¡Oh contigo no se puede hablar! No, no es así, no te fijaste bien" ("Oh, I can't talk to you! It's not like that, you didn't pay attention"; 115). Her understanding of the text is not legitimated. Carolina Maria de Jesus, who does write her own testimony, recalls the joy and empowerment of learning to read: "Percebi que os que sabem ler têm mais posibilidades de compreensão. Se desajustarem-se na vida, poderão reajustar-se" ("I saw that those who know how to read have greater chances to gain knowledge. If their lives fall apart, they'll be able to get themselves together again"; *Diário* 126). Then, the first book she reads and analyzes is about a slave, linking her thinking abilities to understanding racial relations in Brazil.

Taking into account the testimonial subjects' immersion in literate culture and the value they give to the written text, to what extent are *testimonios* purely oral? Just as the testimonial process involves intermediaries between an underrepresented culture and a dominant culture (the unusual individual(s) representing a broad historical experience and then the transcriber), the narrator's original conversation with the transcriber and then the testimonial texts themselves are two intermediate stages between oral and written cultures. The content's origin lies in the voice, yet the text's origin as a concept for publication lies in written culture. Regarding Rigoberta Menchú's *testimonio*, Claudia Ferman describes this as a *mestizaje* of mediums and languages whose "literary discursiveness" does not undermine its orality (166). My point here regards the exigency to uphold the appearance of transparent transcription. Oral inflections in *testimonio* to reproduce the testimonial subject's language work to minimize the transcription's presence. The testimonial text takes on oral elements, disguises itself as oral as the transcriber attempts to relinquish authority to the narrator, and emphasizes the narrator's position outside mainstream written culture even if the narrator's experience entails constant negotiation with that culture. Perhaps one truly oral aspect of testimonial texts lies paradoxically in the transcriber whose task is to fix the testimony in writing: the identification of transcriber with testimonial subject which reflects instances of empathetic identification by oral performers with the hero of the tale (Ong 46).

Poniatowska certainly retains the earthy, Mexican idiosyncratic sounds of Jesusa's language, reminding us that this is what the testimonial subject really said. Jesusa's and any testimonial subject's voice must sound "authentic." As Etter-Lewis points out in her discussion of black women's autobiography, such a situation can actually function to support stereotypes as well as produce a resistance text. She writes that "black autobiographers were forced to invent devices and strategies that would endow their stories with the appearance of authenticity." To avoid alienating the white audience, the black autobiographer could not stray far from black stereotypes (52). Similarly, Sylvia Molloy points out that Juan Francisco Manzano's autobiography "must be incorporated into the white literary establishment (and thus validated by it) if it is to be heeded at all" (397). *Testimonio* is expected to reveal intimate reality, yet the distance between testimonial subject and reading public is enforced, and since the transcriber usually belongs to the same group as the reading audience, the distance widens between transcriber and narrator. The distance lessens the effect of intimacy that would supposedly ensure we are getting the real story. Simply by her identity Jesusa possesses the aura of having been there, [14] but, just as the text legitimizes her identity and her version of the truth, the hegemonic concept of truth that directs either the testimonial process or the interpretive process, or both, threatens to silence that identity by simplifying it. In such a mode, Jesusa embodies the truth simply by her identity, and by her simple identity.

KEEPING UP APPEARANCES

The disguises that result from testimonial discourse's internal oppositions, whereby the texts often must pretend to be what they are not in order to *convincingly* translate one reality into another, ultimately lead to the partial displacement of the speakers' voices, a point developed in my comments ahead on *Me llamo Rigoberta Menchú*. Continuing for now the discussion of Poniatowska's text, the concept of disguise appears on several levels of *Hasta no verte*, from its orality to the figure of the *nagual* and Jesusa's distrust of

---

[14] My using the word "aura" here echoes Moreiras's sense of "auratic practice." See the section "Vengeance and Sacrifice" in Chapter 3.

appearances. In describing how her husband Pedro maintained the appearance of a good husband while in fact he beat her, Jesusa makes one of her typical comments on appearances: "Aparentaba, pero tenía la música por dentro. Parecía ser una cosa, pero era otra muy distinta" ("He pretended, but he was something else inside. He seemed to be one thing, but he was something very different"; 97). When demystifying the *nagual*, according to indigenous beliefs a human's parallel animal form, she complains the belief is only a ruse in order to steal: "Puro cuento y pura conveniencia de las sin-vergüenzas" ("Sheer lies and sheer convenience for the shameless"; 124). She describes the Mexican Revolution as a "guerra mal enten-dida" ("misunderstood war"; 94) whose revolutionaries did nothing for the poor and "me caen como patada en los. . . bueno como si yo tuviera güevos" ("I like them like a kick in the. . . well as if I had balls"; 137). As has become well known, Rigoberta Menchú also refutes dominant discourses about the Spanish conquest (Burgos Debray 170) and *ladino* interpretations of the Bible, used to keep the indigenous submissive (Burgos Debray 245). The need to see beyond appearances is certainly not a new trope, but does reflect the presence of textual disguises on a deeper level, where roles and expected authority relationships are interchanged or blurred. As Tabuenca Córdoba has noted, the locus of the beauty salon in the Obra Espiritual vision that commences *Hasta no verte* serves as metaphor for the disguises present throughout the book since the beauty salon is where one receives a new face (Tabuenca 8). The *testimonio* and *novela testimonial* must disguise their rhetorical side to conform to readings that do not take into account the deeper process producing the text's surface and that take contradictions at face value. Daphne Patai, for example, divorces narrative strategies from deeper truths in her criticism of John Beverley's analysis of *tes-timonio* as a "strategy of subaltern memory." For Patai, falsehoods as tactical choices have "no bearing on the *deeper* questions of truth and trust" ("Whose Truth?" 273). Deeper questions do in fact inspire certain narrative choices. Contradictions in testimonial texts are indeed problematic, but not because they undermine the testi-monial subject's authority in denouncing a social or historical situa-tion. The contradictions arise from the negotiation of that situation. In this regard questionable veracity is especially brought to light in *Hasta no verte*, where elements admitted as partly fictional may contribute to exposing disguises in all testimonial forms.

Jesusa thus cautions the alert reader to the pitfalls of believing the appearance of what he or she is reading, playing with the promise of the real thing desired by a reader complacently interpreting through the paradigm of singular truth according to predefined criteria, a reader mimicking the outward appearance of Jesusa's insistence on one truth: her own truth. [15] Seduced by the possibility of insight into a very different reality, the reader can be fooled into engaging in a set of truths that helped produce the silences motivating *testimonio* in the first place. Jesusa herself participates in a similar contradiction when she insists on her own version of events in the context of undermining official truths. With her insistence on one truth followed by textual examples that contradict her pose, all "truths" become suspect and the reader ought to assume a skeptical pose, doubting this testimony and the process behind it. While this skepticism thus allows a glimpse into testimonial discourse's subversive potential, as Deborah Shaw has demonstrated, continued association of stable truth with social reality draws the empathetic reader back into judging the *testimonio* based on a certain consistency.

Referring again to the instance where Pedro reads to Jesusa and rejects her interpretation (115), we find a reflection on the book's own production and consumption. Jesusa, in the position of listener, initially Poniatowska's role and ours through Poniatowska, supposedly misinterprets what is recounted to her by a reader with a fixed idea of the meaning of the story. This would seem to reinforce Jesusa's criticism of Poniatowska's (and the readers') interpretation and authority, though not her own. Poniatowska may misrepresent the story Jesusa tells her. Indeed, Poniatowska does misrepresent the real Jesusa, Josefina Bórquez, in order to hide her identity and enable her story to be told. In Lucille Kerr's words, she must lie to tell the truth (377). Even when referring to the flesh and blood woman's resistant reaction to Poniatowska's completed text, Poniatowska continues to call her "Jesusa." This flesh and blood Jesusa asserts that Poniatowska misunderstood her entirely, that Jesusa does not recognize herself in what is supposedly her life story told

---

[15] Jesusa's insistence on the absolute truth of her version of events and social codes of course adds greater irony to the orality of *Hasta no verte*. It is Jesusa, the "oral" informant, who defends one true interpretation, more closely associated with written cultures.

from her own lips: "El libro, ella lo rechaza, no le gusta . . . 'Usted inventa todo, son puras mentiras, no entendió nada, las cosas no son así'" ("The book, she rejects it, she doesn't like it. . . 'You make everything up, they're pure lies, you didn't understand anything, things aren't like that'"; "En micrófono" 160). Whether she means this or we have another example of her surly defiance, in Jesusa's/Bórquez's opinion, Poniatowska has conducted a misreading (or mishearing). Both Jesusa as collective character and Jesusa as flesh and blood, legitimated as narrators, act as judges, an authority who determines what is the truth.

Returning to the Jesusa of the text, in the scene with Pedro we nevertheless also encounter a questionable reader-teller-narrator. Jesusa disagrees with his interpretation and in other places emphasizes the fact that Pedro is not what he appears, and therefore is not to be believed. This introduces the possibility of multiple interpretations, multiple "truths" and unreliable narrators. Jesusa/Bórquez may take on gestures expected of her, aware of the authority of this journalist permitted to publish her words, who in turn is aware of the consumer's expectations. Allowing Jesusa/Bórquez to speak in fact exposes the shared authority disguised behind Poniatowska's "gesto ficticio" (fictitious gesture) of giving voice. Her testimony loses authority *when seen as a pose*. At the same time that Jesusa's and Bórquez's combative, strong personality challenges the author it also reminds us of the text's origins: in *Hasta no verte* the narrator is not the one who gives impetus to the project; it is Elena Poniatowska. Until the last page of the book the textual Jesusa is resistant. It is not until Poniatowska decides who can speak and chooses to write in Bórquez's and other women's language that the textual Jesusa's voice gains authority. It is Poniatowska who notices Bórquez's and others' silence and recognizes the limitations of silence as a political strategy.

Does this then mean Bórquez and other women are in fact so much raw material appropriated by Poniatowska, who maintains sole agency in the project? Doris Sommer's critique of reading from leftist intellectual guilt in "Taking a Life" exposes the naiveté and paternalism of such an interpretation. The question of agency Sommer forcefully raises is diabolical in the sense that Jesusa's sometimes contradictory actions or words respond to certain circumstances, as Shaw has shown, to Poniatowska's representation of Bórquez's reaction to the writer, and to Poniatowska's preparation

of the various interviews that comprise Jesusa before the anticipated reading public. Like mediated testimonial discourse's other
inherent contrarieties, the ambiguous agency of testimonial subject
and transcriber simply does not allow definitive conclusions about
who *truly* guides the final text at each moment. Clearly the logistics
of the transcription process undermine the ideal of clear-cut agency.
Neither Jesusa Palancares nor Josefina Bórquez is in charge of the
editing or the decision to write the book, a situation that challenges
the text's legitimacy. At the same time, as Sommer explains, under-
estimating the testimonial subject's ability to manipulate both her
testimony and Poniatowska is equally naive and patronizing to
boot. The informant as well as the transcriber is in the position of
controlling the testimony and its capacity to convince by *appearing*
authentic and unaltered. Jesusa as represented in *Hasta no verte*
seems perfectly aware of disguises, including that of verisimilitude.
Her protestations that Poniatowska is nothing but a bother, including the famous command that ends the novel ("Ahora ya no
chingue. Váyase. Déjeme dormir" 'Stop fucking with me. Leave, let
me sleep.'), put the transcriber, and us, in the place of asking for
more. As Sommer states it: "Jesusa's early refusals to talk are precisely what make us insist on hearing her" ("Taking" 915).

Typical of the contortions to which we lead ourselves in pursuit
of the real truth, we see Jesusa's defiance that leaves us wanting
more does again direct us to the fact that this was Poniatowska's
idea. On the other hand, if Jesusa is hiding some information and
has no investment in the project, why would she lie? Seen this way
her resistant stance contributes to her testimony's authenticity and
legitimacy, rather than undermining them. In "Taking a Life" Sommer asserts that if Poniatowska did manipulate the narrative, she
would have controlled its indifference and shrillness, would have
interpolated an intimacy undermined by Jesusa's tone. Poniatowska, according to Sommer, would have allowed us to imagine "few
or no political and cultural differences between the narrator and
her sororal other" (915). One could, however, see Jesusa's disallow-
ing false reconciliation of differences as a possible strategy by Poniatowska. While Sommer works to demonstrate Jesusa's defiant pose
as evidence of her agency unwilling to submit to idealist, guilt-
ridden, sisterhood-seeking, condescending readers who misread
Jesusa, Jesusa's interruptions and defiance may be attributable to
Poniatowska's agency. These qualities did attract Poniatowska to

Jesusa in the first place and they contribute to her authenticity. Sommer indeed refers to Jesusa's correspondence to Octavio Paz's mythologized Mexican hermeticism as an "authenticity" Poniatowska perceives ("Taking" 915). Here I am not just speaking of an authenticity based on Paz's work, but of an authenticity based on verisimilitude.

Nevertheless, precisely because it is not Jesusa's project, why not play with this privileged woman? The constant possibility of counter arguments demonstrates the circular nature of determining a mediated *testimonio*'s level of accuracy and non-exploitative ideal. I stress again that the weakness of reading for certain veridical qualities does not connote *testimonio*'s failure to communicate facts about a life experience different from our own that challenges our way of viewing certain accepted notions about historical events and privilege. The truths of Jesusa Palancares's narrative include the interpretability of truth, marginalization from hegemonic national history, necessary maneuvers to survive, and the general uncertainty of that survival and of the immediate future. For George Yúdice, this list would incorporate "la construcción comunicativa de una praxis solidaria y emancipatoria" ("is the communicative construction of a praxis of solidarity and emancipation"), and he adds: "De ahí que la dicotomía verdad/ficción carezca de sentido para comprender el *testimonio*" ("From there we see that the dichotomy truth/fiction makes no sense for understanding testimonio"; 216). The question of absolute truth versus fiction (or lies) does not create the key to testimonial discourse, but rather illuminates its slippery definitions and the question's inadequacy in describing the narrator's circumstances. Similarly, the question of whose agency determines the text is less conclusive than the constant ambiguity, the give and take, between transcriber and testimonial subject that eventually leads us away from an idealized notion of *testimonio* and toward the heart of an equally subversive aspect. The text *truthfully* reflects the uncertainty characterizing the testimonial subject's life. If we seek candid insight into the narrator's world, there it lies.

RIGOBERTA MENCHÚ'S APPEARANCES: SILENCE AND COLLECTIVE
IDENTITY

Similar manifestations of the contradictions arising from *testi-monio*'s problematic truth value appear in *Me llamo Rigoberta Menchú*, but with emphasis on issues of silence and collective versus individual identity. Both will link the futility of reconciling all the contradictions through interpretation of testimonial discourse with the broader questions of identity, violence, and critical theories addressed in this book. In addition, the next section explains the relevance of points covered here to the controversy sparked in December 1998 with publicity surrounding the publication of David Stoll's book *Rigoberta Menchú and the Story of All Poor Guatemalans*, where he refutes the truth of several episodes in Menchú's narration. The analysis in the present section accepts the information related in Menchú's testimony to examine the text as it stands, as a rhetorical construction about irrefutable human rights abuses and based on Menchú's interviews about her life in 1982. Afterwards I will turn to the problems raised by Stoll and the reactions to his book. When Menchú met with her testimony's transcriber, the well-connected Venezuelan anthropologist Elisabeth Burgos Debray, she was in France as representative of the Committee for Peasant Unity (CUC) after having lived in exile since 1980. At that point the Guatemalan army had brutally killed her parents and one brother, and she did not know the fate of her other siblings. [16] The late 1970s and early 1980s were especially violent years as the Guatemalan dictatorship repressed guerrilla insurgency and carried out a scorched earth policy against Mayan villages that produced a genocide of "more than a hundred thousand deaths, and more than a million refugees" (Arias, "Rigoberta Menchú's History" 5).

In *Me llamo Rigoberta Menchú*, as in *Hasta no verte, Jesús mío*, the uses of silence provide an appropriate entrance into questions of veracity. Both Elisabeth Burgos Debray and Rigoberta Menchú recognize silence's limitations, though Menchú emphasizes resistant silence and the importance of indigenous languages that lie outside

---

[16] See Menchú's 1998 book about her exile and how she came to know what happened to her other brothers and sisters.

ladino control. This "silence" before the dominant language has served as a survival tactic to preserve her culture, to resist absorption into ladino society and to fight genocide (Burgos Debray 9). At the same time, Menchú must translate her testimony into a dominant language associated with oppression to break silence, an act exhibiting the same contradictions evident in *Hasta no verte*. Moreover, what she reveals and does not reveal affects legitimation and self-representation in ways parallel to Poniatowska's text. In contrast, here we find less emphasis on the spoken quality of Menchú's voice–although present–and on the possibility of rhetorical guises, reflecting the fact that here the tensions exposed in Jesusa's story are buried a bit deeper.

Probably the most well-known characteristic of Menchú's famous testimony is well-guarded knowledge. Menchú reiterates the resistant silence of her people that arises not only from linguistic isolation but also from the careful guarding of secrets about indigenous customs and knowledge. Silence has meant more resources for self-protection: "Cuando empezamos a organizarnos, empezamos a emplear lo que habíamos ocultado. Nuestras trampas. Nadie lo sabía porque lo habíamos ocultado. Nuestras opiniones. Llega un cura a nuestras aldeas, todos los indígenas nos tapamos la boca" ("When we began to organise ourselves, we started using all the things we'd kept hidden. Our traps–nobody knew about them because they'd been kept secret. Our opinions–whenever a priest came to our village we all kept our mouths shut"; 196, 170). [17] As a disguise, a "treta del débil," the silence interpreted by outsiders as ignorance belies the knowledge and developed culture Menchú –partially–reveals in her testimony. Since the Indians have been silenced or their words misused when they did speak, "nosotros tampoco hemos abierto la boca por gusto" ("we haven't bothered to make ourselves heard just for the fun of it"; 196, 170). She does not speak for her own enjoyment, but only out of the necessity to tell enough to satisfy the needs of her testimony, perhaps reinforcing the candid impression of what she does tell, perhaps weakening the overall testimony's verisimilitude through the trope of information withheld. The community guards its secrets well (110) and

---

[17] All translations of quotations from *Me llamo Rigoberta Menchú* are from Elisabeth Burgos-Debray, ed. and intro., *I...Rigoberta Menchú: An Indian Woman in Guatemala*, Ann Wright, trans. (London: Verso, 1984).

does not want these things told (29). Menchú's testimony can therefore never be complete.

Testimonial writing revolves around representing the identity of the testimonial subject and attempts to detail a point of view; however, Menchú can never truly expose her identity. Her resistance to oppression, motivation for the *testimonio*, works against the very process of the text, clearly placing the text and its production as allies of forces that potentially threaten her community. She cannot thoroughly explain, for instance, the *nahual*, [18] a figure closely tied to personal identity, and she certainly cannot reveal her own *nahual* to the transcriber (41). Jesusa's cynical denunciation of the *nahual* as a disguise of convenience contrasts sharply with Menchú's description and supports the distinction between the *novela testimonial's* self-conscious play of truth against fiction the *testimonio*. Menchú cannot explain her identity in the most meaningful manner for her: in terms of her own culture. The oft-quoted last words of the book leave the reader with this sense of incompleteness: "Pero, sin embargo, sigo ocultando mi identidad como indígena. Sigo ocultando lo que yo considero que nadie sabe, ni siquiera un antropólogo, ni un intelectual, por más que tenga muchos libros, no saben distinguir todos nuestros secretos" ("Nevertheless, I'm still keeping my Indian identity a secret. I'm still keeping secret what I think no-one should know. Not even anthropologists or intellectuals, no matter how many books they have, can find out all our secrets"; 271, 247). As in *Hasta no verte* we arrive at the question, what has she revealed and what has she not? To what extent does the strategy of delayed gratification function as a rhetorical tease to engage the reader and maintain Menchú's agency before the transcriber? With truth's instability here, once more its importance lies in the process of legitimation rather than in its opposition to fabrication. Can this other life experience really be communicated? Is not what is communicated a need to reexamine the nature of solidarity through discursive means? Menchú revisits her silences and the consequent incompleteness of her 1983 testimony in her second book, *Rigoberta: la nieta de los mayas*. She reiterates the deliberateness of her silences, more directly addressing intellectuals' appropriation of indigenous culture than in her first narration:

---

[18] Both the *nahual* in *Me llamo Rigoberta Menchú* and the *nagual* in *Hasta no verte* are spelling variants of the same word.

> En esos años la mayoría de los antropólogos, sociólogos,
> escritores de historias indígenas . . . sólo usaban a los indígenas
> cuando querían vender un libro. Para no caer en esa trampa
> guardé los secretos hasta donde pude y los seguiré guardando si
> es necesario. (254)

> In those years most anthropologists, sociologists, writers of
> indigenous histories . . . only used Indians when they wanted to
> sell a book. In order to not fall in that trap I guarded the secrets
> as much as I could and will keep guarding them if necessary.

Intellectual solidarity is not a given, nor does it guarantee empowerment for the testimonial subject's point of view.

As does Jesusa, Menchú characterizes the truth of dominant
discourses as suspect, and consequently the general concept of
veracity as suspect, in contrast with the truth of Menchú's life story,
one with less conspicuous disguises than Jesusa's. To begin with,
Menchú's *testimonio* stands as a negation of the dominant discourses of Church and State as does *Hasta no verte*. For example, her
father warned her not to attend school because of the version of the
conquest they teach there:

> Decían que la venida de los españoles era una conquista, era una
> victoria, mientras que la práctica nos enseñaba lo contrario.
> Decían que los indígenas no sabían pelear. Los indígenas se
> murieron muchos porque mataban a los caballos y no mataban a
> la gente, decían ellos. Todo eso a mí me daba cólera . . . (195-6)

> They said that the arrival of the Spaniards was a conquest, a vic-
> tory, while we knew that in practice it was just the opposite.
> They said the Indians didn't know how to fight and that many of
> them died because they killed the horses and not the people. So
> they said. This made me furious . . . (170)

Similarly, she distinguishes between two Catholicisms: the Catholicism controlled by the regime which teaches passivity in this world
to be rewarded in the next, and liberation theology which relates
the Bible to popular struggles and explains Menchú's involvement
as a catechist. Adding another layer to the translations and mediations at work in this *testimonio*, Menchú's and many of her people's
experience of the Bible is necessarily mediated if they cannot read;
if anything this increases the community's skepticism toward either
interpretation, even if the interpretation is by the "iglesia de los

pobres" ("the church of the poor"): "No necesitamos mucho de consejos o de teorías o de documentos, ya que la vida nos ha enseñado" ("We don't need very much advice, or theories, or documents: life has been our teacher"; 158, 133). Unlike the readers who need the testimony before them to mediate Menchú's story, or Burgos Debray who needs Menchú's *testimonio*, Menchú knows from experience, emphasizing the privilege of an unmediated, concrete experience. Menchú, like Jesusa, distrusts repressive and manipulative versions of history while avoiding application of the same distrust toward her self-representation. As Menchú authors her identity in this way for obvious reasons, her strategy facilitates essentialist interpretations of Menchú's identity that deauthorize the autonomy of her self-representation.

Yet, if Menchú's own skepticism of others' interpretations leads us to approach this testimony with caution, can we believe in any but our own experience? A negative answer would be especially unsavory by encouraging political inertia, regardless of political orientation: thus the indispensability of discarding legitimacy's dependence on easily digestible definitions of truth and identity. Approaching with caution, answering yes and simultaneously realizing Menchú's self-representation is just that, does not delegitimize her *testimonio* but rather refocuses the adjective "truthful" onto a mode of production reflective of Menchú's circumstances. The contradictions with which we must contend include the fact that in order to legitimate support for the Indians, Menchú does not question traditional discourses within her culture. For example, although seemingly more aware of gender-based discrimination than Jesusa, Menchú cannot or does not weaken her defense of indigenous culture with deep criticism of gender roles. Despite her unusual life for a woman, Menchú does not judge the greater freedom males have outside the home or their relatively greater access to education (108). As Sommer has noted, Menchú and Jesusa tend to identify with their fathers, thus gaining "freedom or militancy" by privileging males, or a male model ("Not Just" 129). This does not include sexual freedom, however. Menchú and Jesusa's denial of sexual activity lends to their ambiguous gender identification and further distinguishes them from their communities, but also releases them from the moral questionableness of female sexuality. Menchú's moral stance works to counteract any reaction by her community to women like her, a case where the cultural discourse she defends actually functions to question her activities:

> Una mujer de veintitrés años, como yo, es una mujer muy sospechada por la comunidad, porque no sabe dónde ha estado, dónde ha vivido. Entonces, es una mujer que pierde la sinceridad de la comunidad y el contacto con los vecinos, que son los que se encargan de vigilarlo a uno todo el tiempo. En ese sentido no hay tanto problema cuando los padres están seguros que la mujer es virgen. (86)

> The community is very suspicious of a woman like me who is twenty-three but they don't know where I've been or where I've lived. She loses the confidence of the community and contact with her neighbours, who are supposed to be looking after her all the time. In this sense, it's not such a problem when her parents are sure she's a virgin. (61)

Surely she must have earned the disapproval of men and women in her community, yet any criticism of her for renouncing marriage and motherhood remains obscured. Since Menchú's narration does not state she has lost her people's confidence, just the opposite, this passage assures she has not strayed from traditional expectations during her long time spent outside her neighbors' vigilance. [19] Menchú's moral rectitude is just as important to her legitimation as to Jesusa's, so she must represent those values and counteract any derision directed toward her people's behavior. The need for consistency in Menchú's position to sustain its authority does not allow discrepancies that characterize the apparent conflicts created by action from a marginalized position. Menchú must represent her community at the same time she has left it and learned another language, reaffirming the community as a source of identity. Her standing in the community, where collective identity comes before that of the individual, is perhaps undermined by her singular testimony, so she must displace her voice onto the group. At the same time, that urgency to speak through her community's value on collective agency creates contradictions for other cultures' reading of her *testimonio*, where the narrative must be verifiably one individual's experience.

---

[19] In a speech given on April 2, 1993, in Mexico City, Rigoberta Menchú made a point of saying that in recent years she has come to give equal priority to women's oppression and indigenous people's oppression, marking a change from her testimony from eleven years earlier. In her 1998 book, for example, she makes observations on rape's use in wars and the European conquest of the Americas (186-7).

To use that voice, Menchú invests much in communicating her version of history by learning Spanish. Unlike Jesusa she clearly engages herself in having her people's story told, and her people's resistant silence finds its limits outside their villages when they are taken advantage of for not speaking the dominant language. Menchú's representation of her experience in 1982 may be the closest of those studied here to oral culture in that her isolated community had relatively little contact with writing and Menchú learned Spanish orally. In her community everyone learned orally, unaware even of indigenous written texts (34). This isolation from formal schooling is one point David Stoll contradicts with his evidence–also open to question–that Menchú went to school for some years with Belgian nuns. This is not to mention the war's dispersal of Menchú's community, ending its isolation. Why deny this if indeed Stoll's information is correct? Orality and resistant silence are linked in Menchú's case, as are written culture and silencing, since attending school and learning to write implied losing indigenous culture and the community, including one's native language. As a child Menchú desired an education to express her ideas in writing or in Spanish; she saw it as a chance for something different. Her father, however, saw this as individualistic and a way of removing herself from the community by going to schools run by the government. "Entonces me ponía como ejemplo de que muchos de nuestros primos han sabido leer y escribir, pero no han sido útil para la comunidad. Tratan de apartarse y de sentirse diferentes cuando saben leer y escribir" ("He gave as an example the fact that many of my cousins had learned to read and write but they hadn't been of use to the community. They try to move away and feel different when they can read and write"; 115, 89). "Me acordaba de mi padre cuando nos decía: 'Hijos, no ambicionen las escuelas porque en las escuelas nos quitan nuestras costumbres'" ("I remember my father telling us: 'My children, don't aspire to go to school, because schools take our customs away from us'"; 195, 169). Yet, only through revelation of her family's experience in Spanish and outside their customs do their words become weapons in the outside world (9). Their words carry truth in Menchú's testimony, but only in Spanish, and only partially, since much remains hidden.

While Jesusa chose silence over Spanish in the scene where she angers her father by speaking Zapotec, the urgency of the genocide against Guatemalan Indians requires that Menchú enter into the paradox of linguistically leaving her community in order to give us the feeling of bringing us inside it. Menchú's collective identity as representative of her community creates several more contradictions that undermine the dualism fact/fiction as criterion for judging *testimonios*' value, in addition to those conflicts already seen in Poniatowska's *novela testimonial*. We have already seen that the quotation above where Menchú's describes her unusual situation for an Indian woman questions rather than supports her pose as representative. Also, the multiple interpretations of history and the Bible open the reader's mind to the possibility of questionable truths, although Menchú's testimony does not underscore them as self-reflexively as does *Hasta no verte*. Plus, Menchú's reticence and the contradictory nature of her role as both leader and member of her community, of her singular and her collective identities, emerge from the necessary negotiation of her speaking position.

Despite the evident disparities, Burgos Debray's prologue supports an uncomplicated image of Menchú's representativity since it also legitimates the anthropologist's own project, explaining why the reader should listen to this woman because her testimony's implications reach beyond an individual experience. [20] As with most mediated *testimonios*, in the prologue the transcriber outlines the *testimonio*'s production and a framework to guide our reading. Burgos Debray's prologue clearly presents an image of the ideal transcriber where no tension arises between her and the testimonial subject. This contrasts with the (purposely?) opposite kind of relationship portrayed in *Hasta no verte*. Menchú's words are weapons and the transcriber gives them permanency (16) without altering the content in any major way, since doing so *would* be to betray the testimonial subject (7). She is Menchú's listener and instrument (18), nothing more than the passive medium represented in the Obra Espiritual of *Hasta no verte*. This kind of reading that simplifies Menchú's situation does set the stage for critiques that point out contradictions and link Menchú's authority to fulfillment of a story in uncomplicated terms.

Sylvia Molloy links the imperative for the representativity of the subject in certain autobiographical texts, including those by

---

[20] Significantly, in *Rigoberta*, Menchú notes that Arturo Taracena recommended bringing Burgos Debray into her testimony's project in order to legitimate *Menchú's* project with Burgos Debray's well-known name.

women, to the reading community's preference for seeing "difference *en bloc*" ("From Serf" 406). Because of consistency's importance for credibility and the tendency to homogenize subaltern groups, a statistically critical mass seems desirable in order to produce an authentic and persuasive *testimonio*. Also, testimonial narrators often must represent others because the others did not survive. In either case representativity suits the transcriber's, reader's and often the narrator's purposes. Burgos Debray expresses particular interest in Menchú's collective significance when she writes in the prologue: "Por la mañana al levantarse, un reflejo milenario impulsaba a Rigoberta a preparar la masa" ("The first thing Rigoberta did when she got up in the morning was make dough and cook *tortillas* for breakfast; it was a reflex that was thousands of years old"; 13, xv-xvi). Here Menchú is unreflectingly led by collective, historical impulses. Burgos Debray also writes: "[La vida de Rigoberta Menchú] es ejemplar, puesto que encarna la vida de todos los indios del continente americano . . . Por la boca de Rigoberta Menchú se expresan actualmente los vencidos de la conquista española" ("[Rigoberta Menchú's life] is in that sense exemplary: she speaks for all the Indians of the American continent . . . The voice of Rigoberta Menchú allows the defeated to speak"; 9, xi). To allow this authentic voice to speak alone, Burgos Debray takes great pains to stress her lack of intervention and the text's simple truth. Menchú's voice "[n]os trastorna porque lo que dice es sencillo y verdadero" ("Her story is overwhelming because what she has to say is simple and true"; 10, xii-xiii). Her testimony is straightforward and true despite what must remain hidden and why it must remain hidden. Except for the look of mature suffering Menchú has when she speaks of the horrible things that happened to her family, "[s]u mirada franca era la de un niño" ("her open, almost childlike smile"; 12, xiv). Dependence on truth value and consequently the transcription's transparency to legitimate Menchú's testimony leads to characterizing her as simple and with the look or gaze of a child. A simple child would not be dishonest, but Menchú perceived as a simple child in fact distances us from the complex negotiation between cultures, languages, and power structures that more precisely describes the "true" circumstances readers desire to know through *testimonio*. Her simplification means a manageable, packaged "difference *en bloc*" of marginalized identity that remains on the margins where *testimonio* lends the other agency.

Menchú becomes "sujeto de la historia" ("a subject of history"; 8) [21] and of her text, but within limits. Here is the epic history of all her people, of "all the Indians of the American continent," according to Burgos Debray, . . .except, perhaps, that of Ignacio Bizarro Ujpán?

OTHER TRUTHS AND TRUTHS IMPOSED ON TESTIMONIAL DISCOURSE

Dissenting voices disputing Menchú's authority do not appear within the text itself of *Me llamo Rigoberta Menchú*, but rather in other *testimonios* and the research of the U.S. anthropologist David Stoll. Marc Zimmerman discusses the contrasts between Menchú's testimony and those of Ignacio Bizarro Ujpán, also a Guatemalan Indian who describes many of the events appearing in *Me llamo Rigoberta Menchú*. Bizarro Ujpán, who does not retain many of the traditional customs of Mayan culture, describes life in the *fincas* quite differently, emphasizes alcoholism among the Indians, is disdainful toward Catholicism and speaks positively of his time doing military service. Menchú's representation of course highlights or downplays these issues according to the desired reaction of the reader in support of her cause. Moreover, the collective import of her *testimonio* and her denouncement of genocide do not diminish if she does not reflect all Guatemalan Indians' perspectives. Similar to Shaw's observations regarding *Hasta no verte*, the testimonial process is a negotiation. Zimmerman points out that other research on the situation of Guatemalan Indians shows that Bizarro Ujpán's rather than Menchú's story may reflect the majority of Indians' "reality," although Ignacio does not present himself as representative of his community, does not defer his voice to the "we" of a collective. He does not feel a need to legitimate his life-story as exemplary because he does not strive to communicate a political urgency or authenticity and because he does not speak from within Mayan collective traditions; he does not hesitate to exert his presence as an individual.

The *commentary* to his text places his testimony in a collective

---

[21] This quotation is from the two-page Introduction in the Spanish original that does not appear in the translation.

context. Vera León has written that one of testimonial writing's projects is "la *construcción* de un narrador-informante representante de una totalidad cultural que 'habla' a través de un testigo privilegiado en quien el pasado se hace voz" ("the *construction* of a narrator-informant who is representative of a cultural totality that 'speaks' through a privileged witness in whom the past has a voice"; 188, emphasis added). Menchú's "we" coincides with the testimonial project. Sommer states that the plural testimonial voice springs from translation of an autobiographical project into a colonized culture: "The phenomenon of a collective subject of the testimonial is, then, hardly the result of personal preference on the part of the writer who testifies. It is a translation of a hegemonic autobiographical pose into a colonized language that does not equate identity with individuality" ("Not Just" 111). Yet, along the lines of Sommer's later essay on Jesusa Palancares, can we assume that Menchú's "I" as "we" is only a cultural impulse or is it not also a strategy to strengthen the text's authority? Although from cultures where identity is individuality, do the readers not seek the "we" explicitly or implicitly found in testimonial writing? The readers' and transcribers' simultaneous desire for collective significance in Menchú's story and also for accuracy in her individual history create a situation Menchú negotiated with the narrative license that David Stoll's recent book has exposed.

Stoll's allegations that Menchú invented various events from an eyewitness point of view were not new in 1998. In 1989 Stoll already read a paper about her supposed literary inventions he had discovered while carrying out anthropological research on popular Guatemalan resistence movements (Handley 67). Nevertheless, his book's publication at the end of 1998 provoked a long article in the *New York Times* (Rohter), followed by editorials, letters to the editor, interviews with Menchú and Stoll, and debates among academics on the internet. The debate continues and in 2001 Arturo Arias edited a volume of responses to the controversy. Significantly, it is among academics and other readers of Menchú in the US that this controversy's impact has been greatest. In the end, the controversy, *not* the text or its importance, is based on what Menchú's testimony is for *us*, for *our* western civilization courses, for *our* preconceived notion of truth's function and authentic indigenous culture. On the other hand, although this focus on what Menchú is for us must not eclipse her voice, we also must not overlook the reception in the US of the doubts surrounding Menchú. After all, *testimonios* have been written for privileged audiences in the US, Europe, or Latin America from the beginning. In fact, that audience's implicit presence is crucial to the recent debate, to testimonial writing's production, and to the potential disappearance of Menchú's voice and the disabling of her own self-representational strategies.

Ironically, Stoll, with his some three hundred pages of information that questions the veracity of Menchú's *testimonio*, does not ignore the complex truth of the context in which Menchú narrates her story. In the first pages of his book Stoll writes that, "The underlying problem is not how Rigoberta told her story, but how well-intentioned foreigners have chosen to interpret it" (*Rigoberta Menchú* xiv). The US anthropologist takes on the specific project not of repudiating Menchú personally, but rather of questioning the truth of indigenous peoples' support for the guerrilla. At the same time, however, while Stoll does not show disdain toward Menchú, he does throw into doubt her well-known and personal story's accuracy as a means of forwarding his anti-guerrilla position. He also constitutes one of those "well-intentioned foreigners" of which he speaks. While Stoll does not question the importance of the peace accords, never denies the truth of human rights violations, and does not give much importance to impugning Menchú's person, he does insist on denying her *testimonio*'s representativity to undermine the idea of popular support for the guerrilla.

One problem with Stoll's argument is that even though he appropriately criticizes the search for association with authenticity, in the context of grave collective human rights violations his attention to personal details can easily be interpreted as partial, trivial, or even mean. He carefully scrutinizes Menchú's *individual* life on the premise that because of her *collective* importance, knowing the true facts of her life bring us to the truth of the relationship between the guerrilla and the Indians. That is, he takes as a priori her representativity and the collective nature of her narrative, but then bases his judgment of the collective significance of Menchú's story on whether or not the individual Menchú lived everything as described. He questions each of Menchú's activities, but supposedly not her integrity, in order to also undermine her authority when speaking of the guerrilla. He emphasizes the objectivity of his study and that his objectivity lies reflected in his decision to not include and compare different versions of the events, but rather to "judge" from a foreign perspective which version is more "reliable" (*Rigoberta Menchú* 217). That is, when Stoll admits that there are multiple versions he seems to select the one that makes most sense to him, reserving for himself this privilege. From his perspective, Menchú's schoolmates' memories define, some fifteen years later, what she did during her vacations.

All of this is not necessarily to defend one truth or another. Despite the fact that Stoll indeed has collected convincing data indicating the alteration of some central facts in Menchú's narrative, he as much as Menchú writes his text from a marked perspective. The point here is rather to consider the expectations that mold readings of testimonial texts in general and to highlight the tension between the truth of an authentic identity for the consumer and the truth of a discursive position manipulated by the narrator out of necessity. This tension is not limited to the reception of Menchú's text or to those of her detractors; it illuminates all interpretations of *testimonio* that have obscured or criticized the contradictions inherent in mediated *testimonio* and its purposes of solidarity. Just as Stoll accuses Menchú of simplifying a complicated situation for political expediency, Stoll in fact simplifies the complicated dilemma the testimonial narrator faces and that his book creates. The anthropologist passes over the fact that performed truth still determines the testimonial text's authority, despite its subjective production and Stoll's emphasis that his aim is not to discard the moral weight of the abuses suffered by indigenous groups. In other words, at the same time that testimonial texts are written to obscure discursive maneuvers, they reveal the maneuvers necessary to grant the subaltern the authority lacking in privileged spheres, maneuvers that describe the truth of the subaltern's precarious situation. Deborah Shaw's assertion that approaches to testimonial works, particularly *Hasta no verte*, have often depended upon stable truth and unified identity becomes relevant here as well. The inconsistencies smoothed over by critics of Poniatowska's text—or attacked in Menchú's *testimonio*—reflect the shifts necessary to survive the narrator's circumstances. In *Rigoberta*, Menchú mentions several times the shifts in identity she undertook to escape Guatemala and avoid identification: Indians had to wear the clothes of other ethnicities within Guatemala (159), and Menchú dressed as a *ladino* or tzeltal and took on different names (141, 246). In Menchú's case, the shifts she undertakes negotiate, or subvert, preconceived notions of her truth and the rhetoric of truth in western, individualized subjectivity. As John Beverley sees it, either Menchú creates her own narrative authority and negotiates its conditions of truth, or she is the classical "native informant" ("Real" 276). Her construction of her own narrative clashes with the reading public who guards the separation between *testimonio* and literature precisely because a marginalized speaker is held to higher standards of truth and does not participate in the definition of what *testimonio* should be.

One of the more extreme examples of this appears in a letter to the editor in the *New York Times* which responds to the first article about Stoll's findings. In the letter the anthropologist Roger Lancaster first does not consider *testimonio*'s origins when he classifies it as an "epistolary form," when rarely does *testimonio* take the form of letters. Indeed, the oral origins of *testimonios* like Menchú's have been fundamental to the attempts to define *testimonio*. At the same time, were we to accept his classification, epistolary form connotes a subjectivity and intimacy that Lancaster negates in his definition of *testimonio* as a report of "sociological facts." He chastises Menchú for telling her story in such a way that "force-fits her experiences into the social analysis she wished to dramatize," as if the same could not be said of Stoll, and he adds that "narrative devices like the shading of events that might be acceptable in an ethnographic work or historical novel undercut the authority of a text that purports to tell the unvarnished truth." That is, the ethnologist is permitted the same creativity as the author of a novel when describing another culture. The testimonial narrator, however, does not have rights to the same rhetorical liberty in creating her own self-representation. In a later commentary published in the *NACLA Report on the Americas* Lancaster changes some of his wording, but not his message. He still does not take into account the politics of necessity and survival Shaw outlines, nor the fact that an Indian woman is less convincing to us when, for example, she has had the opportunity to study in a Belgian convent or was perhaps lucky enough not to work on the coastal *fincas* until she was an adult.

Beverley observes in Stoll a similar disparity in the authority attributed to Menchú versus the anthropologist regarding narrative license and the production of knowledge: *testimonio* becomes "raw material that must be processed by more objective techniques of assessment" ("What Happens" 227). Along the same lines, Jorge Rogachevsky also notes that "Stoll wants to reinscribe the authoritative figure of the scholar into the process of narrative construction," which diminishes Menchú's role to a passive one in a set of polarities opposite scholars that "include notions of praxis [scholars] and essence [Indians], history and myth" ("David Stoll"). Our difficulty in recognizing the complex position from which the testimonial narrator speaks determines the nature of that enunciation and reflects our desire to know a simpler truth along the lines of our notion of what is Indian. For example, according to Stoll, without an education beyond what Menchú states in her *testimonio*, or academics' intervention, she could not talk about abstract concepts ("Conundrums"). Arturo Taracena points to this colonial mentality in Stoll's logic, where the indigenous are "infinitely manipulable, always under the influence of a modernity foreign to them" (91). Only manipulated by others or with formal education would essentialized, premodern indigenous subjects master abstract concepts. In Menchú's 1998 book she emphasizes Guatemalan Indian identity's location in the dynamic present, not as a nostalgic myth. The community is not simply "un recuerdo del pasado. No es un mito, no es algo estéril. No es lo que algunos idealizan sin realismo. Es algo dinámico y presente en la memoria de nuestros pueblos. La identidad no es sólo la nostalgia de comer tamales" ("a memory of the past. It isn't a myth, it isn't what some people idealize unrealistically. It's something dynamic and present in the memory of our people. Identity isn't only the nostalgia of eating tamales"; 161). Her identity is not the thousand-year-old reflex to make tortillas (Burgos Debray 13), nor is it the ignorant or the maid, as Menchú states some still prefer to see the Nobel laureate (Menchú 177). Insisting on indigenous characteristics' purity and homogeneity can essentialize their reality altered by atrocities and economic hardship.

Christopher L. Miller observes that anthropology creates as an intellectual tool the very borders it proposes to cross (12). Testimonial readers may cross certain cultural and rhetorical borders that the testimonial narrator cannot legitimately cross through her use of the medium given to her to better her situation. Some defenders of Menchú's version of events have also constructed those borders, even if for reasons of solidarity toward political change. Lancaster fixes certain limits that Menchú cannot exceed since *we* have defined her story as *testimonio* and *he* has determined the authorized definition of *testimonio*. The subaltern narrator can speak for herself through mediation, yet only if she communicates a truth innocent of personal motives and a truth unaltered by influences external to the community. Daphne Patai criticizes Menchú's utilization of the intellectual rhetoric of contingent truth as part of her "careful crafting of an identity likely to be pleasing to her academic supporters" ("Whose Truth?" 276). Although she at least recognizes Menchú's equal ability to wield abstract concepts, Patai takes her to task for doing so to suit her purposes, to be persuasive (Nance 585). Menchú the subject does not submit to status as rhetorical object. As Rogachevsky phrases it, "In the final analysis what troubles Stoll particularly about the Menchú text is that it has the power to define reality" ("David Stoll"). Beverley uses a similar tone: "What seems to bother Stoll above all is that Menchú *has* an agenda" ("What Happens" 221). This is the same resistance Menchú finds in Guatemala "porque una mujer indígena protagoniza pequeños espacios de liderazgo en el país" ("because an indigenous woman is the protagonist of small opportunities for leadership in this country"; Menchú 177). A dynamic, autonomous identity cannot be sold in a jar (Menchú 161), like the merchandise Menchú saw displayed at the World Conference on the Environment in Rio, along with dancing, feather-adorned Indians. What autonomous Guatemalan Indians have in common with our modern lives does not sell as well as the differences.

Metaphor and Metonymy in Women's Self-Representation

Menchú's 1983 testimony and the controversy around Stoll's findings show that, like the dualities of document and fiction, of oral and written, the interplay of individual and collective subjectivities becomes unquantifiable and yet significant through the authority representativity carries with it in testimonial discourse. In contrast with the value placed on Menchú's representativity and her collective cultural perspective, the word testimony itself as memory of the past suggests for the western reader the individual more than does the collective memory recounted in the stories of oral or traditional Mayan cultures. Shoshana Felman sees the guiding question of the testimonial film *Shoah* as, if the testimony is essentially impersonal, having general "validity and consequences," then "why is it that the witness's speech is so uniquely, literally irreplaceable?" (40). Even when the testimonial subject insists she speaks for all her people, as does Menchú, the testimonial text also defines an individual, as we have seen with Stoll's and others' readings of Menchú.

The testifying individual may exist as the nexus where the memories or experiences of various groups meet, as the crossing point of various collective memories. [22] Thus the testimonial text contains a system of relations that translates the singular to the general (Vera León 192); "her singularity achieves its identity as an extension of the collective," not as an individual so typical she can substitute the "we" (Sommer, "Not Just" 108). Without ignoring the important way Menchú's plural identification originates in Mayan traditions she emphasizes, the collective continues to be important in many texts from outside such a cultural perspective on identity. The singular life named and described in the text both contradicts and complements collective authority, producing a narration that resists monolithic truths. Reflecting back on *Hasta no verte*, for Poniatowska Jesusa is at the same time "un fenómeno aislado y solitario" ("an isolated and solitary phenomenon"; "Testimonios" 159) and someone whose language "es un idioma compuesto con toda la gente que yo conozco desde mi infancia porque hay modismos de muchas partes del país. Es el lenguaje en general que utiliza la gente pobre, la gente que trabaja" ("is a language composed of all the people I've known since childhood because there are colloquialisms from many parts of the country. It's the general language poor people use, the people who labor" 159). Jesusa is a remarkable individual distinct from the traditional Mexican woman, yet also a collage, a collective, of many voices. According to Sommer in "'Not Just a Personal Story,'" this collective potential is crucial in distinguishing the *testimonio* from the autobiography, although, as Sylvia Molloy has written, in Spanish American autobiography representativity, collectivity and identity are intimately linked (*At Face Value*).

Readers of *testimonio* must see collective subjectivity as a political strategy–even if one that, with different significance, also reflects concepts of identity indigenous to the testimonial subject's ideology–not as a determinant of homogenized identity that remains

---

[22] Maurice Halbwachs defines the individual memory as the point where many collective memories cross, the memories of the groups to which an individual belongs. See *The Collective Memory* (Trad. Francis J. Ditter, Jr. and Vida Yazdi Ditter, New York: Harper Colophon Books, 1980).

unchanging despite circumstances. When individual versus collective identity becomes a question of which conforms to readers' ideas of truth, Menchú's self-representation lies outside her control and permanently on the margins as the precisely defined Other. When plural versus singular identity is viewed as a political strategy that does not present a neat, coherent, complete and packaged truth, *testimonio* works to indeed cede authority and agency to the testimonial subject.

These conclusions bear great resemblance to recent feminist theories of female identity that eschew assumptions about female collaboration like those underlying some feminist ethnographies addressed earlier in this chapter. Judith Butler, for example, outlines in *Gender Trouble* a shifting concept of "women" that interestingly parallels Menchú's alternate and simultaneous representativity and individuality. According to Butler, among women who may share little, temporary alliances are formed around specific issues for action without assuming universalizing, restrictive boundaries or exclusions for the women involved. Examining women's *testimonio* and works of fiction thus becomes particularly appropriate when tracing commonalities between the paradoxes of mediated testimonial discourse (and of individual and collective subject) and the difficulties of mediating between a non-normative notion of identity and the need for concerted political action. Like the reluctance to study literary vehicles in testimonial texts or *testimonio* alongside fiction, striking a dialogue between Latin American *testimonio* and feminist theories (including those from the US) will surely draw criticism for fear of defusing *testimonio*'s subversive impact. Feminist theories (though not grassroots women's movements) are discourses of middle-class privilege; Latin American *testimonio* is one of oppression by the privileged or hegemonic. We cannot forget, however, that mediated *testimonio* even though ceding space to the subaltern originates in a middle-class initiative for privileged readers. Mediated *testimonio* is about solidarity, not Rigoberta Menchú's forcibly dictating her life-story to a publishing house's typesetter. "To repeat, this decision to interview women in struggle was made by intellectuals; it was not spontaneously generated by those interviewed" (Sommer, "Not Just" 114). In dialogue, testimonial texts that *preceded* recent movements in feminist theory concerned with differences of class and race illuminate theory while gender consciousness can shed light on aspects of women's *testimo-*

nios. While the earlier comments on feminist ethnology addressed women's representation of other women, the merits of examining *testimonio* and feminist theory together stand out especially regarding women's *self*-representation. Here I use Doris Sommer's and Leigh Gilmore's work on concepts of autobiography to discuss individual versus collective self-identification as another fundamental paradox of testimonial discourse that calls for redefining veracity in its role as instrument of authorization for marginalized voices.

In "'Not Just a Personal Story'" Sommer asserts that *testimonio*, and specifically women's *testimonio*, cannot be seen exclusively as a subgroup of autobiography because subsuming the "strikingly impersonal," collective "I" into the autobiographical, singular "I" of the "heroic testimonial norm of male informants" would mean overlooking the blind-spot that conflates history with the lives of extraordinary figures, that continues to separate public and private (109-10), and that excludes certain groups. Connecting the public with the private of course constitutes one of the central feminist platforms so that this effect of women's testimonial writing, as Sommer expresses it, identifies a similar purpose between the two discourses regarding agency in official versions of history. At the same time, Sommer does state we may find it "legitimate" to view women's testimonials as a variation of autobiography since the first-person narration of a life history indeed distinguishes the informant from the rest (110). She describes the ethical dilemma raised by calling *testimonio* autobiographical thus:

> Is [autobiography] the model for imperializing the consciousness of colonized peoples, replacing their collective potential for resistance with a cult of individuality and even loneliness? Or is it a medium of resistance and counterdiscourse, the legitimate space for producing that excess which throws doubt on the coherence and power of an exclusive historiography? (111)

The difficulty of answering either of these questions points to another articulation of the reasons for which Rigoberta Menchú, and Jesusa Palancares, come to occupy shifting positions with respect to collective identity. Significantly, certain readings of women's autobiography may reconcile the conflict.

One such reading is found in Leigh Gilmore's *Autobiographics: A Feminist Theory of Women's Self-Representation*, where she outlines a feminist interpretive strategy she calls "autobiographics" to consider women's self-representation in a way that Jesusa Palancares's and Rigoberta Menchú's *testimonios* seem to demand. Therefore, while Gilmore does not address testimonial writing and writes from the US, and also we do not want to forget Sommer's important distinctions between *testimonio* and autobiography, Gilmore's thoughts repeatedly interlace with Sommer's points and my conclusions in this chapter. Gilmore conceives of an interpretive strategy instead of a definition of women's autobiography because from the outset she concerns herself with shifting identities and "networks of identification"; she does not look for autobiographies to tell truth about women, but rather for them to tell about modes of autobiographical production (13). Learning about the "truth" of testimonial subjects' situations through their modes of talking about those situations makes sense of their contradictions and resists reinforcing their identity as one inherently marginal. Gilmore therefore asserts a law-outlaw metaphor, for instance, as useful for interpretation, but not for defining women's writing because it "tends to reinforce the conception that women are always banished to the margins, and it may naturalize the practices that construct margin and center and then relegate some women to those margins" (22). For this reason she states that the first step in discussing autobiography is to first examine the "discursive legacy of 'truth' and 'lying'" in self-representation and the association of "lying" with women's cultural productions (ix).

With Sommer, Gilmore remaps, to use her term, the shifting discourses women use to describe themselves, reinterpreting "lying" as pushing the limitations on the singular, first-person pronoun. Women in *testimonios* mix features of several discourses because none of them alone completely describes their contradictory situation as "a mother, a worker, a Catholic, a Communist, an indigenist, and a nationalist" ("Not Just" 121). Women autobiographers are aware of a single discourse's insufficiency so they weave various identities together, problematizing definition (Gilmore 124-5). According to Gilmore autobiography is driven by an "authorization complex" whereby authors attempt to situate themselves in relation to "what the dominant culture values and identifies with truth" (226). As explained earlier, simply by its name and its political imperative located in opposition to the official lies it exposes *testimonio* must situate itself in relation to truth, and as seen in the Menchú controversy, that truth must be what is perceived as truth, what is desired by the reader as truth. Interestingly, just as Jean Franco traces the unequal relationship between testimonial interlocutors to the confessors anxious to hear and interpret mystic nuns' visions in the sixteenth and seventeenth centuries ("Si me permiten"), Gilmore asserts that authority in autobiography approximates the truth claim of the confession (107). To convincingly tell the truth a particular structure must be performed in the confession and the confessor's language used to avoid potential punishment (107, 109). When testimonial discourse does not follow dominant structures of truth telling the potential punishment seems to be loss of authority in the apparent loss of credibility.

Both Gilmore and Sommer use metaphor and metonymy to alter the expectations of truth as perceived in testimonial texts. Metaphor and metonymy distinguish the autobiography and heroic narrative dependent on hierarchical one-to-one identity of the self in different forms, from *testimonio* and women's autobiography (Sommer, "Not Just" 108; Gilmore 69). For Sommer metonymy describes a lateral identification that recalls Butler's idea of constantly changing allegiances for political action that do not easily lend themselves to construction of monolithic identity. Lateral identification "through relationship" acknowledges differences, where the reader is invited into "a community of particular, shared objectives rather than interchangeability among its members"; for Sommer insistence on showing relationships constitutes a defining characteristic of *testimonio* ("Not Just" 109, 129 and "Sin secretos" 141-2). For Gilmore the self represented metonymically in relation to others extends through time, depending on a "sustained patterning for meaning," giving the example of the king who must wear the crown frequently enough for the crown to stand metonymically for him (69). The metonym carries meaning in context; the metaphor draws an analogy between essences (78). The metonym recognizes the survival strategies explained by Shaw; the metaphor marks a return to stable truth. [23]

---

[23] In "Traveling Cultures" James Clifford cites Arjun Appadurai's criticism of anthropology's localizing non-Western people as "natives" in a process Appadurai calls "metonymic freezing" that describes representational essentializing (23-4). I mention this to show the different uses metonymy can serve in discussions of marginalized agency and representation. For Appadurai metonymy means individual lives come to epitomize the whole to facilitate an anthropological taxonomy. Here I use metaphor and metonymy to describe self-representation in the way Sommer and Gilmore do, while recognizing other possible connotations of the terms.

The metaphor-metonym contrast proves useful in elucidating both the testimonial subject's relationship to the collective body of which she is a member and also the transcriber's relationship to her. In the metonymic mode we are invited to be in solidarity with the subject without the metaphoric act of being her. Metaphoric identification with her would then mean a misreading of the testimonial "I" in autobiographical terms. Moreiras associates testimonial solidarity with metaphoric identification, but bases his critique of solidarity on the misreadings produced by that metaphoric identification: "Solidarity is precisely the emotional apparatus that enables our metaphoric identification with the other, and a double conversion of the other into us, and of us into the other. . . . Solidarity allows for political articulation, but cannot by or in itself provide for an epistemological leap into an other knowledge, understood as a genuine knowledge of the other" (215). Thus, according to Gilmore and Sommer, the mistaken epistemological leap marks the shift from the metonymic mode to reading in autobiographical terms.

Yet, such a misreading appears in Burgos Debray's prologue to *Me llamo Rigoberta Menchú* and Poniatowska's own testimonies about the writing of *Hasta no verte*. The alternating identification and distancing between transcriber and testimonial subject, produced by a metaphorical reading then finds its embodiment in Carolina de Jesus's *testimonio* where Carolina [24] alternately conflates and separates her double role as transcriber and testimonial subject, as we shall see ahead. The metaphorical reading by Burgos Debray and Poniatowska produces "vicarious identity" and raises the question of empathy. Sommer accurately points out that the testimonial informant's "I" does not invite identification with this radically different experience (108), in the sense of imagining oneself as the testimonial subject. Nevertheless, the reader's identification in the sense of empathy could strengthen the impetus for action in reaction to the *testimonio*, and Burgos Debray's and Poniatowska's framing texts guide the interpretation of the *testimonio* itself toward that empathy. Alberto Moreiras sees a metaphoric interpre-

---

[24] Throughout the book I refer to Carolina Maria de Jesus as "Carolina" not out of false familiarity, nor to fictionalize her along with Jesusa Palancares, to whom I refer as "Jesusa." "Carolina" avoids confusion between "Jesus" and "Jesusa," follows the Brazilian convention of calling by their first name those famous figures who have a common last name, and follows other scholars' lead.

tation as a natural outcome of this empathy or solidarity; yet, complete distancing from the testimonial subject's experience reproduces distancing from her condition. Thus we are simultaneously confronted with the two interpretive strategies of metaphorical autobiography and metonymic women's self-representation and *testimonio*, returning us to Sommer's summary of the ethical ambiguity of metaphorical autobiography: does our reading through autobiographical eyes reproduce imperialist appropriation or open discursive modes of resistance? Does our reading rob or lend agency? Significantly, in this contrast empathy as personal identification comes to be associated with a reading opposed to a feminist one, separating stereotypical female empathy from feminist methodology, contrary to naive concepts of feminist ethnography.

Vicarious Identity's Confusion of Metaphor and Metonymy

There exists a particular gesture of vicarious identity in which dialogue seems to break down, where one hears what one wants to hear, where contradictions become especially acute just as Jesusa's and Menchú's *testimonios* resist identification with them, but where the transcribers adopt their identities, where the impossibility of a neat, delimited identity is overlooked, and where the transcribers find an essential truth that could compensate a lack they perceive in themselves. This is where the transcribers appear to misread as do those who would critique *testimonio* based on its authenticity founded on fixed truths, and where the testimonial subject is threatened with disappearance as she is "privileged" with an essentialized identity that to retain speaking privilege remains on the margins and without agency. In other words, this gesture does not invert center and margin, but ultimately leaves them intact as the testimonial subject's identity becomes essential and essentialized to the transcriber's. This gesture is not simply the familiar ventriloquism of appropriating another voice to wield greater authority on particular issues of concern to the transcriber, but one where the narrator's identity reflects back, brings us back, to the transcriber.

The *nahual* in *Me llamo Rigoberta Menchú* and in *Hasta no verte* symbolically introduces this "vicarious identity." The contrast between Menchú's belief in the *nahual* and Jesusa's incredulity before this same figure reflects both Jesusa's *ladino* perspective and also the less overt, less skeptical portrayal of representation and appropriation in *Me llamo Rigoberta Menchú*. Menchú, unlike Jesusa, considers the *nahual* part of a culture she fiercely defends. [25] In a challenge to the division between essential identity and metonymic self-representation by association, the *nahual* is not a connivance covering hidden manipulations but an integral aspect of identity, a concept of identity as multiple and interactive with circumstances, in this case the natural environment. The *nahual* in this sense illuminates Menchú's perspective on narrative truth in her collective self-representation that interacts with the circumstances of its telling. Essence is redefined as mutation, making individual identity fundamentally variable and therefore incompletely accessible in the testimonial text. Burgos Debray, however, enacts this variable identity as a metaphorical one in her representation of her relationship with Menchú during the interviews. Burgos Debray surpasses the ideal transcriber's deferral to the narrator's testimony when she encounters an integral aspect of her identity in Rigoberta. Beyond characterizing herself as Menchú's listener and instrument, Burgos Debray writes that she situated herself in the place which "corresponded" to her, "luego convirtiéndome en una especie de doble suyo" ("then became her instrument, her double"; 18, xx). Burgos Debray becomes Menchú's double, apparently *losing her own identity*, but indeed *supplementing her own identity* with Menchú's authentically American one: "Ella me ha permitido descubrir ese otro yo-misma. Gracias a ella mi yo americano ha dejado de ser una 'extrañeza inquietante'" ("She allowed me to discover another part of myself. Thanks to her, my American self is no longer something 'uncanny'"; 18, xxi). [26] As Menchú becomes almost a *nahual* for Burgos Debray, familiarizing Burgos Debray's sense of strangeness in herself and providing a link to the American landscape, Burgos Debray comes to understand her own identity through seeing Menchú as an "other within." What begins as a metonymic gesture slips into a metaphoric gesture, leading us back to the "signifier" of Burgos Debray. The testimonial text stems from Burgos Debray's self-perception as absence or lack, what Nance

---

[25] Doris Sommer also independently comes to this conclusion in her essay "Taking a Life," whose later version is "Hot Pursuit" in *Proceed with Caution* (155).

[26] The alteration to Wright's translation here is mine.

terms abjection (577), yet a self-effacing position becomes self-affirming to some extent. It fills silence; it compensates an exclusion (Franco, "Si me permiten" 115); it results from a lack of authority (Ludmer); and it recuperates an identity in Burgos Debray's lost past (Vera León 194). *Whose* past? While Menchú presents *ladinos* as disdaining any mixture of blood that could question their identity as whites, Burgos Debray, living in France, sees *ladinos* enacting the opposite: ladinos exaggerate their indigenous features to set themselves apart from European culture. They feel the need to be different, desiring cultural individuality, and use native cultures to proclaim their otherness and importance before Europe (193, 14). For Burgos Debray, appropriation of what is essentially a multiply subaltern identity (Indian) in fact works to legitimate another identity considered subordinate to European culture: Latin American or *mestizo*.

Burgos Debray performs the same identity shift as does Menchú, in a way preparing us for the text Burgos Debray is introducing. Burgos Debray's shift originates in a nostalgic feeling of not belonging, which considering that Menchú shifts for survival, comes to seem trivial. Yet, that is not precisely where the decisive problem lies in Burgos Debray's repetition. Decisive is how Burgos Debray seems to repeat Menchú's strategy in such a way that erases Menchú's agency and presence–in the framework, not in Menchú's narrative strategies within the *testimonio*. Burgos Debray assumes a performative identity that requires Menchú to represent an essential americanness: a truth, not the different roles Menchú negotiates. This paradox culminates the inherent contradictions in testimonial discourse and the inutility of basing its value on truthfulness. Moving beyond that concept of truthfulness does not mean abstracting the real situations experienced by testimonial subjects until they disappear. In fact, legitimating *testimonio* based on the notion of an essential truth risks sacrifice and disappearance of the testimonial subject in the process of filling an absence or lack in the privileged listener. The "vicarious identity" that brings this conflict together produces a nexus with the works of fiction and critical theory I will address in chapters ahead.

Such appropriation, such a disguise, parallels the legitimating identity Poniatowska finds in Jesusa. In *Hasta no verte*, however, the paradox is more transparent, more ironic. The idea of acting through other identities appears early in *Hasta no verte* when Jesusa

recalls how her dead brother Emiliano went to get her out of the
bars: "Se materializaba, se servía de otros cerebros y me sacaba de
las juergas. Se me presentaba en otro señor y me decía: –Vámonos"
("He materialized, he made use of others' minds and he got me out
of wild parties. He came to me in the form of another man and said
to me–Let's go"; 15). He was only able to act through another identity like both transcriber and narrator. The Obra Espiritual, occu-
pying much of Jesusa's attention throughout her narrative, revolves
around psychic mediation. Psychic mediation works as metaphor
for the ideal testimonial text where the transcriber simply serves as
a body through which one speaks who ordinarily would not be
heard. The medium-transcriber is absorbed into the identity of the
testimonial subject, rather than vice-versa. [27] In one scene in which
Jesusa is first learning to hypnotize a medium the passive medium
labors under the task of mediation. Jesusa hypnotizes the medium,
whose name she does not even recall, in order to have her find
Jesusa's friend Antonio through Jesusa's form:

> No me acuerdo cómo se llamaba la mediunidad que dormí.
> Le decía yo: "Hija", nomás. Era trigueña, gorda. Acabandito de
> dormirse le daban convulsiones y luego comenzaba a hable y
> hable, aunque se veía que le costaba mucho trabajo hacerlo. . . .
>
> Yo me estaba divirtiendo. Pero aquella pobre alma se fue
> volando tras de Antonio porque es el alma la que se le sale. Des-
> de donde andaba el alma contestó en la bocina de la mediu-
> nidad. (166)
>
> I don't remember the name of the medium I put to sleep. I
> just called her "Child." She was brown-haired, fat. As soon as
> she fell asleep she had convulsions and then started talking and
> talking, though you could see that it was really hard for her . . ..
>
> I was having fun. But that poor soul went flying after Anto-
> nio because it's her soul that goes out. From where it was wan-
> dering, her soul answered through the medium like through a
> speaker. [28]

This quotation could represent the difficulties of transcription ("se
veía que le costaba mucho trabajo hacerlo" 'you could see that it

[27] Tabuenca Córdoba's paper on *Hasta no verte* also explores the *Obra Espiritual* as metaphor for transcription, although with different emphasis.
[28] ". . . it's her soul that goes out" is from the Heikkinen translation (168). See
note 9.

was really hard for her') through the passive medium, her body nothing more than a speaker box mesmerized by Jesusa and a body that has lost its own form; however, it also suggests Poniatowska's "hacer hablar." Jesusa makes the medium speak in the way Poniatowska does to Jesusa, but in a manner that portrays the relationship as one of cruel manipulation. "Hija," the name Jesusa uses in lieu of the medium's name, is either affectionate or recalls condescending treatment of maids by their mistresses, as Poniatowska points out in her introduction to *Se necesita muchacha*. Poniatowska assumes Jesusa's form and Jesusa acts through Poniatowska to lure the audience; Poniatowska uses Jesusa as a better vehicle to communicate her position. This superimposition of one over the other prohibits a metonymic relationship: one individual seems to disappear. Jesusa's skepticism of the *nagual* exposes as a disguise the appropriated identity of mediation since the animal mask is adopted in order to steal. In order to steal a voice? Why does Poniatowska speak through Jesusa?

The *novela testimonial* and *testimonio* are of course modes of speaking or acting with others' help in order to spark political consciousness and work in solidarity. Not only does the transcriber-author act as intermediary, as medium, for the informant; the informant voices, mediates, legitimates the transcriber-author's project. Speaking vicariously through another identity enables and legitimates. Acting through another identity is associating oneself metonymically with what that identity represents; it is reclaiming for oneself the characteristics of the other, a gesture Vera León signals as part of the "deseo-de-ser-el-otro" ("desire-to-be-the-other") of modern literature (188). In the case of testimonial texts, speaking through someone who is witness legitimates a message that an author from another background may not be authorized to advocate. Although Elena Poniatowska may want to publicize the plight of poor women and certain opinions she shares with her testimonial subject, Jesusa's critical voice is convincing for she *must* know through her subaltern condition; she is witness. For Felman, testimony is "an utterly unique and irreplaceable topographical *position* with respect to an occurrence" (41). When does reclaiming for oneself the witness's characteristics, where does locating oneself in the witness's topographical position, shift from a metonymic to a metaphoric interpretation?: when the transcriber perceives a personal lack, where the transcriber feels her own displacement. For this reason "vicarious identity" seeks stable meaning and location.

The witness is located in a certain "topographical position" that lends his or her testimony certain value, certain authority, certain identity. The witness's very identity as a representable concept is legitimizing because it is irreplaceable, even considering the testimonial subject's representativity (interchangeability). Metaphors of location like that of Adrienne Rich's well-known politics of location attempt to establish associations and locate the subject within structures of power by describing her topographical position, in Rich's case, as a white, Jewish, middle-class, North American lesbian. Location as Rich uses it means the place from which we come, the different aspects of our identity that form our perspective (219-20). Thus, a politics of location is a politics that attempts to base itself on the daily life of our identities through structures of power. One could also say it is a politics of association: with whom are we going to associate? With whom will others associate us? The "gesto ficticio" of the Bishop of Puebla, Bartolomé de Las Casas, José Hernández and Poniatowska is a gesture of association with those who they are not, an association with a certain location, a politics of association and vicarious location. This politics can be a gesture based on association with another in order to give voice to the subaltern and it can also constitute not just an association, but a location, a "vicarious identity," in that Poniatowska and Burgos Debray perceive an enrichment of their own identities as Mexican and Latin American, respectively. The politics of locating oneself differently is thus a disguise; [29] it is a linguistic disguise donned through language. For this reason Jesusa rejects a language that places her, that locates her, in an inferior position; and for this reason her father does not want her to locate herself in a language outside his control. For this reason Menchú's community locates itself in indigenous languages.

Poniatowska chooses to speak through Jesusa's language because Jesusa "no reúne las llamadas cualidades femeninas, no es abnegada ni sumisa ni siquiera madre, al contrario, y cuando le dan un trancazo es porque ella ya dio dos" ("does not bring together so-called feminine qualities, she is not self-sacrificing nor submissive, not even a mother–to the contrary; and when they give her a blow

---

[29] The Spanish "disfraz" would better describe what I mean here since it does not carry with it the purposefully deceitful or even malicious connotations of "disguise."

it's because she gave them two"; "La literatura" 27); because in servants' Spanish Poniatowska discovers "otro sentido a las palabras" ("a new meaning to words"); because Poniatowska recognizes the problematic of legitimizing oneself when one speaks about the subaltern. Interestingly, Poniatowska worked briefly for Oscar Lewis, for whose work legitimation is relevant considering the criticism his methods and theory of a "culture of poverty" have received, although she denies the few weeks she had spent as one of his assistants influenced her own work. [30] Nevertheless, the subaltern does not have access to publishers, perhaps not even to the written word; he or she depends on the transcriber-reader who offers the gesture of giving voice. Upon locating herself in Jesusa's *language*, Poniatowska associates herself with, reaffirms herself in, another identity: "después de identificarme largamente con la Jesusa y repasar una a una todas sus imágenes, pude decirme en voz baja: 'Yo sí pertenezco'" ("after identifying myself over time with Jesusa and reviewing her images one by one, I could say quietly to myself: 'I do belong'"; "Hasta" 8), clearly comparable to Burgos Debray's understanding of her American self through her friendship with Rigoberta. Although Jesusa and Poniatowska gradually build a friendship, from Poniatowska's point of view it seems that her identification with Jesusa brought her closer to self-knowledge than to Jesusa, that she depended on this relationship to a greater degree than did Jesusa: "Empecé a vivir un poco de miércoles a miércoles. Jesusa en cambio no abandonó su actitud hostil" ("I began to kind of live from Wednesday to Wednesday. Jesusa on the other hand did not abandon her hostile attitude"; "Hasta" 5).

Poniatowska speaks of her feelings of marginalization as an "hija de eternos ausentes" ("child of the eternally absent") of Polish origins. Through Jesusa who embodies "lo mexicano" ("that which is Mexican") the author attempts to find the Mexican in herself and to eventually belong. The paradox of this vicarious belonging emerges when Jesusa negates her own Mexican identity: "Si yo tuviera dinero y bienes sería mexicana, pero como soy peor que la basura pues no soy nada" ("If I had money and possessions I'd be

---

[30] Personal interview with Poniatowska on June 5, 1993. Lewis believed in the authenticity of his portrayal of the Sánchez family in *The Children of Sanchez*, where the subaltern ostensibly speak for themselves. His authenticity, however, is undermined by the editing process and the written parts added by Consul that were not of an oral nature (Franco, "Si me permiten" 114).

Mexican, but since I'm worse than garbage, well I'm nothing";
218). As Daphne Patai comments, "the researcher's desire to act
out feminist commitments, relinquish control, and involve the
researched in all stages of the project" can reflect the researcher's
"own demand for affirmation and validation" ("U.S. Academics"
147). Bell Gale Chevigny posits that Poniatowska found an empty
space in her position of privileged woman and that Poniatowska's
identification with Mexico and a woman without resources is an
"authorial self-creation" (213). With reference to the privileged
woman Poniatowska has written: "no es la mujer en el poder ya sea
político o artístico la que le hace justicia a sus compañeras de sexo"
("it is not the woman in political or artistic power who treats her
fellow women justly"; "La literatura" 23). At the same time that
Poniatowska includes women's writing among those of the oppressed,
she acknowledges the silencing among women and the power that
the woman writer possesses with her access to the written word
through which she utilizes and participates in the structures of
power. Therefore, for a woman writer who *has* dedicated herself to
questions of justice and inequality the adoption of Jesusa's voice is a
comprehensible political strategy. There exists the necessity to distance oneself from those women presented as traitors, [31] and to distance oneself from the misuses of ventriloquizing, misuses Jean
Franco has pointed out: "el indígena y la mujer han sido necesarios
para sostener la posición patriarcal" ("Indians and women have
been necessary to sustain patriarchal status"; "Si me permiten"
114). Dominant as well as resistant discourses have chosen to speak
through subaltern voices; Poniatowska and other *testimonio* transcribers wish to introduce these voices as resistant to dominant discourses. The collective attitude of privileged women leads to guilt
and distancing from the transcriber's own identity.

Nevertheless, Poniatowska's identification with Jesusa is not without certain distancing as well, creating a marked tension between a

---

[31] Molloy indicates a similar phenomenon in the case of Manzano's autobiography, written at the request of Domingo Del Monte, his sponsor (395): the autobiography would be useful to Del Monte because it "would reflect (*vicariously*, through
the slave's testimony) the opinion of an enlightened middle class that wished to distinguish itself from its more obtuse contemporaries" (400; my emphasis). Although
I wish to accentuate the consequences of women writers' identification with other
women's *testimonios*, Molloy's observation and her coincidental choice of words
support my point about Poniatowska. Del Monte, however, never comes to speak
through Manzano in order to compensate a personally felt absence of identity.

metaphoric and a metonymic reading of Jesusa. The silence maintained by Jesusa before Poniatowska in some matters and the fact that she withholds information distances her from the writer. Moreover, at the same time that the servants' language in the testimonies of *Se necesita muchacha* fascinates Poniatowska for its subversive possibilities, "[s]u español no es nuestro" ("their Spanish is not ours"; "La literatura" 27); it is another's language. Cynthia Steele observes a "radical sense of otherness" in Poniatowska's works through the association of servants with the sensual, with approximation to nature, and with taboo body fluids (315). The woman of few resources is someone with whom we want to identify ourselves, but who we are not, nor do we want to be.

Poniatowska writes Jesusa's life but also "reads" it, interprets it and thus, appropriates it. Vera León writes that the transcription of oral testimony is the inscription of a reading, an interpretation that results in appropriation through writing the oral (188). To some extent Ricoeur's hermeneutical idea of appropriation corresponds to the way Poniatowska finds an identity by speaking through Jesusa, although it also suggests the ideal of the transcriber as a reader and listener who believes what she hears and relinquishes herself to the narrator: a passive adoption of the narrator's world. Daniel Chamberlain links interpretation to Ricoeur's idea of the revelation of a world to the open reader who appropriates by making "one's own what was initially 'alien'" (Chamberlain 30; Ricoeur 185). Ricoeur also writes: "Appropriation is the 'process by which the revelation of new modes of being . . . *gives* the subject new capacities for knowing himself'" (192). Here is the self-reflective quality that Sommer criticizes in reader-response theory, but a reading very much part of the framework for *Hasta no verte* and *Me llamo Rigoberta Menchú*. The reader receives a "new mode of being" from the text, which at the same time makes the reader reveal aspects of the self in order to experience a different reality. She assumes the identity of the text she is reading. Burgos Debray received a greater understanding of her "American self" through her supposed relinquishment to Menchú's testimony and Poniatowska better understood and represented her Mexican identity through her friendship with Jesusa. Nevertheless, appropriation in Ricoeur's sense incorporates relinquishment, a letting go and allowing oneself to be carried off by the text; appropriation thus is the means by which revelation reflects belief in a text (Chamberlain

31). This hermeneutic theory assumes a text with one ideal meaning to which the reader is carried off; it assumes a text that does not lie, but whose truth the interpreter uses as her own. What about when a text "lies to tell the truth" (Kerr)? We have seen how Jesusa's and Menchú's mediated *testimonios* resist stable, essentializing interpretations and therefore complicate desires for appropriation or arrival at an easily communicable identity. Yet, what occurs when the reader is also literally the writer, when the writer is both observer and observed? Such is the nature of Carolina Maria de Jesus's *Quarto de Despejo*.

Carolina Maria de Jesus's *Quarto de Despejo* and the Conflation of Transcriber and Narrator

Carolina Maria de Jesus is both narrator and transcriber of her experience in São Paulo's *favela* 'slum' of Canindé. This does not simply mean in fancy terms that she is literate and therefore able to write her own *testimonio* without a transcriber. Carolina creates the representative narrator's identity and the transcriber's disguise, in addition to the layer of editing through the journalist Audálio Dantas, who pushes to publish her diaries. *Quarto de Despejo* does not parallel exactly the mediated format of the Burgos Debray and Poniatowska texts because Carolina's editor is not present at the creation of her diaries, although the two had already met when she wrote the entries published in later volumes. Dantas's role in this sense is like that of editors for *testimonios* by more privileged authors, but Carolina's economic and racial marginalization mean her diaries' publication depended on Dantas's intervention. This and his liberal cuts to Carolina's original text make the relationship important to explore after my observations about the text itself.

Yet, the roles of ethnographer and narrator *are* both present at the text's creation in the complex position Carolina must negotiate, where she alternately identifies with her fellow *favelados* 'slum dwellers' and distances herself from them. While Jesusa emphasizes her individual independence within Poniatowska's framework that emphasizes her collective importance, and while Menchú relates the collective importance of her story before a reading public in disagreement over the relationship between her "I" and "we," in *Quarto de Despejo* Carolina clearly is balancing individual and collective self-representations and outsider/insider status. In addition to further illuminating the narrative strategies a disenfranchised social position influences, Carolina's double role supports the idea that the process of creating testimonial texts is inherently conflicted and contradictory, even when a transcriber does not intervene. She is both part of the community, suffering the same hardships as everyone, and an extraordinary individual who separates herself from the rest in order to expose the reality of extreme social injustices, as well as some less transcendental injustices committed against her by neighbors. Her self-identification fluctuates between representative example and judging observer, yet her dominant individuality emphasizes her personal motivations for writing her diaries and provides an interesting parallel with the process of vicarious identity and collectivity. Moreover, her diaries follow her struggle with the terms under which she can determine her own future.

Carolina's diaries are not considered an autobiography or a *novela testimonial*, but rather a *testimonio*, although her double role further blurs the boundaries among these terms. Her individual history is embedded within a testimony of *favela* life, any personal motivations hidden behind or mixed with a message meant to increase political awareness of a collective reality. In this sense *Quarto de Despejo* shares a political purpose with *Me llamo Rigoberta Menchú*, and perhaps with *Hasta no verte*, to represent a marginalized community to inspire empathy and political action. Also, both Menchú and Carolina's self-representations can potentially undermine the explicit, collective project. The two testimonies diverge, however, when Carolina's personal motives for writing lead her to deliberately distance herself from the other *favelados*, even as she speaks against the conditions she shares with them, and to condemn not only the policies that create the *favela*, but also the community itself. Like Jesusa, she is lonely.

For personal aims, Carolina speaks as an individual, but also through the community of *favelados*: she wants to get out of the *favela*. The pride in the community evident in Menchú's testimony does not exist here, just the degradation caused by poverty. Attachment to the neighbors is association with the injustices of slum life and racism, which Carolina certainly shares, but the object of the diaries is to pull her own self from that situation. She does not want to write herself a marginalized identity that keeps her on the des-

perately impoverished margins. As Carlos Vogt, as well as Robert
M. Levine and José Carlos Sebe Bom Meihy, explain, Carolina
pulled herself from the slums through the transformation of her
experience into a "diário-reportagem" 'diary-report.' On its publication in 1960 her book was an instant success that led to reports in
international magazines, translation into thirteen languages, dinners
with important people and the funds for Carolina to buy a house
outside the *favela*, where she had collected papers and scraps to
earn a living. Her popularity diminished with the end of populism
and the rise of the dictatorship in 1964; after financing another
book which failed, Carolina was seen collecting paper again and she
complained that none of the paper buyers want to do business with
"uma estrela" 'a star.' Her testimony suited the purposes of official
discourse at the time: the criticisms Carolina directed at politicians
and the Catholic Church happened to fit into the politics of the
period. The official discourse was legitimated by speaking through
the voice of a *favelada*.

Conscious of veracity's importance for her authority and her
climb out of Canindé, and anticipating the reader's reaction to the
diaries' contents, Carolina writes, ". . .Ha de existir alguem que
lendo o que eu escrevo dira. . . isto é mentira! Mas, as miserias são
reais" ("There is probably someone reading what I write who is saying. . . this is a lie! But the miseries are real"; 38). Later on, "Se eu
escrever que o Valdemar é bom elemento quando alguem lhe con-
hecer não vai comprovar o que eu escrevi" ("If I wrote that Valdemar is a good guy, when someone meets him he isn't going to agree
with what I wrote"; 60). Carolina writes her diary not only to publicize the reality of poverty, but also to defend herself against her
neighbors, since according to her she is stigmatized precisely for
revealing the truth about them. They are aware of her writing activity and ask her to remove their names, but she insists that the
description of what they do to her strengthens her arguments (14-
15). In fact, Carolina rejects books read to escape reality (108, 110).
The only writing worth while is hers since it is realistic. When she
reads the fable of the frog and the cow, her identification with the
frog who wanted to grow as big as the cow easily refers to Carolina's real-life situation. She is warned, however, that it is unadvisable
to write reality by the shoemaker who asks if her book is communist (91). In addition, the very act of writing helps her escape reality
at the same time she supposedly represents it in her diaries:

"Enquanto escrevo vou pensando que resido num castelo cor de ouro que reluz na luz do sol" ("When I am writing I think I live in a golden castle that sparkles in the sunlight"; 49).

Carolina wields words as weapons as does Menchú and reiterates the pen's power over the sword: "Não tenho força física, mas as minhas palavras ferem mais do que espada. E as feridas são incicatrisaveis" ("I'm not physically strong, but my words hurt more than a sword. And the wounds are incurable"; 39-40). As strong as the biting directness of her words are her metaphors, since Carolina consciously attempts to create a literary text, despite her insistence on the contrary.[32] The title of the book comes from her comparison of São Paulo to a house; when Carolina is in the center of the city she feels like she is in the luxurious "sala de visita" 'sitting room' and when she is in the slums "sou um objeto fora de uso, digno de estar num quarto de despejo" ("I'm a useless object, fit for the garbage room"; 29). She also compares the city to a queen richly dressed except for cheap cotton stockings (the *favela*) and to a body whose ulcers (the *favela*) are not superficially visible to tourists. The city hides its ugly reality that Carolina exposes along with the reality disguised by carnivalesque politicians (112) and priests. With a flippancy like that of Jesusa she writes: "Fico pensando na vida atribulada e pensando nas palavras do Frei Luiz que nos diz para sermos humildes. Penso: se o Frei Luiz fosse casado e tivesse filhos e ganhasse salario minimo, ai eu queria ver se o Frei Luiz era humilde" ("I keep thinking about life's tribulations and about Brother Luiz's words, who tells us to be humble. I think: if Brother Luiz were married and had kids and earned minimum wage, then I'd want to see Brother Luiz humble"; 72). She names names, revealing the truth behind the carnival masks with which politicians and the Church disguise themselves. With facts, names and dates she builds her case.

In building that case, she must speak both for and against the *favelados* since she both publicizes the plight she shares with her neighbors in poverty and also states her case against the persecution she feels from them. Her motivation for writing is to denounce life in the *favela* and her neighbors, and to get herself out of the *favela*, which indeed she achieves. Carlos Vogt compares *Quarto de Despe-*

---

[32] Carolina wrote poems and novels that she tried to have published. See Levine and Meihy's book and their material in Carolina's unedited diaries.

jo with Saint Michael's book of judgment where he threatens to expose his neighbors' erred ways (210). Levine and Meihy point out she felt "a responsibility to act as an agent of stability and decency within the turmoil of the *favela*" (*Life and Death* 43). Carolina's writing simultaneously gives her voice and silences her since her act of writing isolates and stigmatizes her in the community: ". . .Eu percebo que se este Diário for publicado vai maguar muita gente. Tem pessoa que quando me vê passar saem da janela ou fecham as portas. Estes gestos não me ofendam. Eu até gosto porque não preciso parar para conversar" ("I feel if this Diary is published it will offend a lot of people. There are people who move away from their windows or shut their doors when they see me go by. These gestures don't offend me. I even like it because I don't have to stop to talk"; 66). As in the other testimonial texts already discussed, silence protects Carolina while she must break it to have her testimony heard. She disguises the criticisms directed at her neighbors behind silence, although they certainly suspect what she is up to in her diaries. She does not directly confront their collective persecution toward her (as she characterizes their behavior), but appeals to higher authorities in the form of publisher and public. The moral high ground she takes in the quotation above and throughout the diaries augments her project's importance; she has better things to do, i.e., her writing.

As with Jesusa and Rigoberta, her pose of moral superiority distinguishes her and supposedly creates a more dependable informant. Nevertheless, in a contradiction seen in the other testimonial texts, she admits that for her own purposes, for the disguise she dons, she must keep some information secret. "Eu tenho uma habilidade que não vou relatar aqui, porque isto há de defender-me. Quem vive na favela deve procurar isolar-se, viver só" ("I have a talent I'm not going to relate here, because this is supposed to defend me. Whoever lives in the favela should try to isolate herself, live alone"; 40). She does not want the reader to know certain negative facts about her, yet seems to displace the reason for this onto the environment of the *favela*. In this manner it is not because of her personal motivations and manipulations that she must keep quiet, but rather because of the pernicious life of the slums, which then reflects back on her neighbors and her self-defense. Those who live in the *favela* should isolate themselves, since people talk. Her isolation through writing leads to a solitude she shares with Jesusa, a solitude and silence both imposed by a way of life and used to maintain independence. Her main occupation of collecting paper leaves her alone much of the time and is symbolic of her secondary but transcendentally more valuable occupation of reading and writing. Her refusal to commit herself to any man links her work on the diaries to solitude in that "um homem não há de gostar de uma mulher que não pode passar sem ler. E que levanta para escrever. E que deita com lapis e papel debaixo do travesseiro. Por isso eu prefiro viver só para o meu ideal" ("a man doesn't like a woman that can't go without reading. And that gets up to write. And that goes to bed with pencil and paper under the pillow. That's why I prefer to live alone for my ideals"; 41).

In her loneliness Carolina often adopts a removed, ethnographic perspective in order to fulfill her ideal of recording reality. She refers, for example, to the confidence she inspires in those to whom she listens, a confidence that can eventually grow between testimonial subject and transcriber and which Poniatowska and Burgos Debray describe: "Percebi que êle confia em mim. As pessoas sem apoio igual ao carteiro quando encontra alguem que condoi-se dêles, reanimam o espirito" ("I felt that he trusts me. People like the mail man who have no one to help them have their spirits lifted when someone sympathizes with them"; 66). She speaks of the observed as if she did not belong to the *favela*: "A favela ficou quente igual a pimenta. Fiquei na rua até nove horas para prestar atenção nos movimentos da favela. Para ver como é que o povo age a noite" ("The favela was hot like pepper. I stayed in the street until nine to pay attention to the favela's movements. To see how the people act at night"; 63). She acts as if she had never seen the "the people at night," as if she were just visiting. This is to her advantage since although her personal experience as *favelada* lends authority to her testimony, her characterization of the *favelados* in general is negative. Even though she attempts to attribute the bad behavior she records to the inequality of a corrupt system handed down from above, she distinguishes herself from that behavior because if she is too closely associated with the others her integrity as reliable testimonial subject will become questionable. Her self-representation gains complexity and relevance to the contradictions inherent in testimonial transcription when she then contradicts this objectivity.

Her objectivity is particularly compromised when she mixes her roles as participant and transcriber, functioning as mediator in the *favela*, both forming part of the events and emphasizing her distance. These moments offer an ironic conflation of metaphoric (mediator and narrator *really do* share the same identity) and metonymic relationship between transcriber and testimonial subject. The community's annoyance at her mediation comments on the negative role of transcriber or ethnographer as meddler and also provides contradictions that undermine Carolina's authority in the text. There are at least four instances where she intercedes on one side or the other in disputes. She is called an "entrometida" 'busy body' (42) and after one instance, when she returns to her shack, everyone is looking at her and one of the participants in the fight yells at her: "Negra ordinaria! Você não é advogada, não é reporter e se mete em tudo!" ("Low-class black woman! You're not a lawyer, you're not a reporter and you stick your nose in everything!"; 135). Yet, Carolina asserts hypocritically, "Não interfiro-me porque eu não gosto de polemica" ("I don't interfere because I don't like controversy"; 64). Reflecting the dilemma of the transcriber or ethnologist through the conflicts of her own double role, she insists on her position as objective, separate observer while she also implicates herself in the activities she observes. As insider her authority to mediate is not recognized by the community because she is not a lawyer or reporter, but she does mimic Burgos Debray's and Poniatowska's readings. The observer or listener cannot be passive medium; she affects and participates in that which she is studying, altering the resulting information or *testimonio* by her presence.

The fact that the *favela* community itself does not authorize one of their own to mediate their affairs or advocate on their behalf, since she is neither lawyer nor reporter, emphasizes the ultimate purpose of Carolina's *testimonio* and *testimonio* in general. According to Dantas he is editing a book with which the *favelados* can identify, as well as one for intellectuals, yet which of Carolina's neighbors will acknowledge this "authentic" text, much less be able to buy or read it? Like other *testimonios, Quarto de Despejo*'s truth serves the didactic purpose of correcting dominant discourses to educate Brazil's intellectuals: "Carolina fêz uma coisa simples, tão simples que causa espanto. Disse a verdade que . . . oferece uma lição a grande parte dos nossos intelectuais" ("Carolina did something simple, so simple it's frightening. She told the truth that . . . teaches a lesson to most of our intellectuals"; 5). This idea is repeated within the diary itself: "O Brasil precisa ser dirigido por uma pessoa que já passou fome. A fome tambem é professora" ("Brazil needs to be led by a person who has experienced hunger. Hunger is also a teacher"; 23). Therefore, this lesson must be taught through the voice of a person who has suffered hunger, a witness. However, in this text she is problematically a person who shuns her representation as the emblematic identity of all the *favela*'s hungry voices in order to cross the boundary dividing her from those with enough to fill their stomachs. The border that intellectuals would like to open to know the other side is two-way. This becomes particularly evident when after gaining fame she is criticized for not knowing or remaining in her assigned role, and for her conservative morality that annoyed progressives (Levine and Meihy, *Life and Death* 55-7). Like Menchú she was denied autonomy beyond the text's rhetorical confines and readers' desires.

This leads us back to the editor Audálio Dantas. My focus here is on Carolina's narrative contradictions and self-construction, but Dantas's presence of course cannot be overlooked for two reasons relevant to my discussion, aside from the obvious question of his influence on the diaries' published form: his framing introduction and his embodiment of the reading audience before whom Carolina must negotiate her self-representation. Her awareness of an audience and inherent dialogue with the future reader lie at the root of her divided pose, at times that of representative *favela* inhabitant, at times that of ethnographic observer. She must defend herself before authority and search to legitimate herself and her project. She must communicate a different reality to a literate audience, must consider how to persuade, how to mediate, how to speak both through her own voice and that of the *favela*. The ethnographic and legal discourses inherent in all *testimonios* therefore permeate her text.

Despite the fact that Carolina writes down her own diary and is always the sole author on the title page, she does remain dependent on Dantas to publish her work, before whom she must legitimate herself in much the same way that Menchú and Jesusa must defend their version of the past before those with access to publishing. Her daughter Vera recalls Dantas saying "I had to correct the parts that were confusing and to lighten up the parts that were too serious" (Levine and Meihy, *Life and Death* 103). Levine and Meihy have, however, found evidence that Dantas's editing lay in elimination, not in rewriting. He is concerned to prove that his intervention did

not exceed "algum trabalho de composição" ("some organization"), which in fact means cutting thirty-five original notebooks to
the 160-page published version (Vogt 207), or cutting two-thirds of
the original writings (Jesus, *Unedited* 205-6).[33] The eliminated parts
tend to criticize racism and political figures (or Dantas) too strongly
for the tastes of the editor and a mainstream audience (Jesus,
Unedited 186, 206). Thus Dantas represents the public whom Carolina must persuade before its resistance to the full impact of her
message. Dantas does not position himself metaphorically in relation to Carolina, nor creates a vicarious identity.[34]

In the introduction, Dantas's minimization of his manipulation
of the text in fact constructs Carolina as a simple woman whose language is radically different, and consequently authentic, from those
of intellectual readers, who must therefore act on her behalf, if at
all. Downplaying editorial intervention serves in this case to essentialize Carolina's identity as "other." As we have seen, both editor
and writer seek to legitimate their roles before the reader. In fact,
Dantas appeals to the authority of the "grande poeta" 'great poet'
Manuel Bandeira from an article that Bandeira wrote on *Quarto de
Despejo* entitled "A Humilde Verdade" 'The Humble Truth.' The
poet testifies (as expert witness?) that there are "nestas páginas certos erros certas impropriedades de expressão, certos pedantismos
de meia instrução primaria, que são de flagrante autenticidade,
impossíveis de inventar" ("in these pages certain mistakes, certain
errors of expression, certain pedantries from an incomplete primary
education, that are flagrantly authentic, impossible to make up"; 6).
By establishing a limit on possible linguistic invention by the editor,
Bandeira characterizes Carolina' writing as radically different, thus
emphasizing the reader's separation from the narrator when the
diaries also attempt the opposite, producing the conflicting purposes of Carolina's voice in the diaries themselves.

Else Ribeiro Pires Vieira's analysis of *Quarto de Despejo*'s framing texts also raises Carolina's "dual being" that she does not

---

[33] The unexplained ellipsis throughout the text are sometimes signs of this editing work, sometimes Carolina's sign for the passage of time (Jesus, *Unedited* 186).

[34] The fact that Dantas is male indirectly draws attention once again to the feminist theories of oral testimony and field work that wish to eliminate the separation
between ethnologist/journalist and testimonial subject but that ignore the remaining power relationship between the two. Dantas's gender does not lead us to easily
expect an idealized notion of the relationship.

resolve (117), but with greater emphasis on Dantas's and Carolina's convergence (or metaphorical exchangeability): "It could be said that the other, the reporter, was already inside Carolina and vice-versa" (113). Indeed, Vieira identifies important parallels between the two, where Dantas used Carolina for self-promotion the way Carolina used the *favelados* (116). Also, like a pharmakon Dantas enables Carolina's writing and partially silences it through editing (115, 117), like any mediating transcriber, and like Carolina's own approach to the *favelados*. In fact, what first called Dantas's attention to Carolina was her yelling out that she would put neighbors with whom she was arguing in her book, reminiscent of Poniatowska hearing Josefina Bórquez's feisty outburst for the first time. The relationship between Dantas and Carolina does not, however, take on convergence beyond the typical ventriloquism that legitimates the intellectual transcriber's point of view through an authentic *favelada*. This is because her duality becomes more wrapped up in her identity than does his mediating role. Dantas seeks legitimation and self-promotion, but not a personal or national identity for himself. Carolina is constructing her subjectivity as both writer and *favelada*. She is part of the *favela* in a way that Dantas is not part of her. Furthermore, the negotiation of her dual self-representation already began before she met him, which makes problematic the bilateralism Vieira describes in their convergence: "Audálio Dantas transformed Carolina's writing, Carolina transformed with Audálio" (116). This "bilateralism" leaves Carolina as the only one subject to change as he alters her diaries and she reacts to his presence. While Carolina does include Dantas's presence in entries after their meeting, her unresolved contradictions and self-representation pre-date Dantas's intervention. Moreover, in her later books she adopts a removed, ethnographic voice less than before because she no longer lives in the *favela*. She does, however, retain her denunciatory, and at times sensationalist, journalistic mode, particularly regarding social class and race in *Diário de Bitita*, but from the perspective of individual experience.

Vieira's approximation of Dantas and Carolina seeks an "in-betweenness" that breaches the divide between the subaltern and the intellectual through equal displacements of identity. Testimonial discourse in general attempts to cross cultural barriers, yet the texts seen here question that possibility. The text of Menchú's life story shows the hazards for the testimonial project of her crossing cultural barriers, of her leaving her community to work with *ladinos* and learn Spanish (Sommer, "Sin secretos" 139). Poniatowska wishes to cross a barrier that separates her from feeling truly Mexican and that separates her from the vast majority of women in Mexico. Carolina wishes to cross the barrier that prohibits her from leaving the *favela* and feeding her children every day. All attempt to cross barriers of communication through translation of a marginalized experience for a privileged audience, except the possibility of such communication is questioned in the testimonial text itself and in the process that creates the published testimony. In fact, the truth of the narrator's circumstances reflected in her negotiation of self-representation becomes lost in the problematic possibility of finding the truth of the facts recounted and in discussions of the delegitimizing effects of manipulated truth. The narrator's strategies to legitimate the text can elicit critical reactions that negate legitimizing efforts.

Using three examples of variations on testimonial texts by women, we have seen how the search for textual legitimation links several key elements of all three works: resistant silence; orality; truth as a tool toward textual authority and its particular relevance to *testimonio*; the tension between individual and collective identities; and the transcriber's and the testimonial subject's self-representation through metaphoric and metonymic modes that produce certain associations and "vicarious identities" that change the subject–in the sense of speaking subject and of the text's focus. Most importantly, we have seen testimonial subjects' active negotiations of textual authority across social boundaries and the essentializing constructions of marginalized identity, which threaten the speaker's status as subject. Her testimonial subjectivity is subject to change: the testimonial process changes her self-representation as she actively negotiates the shifts in her circumstances. She receives change and manipulates it.

As a testimonial *novel, Hasta no verte, Jesús mío* more self-consciously exposes the complexities of the transcriber-speaker relationship than do the other works. Poniatowska novelizes a resistant woman's testimony, both emphasizing her distance from Jesusa's experience and also filling an absence in her own identity as she perceives it. Burgos Debray positions herself as nothing more than conduit for Menchú's intensely political testimony, yet in the introduction indicates that Menchú's story and the process of transcription serve to fill an absence she also perceives in her identity. Carolina assumes both roles, reflecting two dynamics, almost two parallel stories, in her diaries. Carolina the representative informant and Carolina the transcriber as one and the same literally conflate two women in almost a parody of the previous transcribers' tendencies to read themselves in the informants' lives. The fact that this conflation breeds conflicting goals reveals the reading as a misreading that works against the unstable, non-essentializing self-representation that the testimonial narrator must balance with the boundaries established by the testimonial process.

Metaphors of the transcription process within the texts themselves lay bare the struggle for legitimation in the *testimonio* and the *novela testimonial,* a critical process not only for these genres in general, but also for an analysis of difference in feminist theory. Many issues brought up in this chapter apply to similar works by men, but crucial are the consequences for feminist perspectives and the insights brought by feminist perspectives on this type of relationship. The potentially exploitative relationship between a privileged woman and a marginalized woman becomes an instrument to shift authority to the marginalized, a shift that can reflect a desire to shift authority from male hands to female hands. In such a case identification between the two women becomes integral to the transcriber's endeavor. As we have seen, however, this ceding of authority is problematic even when partially achieved and some feminist theories of self-representation aid in clarifying the problems. The next chapter investigates how similar situations arise in non-testimonial narratives where authority relationships between women, or between a marginalized woman and a male "intermediary," reflect and broaden arguments from this chapter. While the *testimonio* and *novela testimonial* as genres emerge from a particular political imperative and specific, urgent, extra-textual circumstances, fictional texts can serve to further enrich our understanding of the authority relationships underlying testimonial texts and place *testimonio* as central, not marginal, to Latin American narrative.

CHAPTER 2

FICTIONS OF TESTIMONY: ESSENTIALIZED IDENTITIES
AND THE OTHER IN ONESELF IN TWO WORKS BY
CLARICE LISPECTOR

> Hasta aquí hemos analizado el contenido de este pro-
> ducto que llamamos novela-testimonio. Ahora veamos
> cuáles son los pasos que deben seguirse para su elabo-
> ración. Ojalá no tenga esto nada que ver con una re-
> ceta culinaria.
>
> Until now we have analyzed the content of this prod-
> uct we call novel-testimony. Now let us see what steps
> one should take for its creation. I hope this has noth-
> ing to do with a cooking recipe. [1]
>
> Miguel Barnet, "La novela-testimonio: socio-
> literatura"

> Bien dijo Lupercio Leonardo, que bien se puede filo-
> sofar y aderezar la cena. Y yo suelo decir viendo estas
> cosillas: Si Aristóteles hubiera guisado, mucho más
> hubiera escrito.
>
> Lupercio Leonardo spoke well when he said that one
> can philosophize and season a dinner. And I tend to
> say, seeing these little details: If Aristotle had cooked,
> he would have written much more.
>
> Sor Juana Inés de la Cruz, *Respuesta a Sor Filotea*

THIS chapter's intentionally ambiguous title reflects the complex
and often contradictory rhetorical manifestations of subjectivity, representation, and legitimation in the testimonial texts of the
last chapter and the works of fiction in this chapter. "Fictions of
Testimony" alludes to both the problematic nature of truth in the

---

[1] All translations in this chapter are mine, unless otherwise noted.

testimonio and *novela testimonial*, and also the testimonial elements of two novels by the Brazilian author Clarice Lispector, analyzed in this section. By "testimonial elements" I mean a range of textual characteristics and outcomes of the *testimonio* and *novela testimonial* as I have presented them, such as the problem of representativity, testimonial discourse's reliance on stable truths it also wishes to undermine, and reliance on the testimonial informant as "vicarious identity" to compensate a lack perceived by the privileged transcriber. Testimonial elements in some fiction can closely simulate and even parody the transcriber-informant relationship or raise related issues through relationships of authority and legitimation even when the narrated situation does not reproduce an oral interview format like that of testimonial texts. With my title I attempt to indicate the two directions in which one can read *testimonios* with fiction: works of fiction serve to highlight, comment and play ironically upon the testimonial project while the *testimonio* and *novela testimonial* provide a provocative framework that highlights the politics of writing another life in those works of fiction. The significance of *testimonio* is its paradoxical process in the service of solidarity, stimulating examination of critical strategies and the very act of authorship that writes and absorbs or appropriates an other. As Alberto Moreiras notes, "[Testimonio's] tenuous abandonment of the literary . . . has paradoxically enabled us to see, under a better light, the deep implications of literary discourse with power-knowledge effects" (216). Thus testimonial discourse *should* be read with literary discourse while keeping in mind their distinctions in process, in readership, and in what they ask of the reader. The irony described by Moreiras surfaces particularly in literary texts when a privileged character gradually comes to usurp the role of the subaltern character who constitutes the text's rationale or inspiration, or literally pre-text, as is the case in testimonial discourse.

By examining elements comparable to testimonial texts I do not assume that either of the works of fiction studied here consciously responds to testimonial writing or originates in actual conversations. [2] By also asserting that the works of fiction I have chosen indirectly question the *testimonio*'s pretense of ceding space to the subaltern, I do not discard the imperatives that produce testimonial

---

[2] Clarice Lispector was, however, conscious of the Western ethnographic perspective, most evident in her story "A Mulher Mais Pequena do Mundo."

works but also have in mind Latin American literature's frequent engagement with social and political issues. [3] One example of this appears in a novel by Clarice Lispector discussed in this chapter, *A Hora da Estrela 'The Hour of the Star,'*: "Esta história acontece em estado de emergência e de calamidade pública" ("This story takes place in a state of emergency and of public calamity"; 8). Lispector then indicates her story leaves an open question; who will answer the question: you? On the one hand, the *testimonio* as the eyewitness account of oppression wields a potential political tool for change, as Rigoberta Menchú's testimony shows. On the other hand, I agree with Gayatri Spivak when she states that, "what I find useful is the sustained and developing work on the *mechanics* of the constitution of the Other; we can use it to much greater analytic and interventionist advantage than invocations of the *authenticity* of the Other" ("Can" 294). Doris Sommer reflects this thinking when she posits that the "question, finally, is not what 'insiders' can know as opposed to 'outsiders'; it is how those positions are being constructed as incommensurate or conflictive" (*Proceed* 8-9). Brett Levinson enacts both points when he works on the mechanics of constituting the Other in Latin American orientalism and de-orientalism, resulting in the call for a third Latinamericanism conscious of these mechanics. Interestingly, Spivak uses "invocation" to describe the manipulation of the other's authenticity, a word that evokes the religious connotations of sacrifice and appropriation addressed in Chapter 3. By "invocations of authenticity" Spivak refers to intellectuals' representations of the oppressed's concrete and therefore "authentic" reality and shows how intellectuals ignore their own role in that reality, also an issue to which Chapter 3 returns. The difficulty of representing that authenticity without reflecting back on the writer creates the necessity of examining the mechanics of truth's function in language since, as Leigh Gilmore and Hayden White have pointed out, equating physical, concrete people and events with their representations gets us into trouble when seeking a singular, "real" truth. As in the first chapter, my conclusions here indicate the effects of the power relationships, lin-

---

[3] Although this statement is practically self-evident and has been elaborated by many a critic, Cristina Ferreira-Pinto's 1997 article, "Escrita, Auto-Representação e Realidade Social no Romance Feminino Latino-Americano," provides a recent example, and one focused on women's novels, including a Brazilian perspective (*Revista de Crítica Literaria Latinoamericana* 23.45 (1997) 81-95).

guistic devices and linguistic deviations through which a subaltern voice must pass. Levinson might characterize these relationships, devices, and deviations as hegemonic mirrors rather than counter-hegemonic conduits, mirrors used to reflect and represent the marginal in ways that disable attempts to escape dominant paradigms. The works of fiction, not surprisingly, exhibit consciousness of these mediations, mediations personified by the testimonial text's transcriber and intensified in the author of fiction's acute concern with language's limitations.

In Miguel Barnet's essay "La novela-testimonio: socio-literatura," one of the seminal essays on the testimonial novel as an institutionalized genre, the Cuban ethnologist and author attempts to de(-)limit "oppressive, misleading" notions of the novel by focusing on the fiction author's relationship with reality and the dynamic, social function of recounting (280), thus implicitly linking his concept of the novel with orality. The novel's author should represent reality, which in this essay influenced by socialist realism seems singular and certainly describable. Therefore, the literary author assumes the task of defining the surrounding world. From this intent to name, define, and synthesize "la mayor cantidad de elementos puros posibles" 'the greatest number possible of pure elements' emerges the ideal novel, and most especially the *novela testimonial*, as a founding literature (284-86). Foundational literature therefore reunites the pure and the essential toward an understanding of a national identity, a truth based on representable reality in transparent language. According to his broadened definition of the novel and *novela testimonial*, Barnet does not limit testimonial genres to texts based entirely or even partially on the ethnographic interview since literature should equally portray national reality, although he *does* point to his own *Biografía de un cimarrón* 'Biography of a Runaway Slave,' based on such interviews, as a "modelo ideal" because the informant Esteban Montejo stands out as extraordinary individual *and* exemplary representative of a transcendental historical moment (287). He articulates in this ideal the two roles testimonial subjects juggle, as we saw in Chapter 1. Barnet uses Carpentier's *El reino de este mundo* '*The Kingdom of This World*,' a third-person fictional narrative, as an example of the *novela testimonial*, since the protagonist Ti Noel "no es real, pero cumple la función de *griot*, de un protagonista de la novela-testimonio" ("is not real, but accomplishes the function of *griot*, of a protagonist of the novel-testimony"; 288). Ti Noel's experience tells us something about the national context, and should "establecer un diálogo con su tiempo, funcionar integralmente" ("establish a dialogue with his time, function integrally"; 288). Ti Noel and Montejo's representativity contribute to a founding literature and to the understanding of a collective, national identity. Ti Noel is a character who "exists" (300). Hence, for Barnet a fictional character's representation of and dialogue with his time and people, and his enactment of the testimonial informant's role as *griot* are sufficient to blur the border between *testimonio* and (an albeit narrow notion of) literature by essentially defining testimonial writing as one of national identity, not just of marginal identity, even though Barnet may see the two merge in revolutionary Cuba. Thus, a fictional figure "exists" if he truthfully represents some aspect of the nation, the nation as stable and perhaps prescriptive concept. [4]

Barnet's concept of discernible truth and reality and his confidence in language's ability to accurately capture them, even for subaltern narrators, leaves him in a position of (re)producing dominant, official truths to counteract "oppressive, misleading" concepts of literature. The testimonial informant's (or fictional character's) authority remains dependent upon preconceived collective identities, even if he or she is an extraordinary individual. Barnet's definition of the *novela testimonial* thus oversimplifies the testimonial process, yet his incorporation of fiction directly or obliquely reflecting testimonial concerns into discussion of testimonial discourse is useful and justifiable for reasons distinct from or even opposite to those asserted by Barnet. Struggling with language and writing as media to communicate marginalized reality constitutes a central task of *testimonio* and much Latin American literature. The literary works studied in the next pages represent situations that act out linguistic struggles arising from language's mediation between

---

[4] Barnet's conflation of *testimonio* and fiction along the lines of national identity of course brings to mind studies of Spanish American founding fictions of the nineteenth century, such as those of Doris Sommer (*Foundational Fictions* (Berkeley: U Cal P, 1991)) and Nicolas Shumway (*The Invention of Argentina* (Berkeley: U Cal P, 1991)). One could say that in both Barnet's essay and the nineteenth century writing that attempted to create a sense of unity and common direction for nascent nations, national identities are mapped through blurring fact and fiction, where fiction wishes to come across as describing reality faithfully, legitimating its unifying message.

consciousness and the world (White 29), and the closely related partial failure of the testimonial project.

My exploration of testimonial discourse's contradictions, tensions and imperfect fulfillment of the wish for the true story, in addition to my incorporating testimonial discourse and fiction into the same theoretical framework, does not deny *testimonio* as a profoundly political and radically resistant project, but does recognize its mediated fulfillment of those expectations. We are to believe that testimonial texts were written outside the disciplinary discourse of literature, so that an analysis of "literary" tropes in these *testimonios* would become unjustified and even damaging to the *testimonio*'s integrity, and therefore to the informant's integrity. Kimberly Nance takes a similar point of view regarding damage to the reader's critical role (577). Examining meanings contained below the surface of the text, meanings that contradict the explicit purpose of the text would suggest a disguise or dissimulation that repressive, hegemonic discourses utilize, literature being one of those discourses viewed to be a hegemonic tool (Levinson 183). As we have seen, however, disguises have served as resistance. Recourse to the extraliterary does of course remain a vital and *rhetorically* distinguishing characteristic of *testimonio*, as Moreiras maintains: "the cultural significance of testimonio includes an extraliterary dimension that is just as irreducible [as the aesthetic dimension]" (212). Its "cultural significance" and authority as an important discourse rely on a particular process of elaboration and rhetorical allusion to that process, plus the urgency of a historical crisis situation.

Awareness of *testimonio*'s reference to the extraliterary alters readers' responses, either inspiring political action or higher expectations of a truthful performance, both demonstrated by the response to Rigoberta Menchú's narrative. For Beverley the *response* elicited by the two distinguishes *testimonio* from the "field" of literature ("Real" 279). In a similar vein Claudia Ferman asserts that through devices she calls "conditions of authentication," readers of *testimonio* are asked to make "acts of faith" to believe the story. Readers of fiction, on the other hand, are asked to suspend their disbelief and identify with the narrator (156-7). Sommer has shown, however, that some fiction by minority or "particularist" writers discourages that identification with the narrator in order to maintain difference and a space of democratic negotiation (*Proceed* 2). *Testimonio* maintains that difference as well and does require "acts of faith," but also acts of empathy that dispose readers to those leaps of faith. Nance defines testimonial discourse by its impetus for social or political change, dependent on readers' actions, but also by its threat to the readers' comfort, which provokes evasive reading strategies (Nance). This call to action faced with resistance parallels the difficulty in defining *testimonio*'s distinction from fiction based on the readers' degree of identification with the narrator or their degree of passivity and distancing. In other words, while there are predominant tendencies one way or another, as the above scholars have noted, the degree of identification with the testimonial or fictional narrator does not guarantee a stable distinction between *testimonio* and fiction, considering the variation in texts of both genres. Readers do, however, adopt certain *expectations* for most texts labeled testimonial, and ultimately readers' involvement in the text based on expectations, by invitation or self-invitation, through activism or a feeling of entitlement to judge the text, that marks testimonial writing regardless of that involvement's outcome.

In contrast to extraliterary reference and readers' expectations, outsider status can no longer constitute part of testimonial *discourse*'s definition, even if the narrator remains outsider. According to Nelly Richard in "Bordes, diseminación y postmodernismo," mainstreamed *testimonio* has come to occupy the center through the academy's consumption, serving what Levinson might call a de-orientalist function where the *testimonio*'s rhetoric ultimately reflects back on the privileged. *Testimonio* as much as literature has come to occupy the center as a consumer object, linking the two in terms of access to the order of canonicity and thus a potentially reduced subversive impact. For this reason *testimonio* cannot be separated from literature on ethical grounds, as artificially untainted by authorial, ethnographic, or academic manipulations. After all, *testimonio*'s purpose *is* to reach a mainstream audience through transcription and publication; that is the strategy chosen by *testimonio*, as Camacho de Schmidt puts it (41). In its current mode of production we expect too much: we expect testimonial writing, like the testimonial subject herself, to retain an authentic difference and also accessibility, allowing the reader a certain passivity. In fact, the alternative of maintaining *testimonio* on the outside contributes to the fetishization of marginalized identity that permanently disenfranchises the represented group. Thus, while keeping in mind testimonial discourse's distinct originary process and the need to avoid divorcing it from action, denying its status as *representation* mediated by language and denying its informant any creative abilities and motives, that is, refusing its kinship to literary representations of marginalization, repeats the imposition of preconceived truthfulness that threatens once again the informant with objectification. Carrying that project closer to its objective requires a critical reading of testimonial discourse's current medium in order to investigate moving beyond the medium's limitations, and readers' limitations (or resistance as Nance would state).

In his essay "What's Wrong with Representation?" Santiago Colás demonstrates *testimonio*'s process as one of representation that does not guarantee, nor need guarantee, the transparent transmission of realist truth in order to resist hegemonies that silence the marginal. In the context of ethnography, Kamala Visweswaran advocates a feminist ethnology based on experimental ethnography that acknowledges ruptures and incomprehensions and incorporates literary elements (20, 100). Her objective is to move away from declarative or official historiography founded on transparent realist narrative (61). As Janet L. Finn has written:

> [The works discussed] raise questions about the "truth" value of the novel and the ethnographic text in representing cultural experience. By calling a work fiction, does one remove it from the realm of argumentation? Does that diminish its power to contest the history and practices to which it responds? In what forms can knowledge be packaged to best challenge the histories of misrepresentation by dominant groups? . . . Lacking in this understanding of culture [in recent critical writings] is a sense of urgency and struggle on the part of less powerful subjects to inscribe their own stories in this "politics of identification." (133)

Similarly, Colás responds to George Yúdice's insistence on realist representation and truth value as sources of *testimonio*'s authority by pointing out how Yúdice's emphasis on Rigoberta Menchú's community's materialism "restricts the meaning of 'other' to that materiality, sensuous being, or body fetishized in poststructuralism" (166). Other parts of Yúdice's work on *testimonio* de-emphasize absolute truth and reflect greater sensitivity to the process than evidenced in this quotation. At the same time, Yúdice's reading quoted in Colás follows the framework established by Burgos, a framework that sets up a metaphoric reading. The fetishization Colás describes, based in part on the *testimonio*'s truth value, is linked to narrative processes in works of fiction. When Colás affirms that Indian *testimonio* actually stems from the *destruction* of the harmony with materiality emphasized by Yúdice and the division between "an Indian's self-consciousness as a human and the inhuman material conditions of his or her life," Colás continues: "To this extent, the opposition constructed, along an axis of representation, between *testimonio* on the one hand and boom, poststructuralist, or other kinds of literary representation on the other, begins to blur" (166). In other words, reality is the violation of the ideal truth used to describe a certain cultural identity. If reality is not the ideal described, the ideal becomes a fiction no more or no less reminiscent of reality than the fictional writing of reality. Moreover, one could argue that while the testimonial fiction may obscure an evolving reality, a fictional representation exposing the obscuration caused by idealization may ultimately prove more "truthful" as well.

While the combination of *testimonio* and works of fiction may appear to undermine *testimonio*'s political impact as a discourse that challenges hegemonic and elite literary discourse and official history, the revelations created by this intertextual reading indeed expose ways in which *testimonio* subverts hegemonic assumptions of identity and agency beyond a truth value that can limit the possibilities of the informant and reinforce her location on the margins. Colás writes from the perspective that *testimonio*'s use of representation as failed transparency is as essential to its political power as its role in bringing to public, dominant discourse alternative versions of history.

> The resistance value of the testimonio as cultural practice and artifact, far from resting on either the absolute identity between a people, their representative, the interlocutor, and the foreign sympathizer, seems rather to derive from the tension generated by the disjuncture between these different subjects. It is not the testimonio's uncontaminated positing of some pure, truthful, native history that makes it so powerful, but rather its subversion of such a project. (170) [5]

---

[5] Camacho de Schmidt notes that "tension generated by the disjuncture between these different subjects" (Colás) in one sense is a selling point: "a mayor tensión cultural entre emisos y receptos, mayor interés del receptor" (39). Colás's reading of the tension between different subjects as subversive does not in the con-

Thus, objections to combining testimonial and literary discourse so that one enlightens the reading of the other are based upon an idealistic reading of *testimonio* that like Levinson's de-orientalism sees *testimonio*'s subversive potential within a role for the speaker whose truth is established and maintained by the system to be subverted. Strict separation of *testimonio* and literature on ethical and political grounds overlook the ethical and political grounds on which *not* to do so: testimonial subjects' mastery of rhetorical complexity and *testimonio*'s indeed subversive nature as a discourse that ultimately challenges assumptions about authenticity and exposes its own circularity that turns back upon privilege.

Reflecting the *testimonio*'s dialogic form, I therefore set up a dialogue between fiction and testimonial texts: the lessons of *testimonio* form a framework for fictional texts and the fiction I examine in this chapter comments and plays ironically upon several facets of *testimonio* and its critical analysis. Beyond this, it is worthwhile to consider how Barnet's concept of the *novela testimonial* as a founding fiction may be appropriate to women's writing in a different sense from that intended by Barnet. Texts that might qualify as founding fictions of women's experience recount a collective "historia de las gentes sin historia" 'history of the people without history' of which Barnet speaks; however, women's founding fictions recount a collective history that may not seem to carry transcendent meaning for the kind of national identity to which Barnet refers. Hence Barnet dismisses the cooking recipe as a paradigm for his prescription for the *novela testimonial*, while the cookbook has been considered a founding "genre" for women's writing and women's collective history. His easy dismissal is especially ironic if we follow Debra Castillo's concept of recipe as dialogue, relating the recipe to her writing: "I said at the opening of this book that my strategy was to give you this piece of writing like the first step in an exchange, like a recipe for use and modification, as the continuation of a dialogue opened in the first taste of a food we both savor" (305). The exchange of recipes as a grassroots dialogue would seem to correspond well to several political aspects of Barnet's definitions

---

text of the rest of his essay appear to refer to the enforced otherness of a marketable testimonial identity, but rather to a disjuncture between the subjects' projects where the informant asserts her own agency and upsets her easy packaging.

of the *novela testimonial*. The broader significance of women's experience, and what their texts could indeed reveal, has been overlooked, as Sor Juana's quotation in my epigraph suggests. She vindicates a domestic chore as creative, productive and philosophical in the effort to valorize her intellectual development. *Hasta no verte, Jesús mío, Me llamo Rigoberta Menchú* and *Quarto de Despejo* are certainly embedded in the greater political context as critical voices, and also as women's voices, including when the narrators tend toward a non-sexed self-representation. The works of fiction in this chapter do not incorporate broad, historical events–sometimes the extreme opposite–but do incorporate transcendent social relations that define a collective experience, especially that of women: the relationship between maid and mistress and how the maid's identity is interpreted for her, and the almost invisibility of the anonymous poor barely eking out an existence.

Although there are other fictional narratives that illustrate my assertions, this chapter focuses on two novels by Clarice Lispector that most profoundly explore relationships of privilege. Her *A Paixão Segundo G.H. 'The Passion According to G.H.'* from 1964 has as its starting point a maid's departure. Representations of maids aptly reflect in exaggerated form the dilemmas of writing another identity that compensates an absence in a privileged subject's self-perception since maids' roles are traditionally an absence of identity to be filled by the employer. The employer determines the limits of the maid's presence, making her a projection of the mistress's desires by carrying them out as extra hands for the employer. My discussion of *A Paixão* continues in the next chapter's observations on violence and sacrifice, so Lispector's *A Hora da Estrela 'The Hour of the Star'* forms the heart of the present chapter.

A Hora da Estrela is Lispector's last novel, published in 1977. Macabéa constitutes a protagonist whose existence does not even reach the recognition of maid. She rather seems to be nothing, the truly subaltern that constitutes an impoverished majority. For this reason, her narrator's desire to live through her becomes especially ironic, almost parodying Barnet when he writes that "América requiere de la obra de fundación. América necesita conocerse, sustentarse" ("America requires a foundational writing. America needs to know itself, sustain itself"; 301). Like Macabéa, Lispector's slender volume in simple language looks poor and malnourished from lack of big words, but in reality offers vast complexity and ambiguity. Lispector's male narrator Rodrigo S.M. is accordingly ironic, revealing presumptions about gender that provide an additional layer of critique to idealized notions about women's better capacity to weaken barriers of difference. Although Lispector's protagonist does not prostitute herself (she is too ugly and too oblivious of sexuality at all), the novel subtly alludes to a vaguely sexual side to the narrator's attraction to Macabéa.

By founding stable identity on displacements, tracing gestures that falsely lend agency to the disenfranchised protagonist, and repeating metaphors seen in the first chapter, these two works of fiction describe the privileged character's attempt to name and self-define him or herself in identification with or legitimation through the marginalized. Where in fictional representation do metonymic relationships slip into metaphor? How do these works of fiction represent the desire for truth exhibited by readers of *testimonio*? In addition, these texts interweave the attempt to address "woman." How do consciousness of women's situation and the need to legitimate oneself as a woman affect representations of self and other women? How do they affect fictional representations of racially and economically marginalized women and of power relationships between women?

THE OTHER AS ESSENCE AND ABSENCE IN LISPECTOR'S *A PAIXÃO SEGUNDO G.H.*

The relationship between maid and mistress, so common in Latin America, constitutes one central aspect of the domestic experience of women writers who predominantly come from the upper classes and appears frequently throughout Latin American women's writing. By their presence, domestic workers have allowed privileged women more time to write, so while some *testimonios* mediate the experience of domestic servants themselves, such as *Se necesita muchacha*, fiction also suggests the maid's experience indirectly through the writer's sense of the maid's authority. In Lispector's *A Paixão Segundo G.H.* the maid's thoughts remain closed to the reader. Her mistress interprets her body and the signs she left behind. This text's relevance to testimonial discourse also stems from the racial and class differences that characterize both the transcriber-informant relationship and the mistress-maid relationship. Cornejo-

Parriego has described the latter relationship in Poniatowska's "Love Story" as the representation of a lingering colonial relationship between a *criolla* and a woman of color, a relationship that undermines notions of automatic solidarity between women and forces us to approach women's identity from a postcolonial awareness of that identity's plurality and fluidity (15). Although *A Paixão* is not about the overt gesture of lending voice to marginalized women, the maid's absence and the space of her empty room serve as catalysts for the narrator's introspective approximation to others, just as the maid allows the middle-class woman time to write. *A Paixão* originates in the overwhelming presence of the maid in the *criolla*'s thoughts, the maid's silence given the "breve rótulo" [6] not by her own words but by the mistress.

As already mentioned, the novel begins with the recent departure of the maid, Janair. She exists materially only in a drawing she created and in her mistress G.H.'s memory and reflections. The entire novel's events consist of the woman G.H.'s entrance into the maid's room of her apartment, expecting to find a mess. After contemplation of what she really finds, G.H. opens the wardrobe door from where a large cockroach appears. G.H. slams the door on the roach and during her prolonged consideration of the roach's being and her own, she tastes the roach's oozing matter in a kind of communion. G.H.'s short but life-changing journey to this room leaves her searching for essential, prelinguistic, even prehistoric, truth. Janair has vacated her room, leaving a rough, charcoal drawing on the wall, in reality a form of writing, we are told. This writing without writing hints at a truth beyond the superfice on which G.H. lives her life, symbolizing a prelinguistic essence G.H. comes to seek, but also Janair's only first-person testimony, left to G.H.'s interpretation. The nudity of the man, woman and dog in the image goes beyond nakedness, since their outlines contain no marks to describe their nudity. They are nothing more than empty contours, as is G.H., whom the drawing of the woman represents. G.H. interprets Janair's testimony as reflecting back on her. Although *A Paixão*'s complexity extends well beyond those aspects I elucidate

---

[6] Here I allude to my reference to Sor Juana in Chapter One's discussion of silence. Sor Juana writes that silence in order to be effective must include an explanation for its silence, a "breve rótulo" that indicates the silence does not mean nothing to say.

here, G.H.'s encounter with the drawing, the roach and her self in a dry, bright maid's room merits mention for its relevance to reflections on testimonial texts through truth, paradox, silence, attempted reversals of power, self-knowledge through a radically different being, and the possibility of communicating one's own and another's experience–the latter clearly one of *testimonio*'s fundamental aims.

Before entering the maid's room at the end of a back hall, G.H. existed as an ectoplasm, an image projected to others, a façade of which she denudes herself upon going "out" into the world of the unknown corner of her apartment (17, 22, 42). Janair's drawing, however, indicates that the maid in the back room was not fooled by the façade and perceived the empty truth behind the image. The room's clean surfaces that do not submit to G.H.'s desire to correct the dirt she expects the maid has left irritate her since they reflect nothing but herself: "agora estava descobrindo com irritação que o quarto não me irritava apenas, eu o detestava, àquele cubículo que só tinha superfícies: suas entranhas haviam esturricado" ("now I was discovering with irritation that the room did not just irritate me, I hated it, that cubicle that only had surfaces: its innards had dried up"; 29). Her "exit" into the room marks the initiation of her search for the truth that she has lost, and that the maid and the cockroach possess. The questionable, racist discourse that subtly compares the maid to the roach, a less advanced life form no matter how glorified by its proximity to the essence of life, is later exploded in *A Hora da Estrela* where the narrator seeks the truth through his abused, humiliated protagonist. Previous to the epiphany to which her thoughts lead her in the abandoned room, G.H. existed only in the negative; the image she projected was what she was not. "Como eu não sabia o que era, então 'não ser' era a minha maior aproximação da verdade: pelo menos eu tinha o lado avesso" ("Since I did not know what I was, 'not being' was my closest approximation to the truth: at least I had the flip side"; 22).

G.H.'s confrontation with reality from a marginal perspective outside her own forces her to confront her own emptiness and the infinite potential of "ser" 'being' opposed to "não ser" 'not being.' The gesture of opening discursive space that ultimately reflects dominant discourses in mediated testimonial writing appears in another form in G.H.'s experience. As she opens herself to the other's existence and meaning, the text is about her existence and one wonders to what extent privilege is undermined when the medium cannot completely abandon paradigms that define privilege. G.H. declares that she lacks substance, lacks origins which she lost two minutes after birth, so that her journey to the truth involves an excavation through layers of time to find origins and fundamental significance (20, 45). She also lacks children, unlike the cockroach, and therefore cannot die; her death would be final since her life would not perpetuate through offspring (78). G.H.'s identification with the roach through what she imagines to be their mutual contemplation, a link to prehistoric, essential life, will compensate these lacks. Reminiscent of Burgos's seeing herself in Menchú, "eu olhara a barata viva e nela descobria a identidade de minha vida mais profunda" ("I had looked at the living cockroach and in her I discovered the identity of my deepest life"; 38). The roach lends G.H. the possibility of renewal: "Mas se seus olhos não me viam, a existência dela me existia. . . . Ela fertilizava a minha fertilidade morta" ("But if her eyes did not see me, her existence existed me. . . . She fertilized my dead fertility"; 50). Without the other she cannot exist. Without the other *as* other, as a completely different form of life, she cannot exist. The revelation of this lack reveals love, the passion G.H. had never felt previously (97). In the process of her consequent adoration of the roach (the novel ends, "E então adoro._____" 'And so I love._____') hierarchy and privilege become inverted; the loved other is assigned a superior position, as Barthes has noted (83).

Before the transformation, G.H. plans her day's activities in a traditional hierarchy just as she encloses, sets boundaries, and organizes her identity in its image. Moving from the maid's room to the living room, she imagines herself "rising horizontally" (23-4). Her disillusionment with the maid's room begins with its unexpected nonconformity to this imposed organization since its space is unorganizable and has no beginning or end, but most of all it seems to lie "em nível incomparavelmente acima do próprio apartamento" 'on a level incomparably above the apartment itself,' like a minaret (44, 30-1, 26). The destruction of rigid layers and classes constitutes an infernal, confounding disorganization in the dry room that contrasts with G.H.'s humid apartment (26).

Recognizing her insufficiencies and ceding authority in this new arrangement, G.H. portrays herself as the passive receptor of signals the world transmits to her and she transcribes phonetically

(15). She becomes an odd transcriber of a physical pre-language that she can only express inadequately in language. G.H. thus requires particular courage to "say": "Será preciso coragem para fazer o que vou fazer: dizer. E me arriscar à enorme surpresa que sentirei com a pobreza da coisa dita" ("It will need courage to do what I am going to do: to say. And to risk feeling the enormous surprise at the poverty of the spoken word"; 14). Words exist in poverty of significance, yet for G.H. the person who lives in poverty approaches the meaning of existence the word cannot.[7] In fact, words are so impoverished in their potential to communicate a marginal existence that *A Paixão* constitutes, like *A Hora da Estrela*, nothing more than a silence, a failed testimony, the transcriber's interpretation of signs left behind. Silence emerges initially from the maid's absence at the same time the text depends on her existence and the appropriation of her space through G.H.'s interpretation and interiorization of the drawing and the clean room that contradicts G.H.'s assumptions. The text depends on silence, not on breaking it. The maid does not exist in the text outside her reflection in G.H. and G.H. realizes that "Janair era a primeira pessoa realmente exterior de cujo olhar eu tomava consciência" ("Janair was the first real outsider of whose gaze I became conscious"; 28). Janair's final gesture before leaving confronts the mistress with an exterior perspective of herself that threatens her contained identity and privileges. The other's presence functions as catalyst to question G.H.'s contained life, an existence framed between ironic quotation marks. G.H. listens to the "som inaudível do quarto" 'inaudible sound of the room,' but only to absorb the other into G.H.'s own consciousness, into her own voice, into her own growing self-knowledge. Only through G.H.'s reflections on her own existence can we imagine Janair's situation. Implicitly equated, Janair and the cockroach share silence.

The novel then returns to silence at the end point of G.H.'s "viagem" 'voyage': she comprehends her own silence, her own lack, and her own insignificance in the failure of her own voice. Her language is incapable of communicating the reality she perceives in the space of the other, the maid's room, and in confronting the other, the cockroach. Grasping an outside perspective, she sinks deeper

---

[7] See the reference in the first and third chapters to Gayatri Spivak's commentary on intellectuals' valorization of the oppressed's "concrete reality."

into self-reflection: "só posso alcançar a despersonalidade da
mudez se eu antes tiver construído toda uma voz. . . . É exatamente
através do malogro da voz que se vai pela primeira vez ouvir a
própria mudez e a dos outros e a das coisas, e aceitá-la como a pos-
sível linguagem" ("I can only reach the impersonality of muteness if
beforehand I have constructed a whole voice. . . . It is exactly
through the voice's failure that one is going to hear one's muteness
for the first time, and that of others and of things, and accept it as a
possible language"; 112). G.H.'s depersonalization results from her
failed attempt to construct her own voice and from interiorization,
yet suggests the greatest exteriorization at which one can arrive, by
assuming another's voice or gaze:

> A despersonalização como a grande objetivação de si mesmo. A
> maior exteriorização a que se chega. Quem se atinge pela desper-
> sonalização reconhecerá o outro sob qualquer disfarce: o pri-
> meiro passo em relação ao outro é achar em si mesmo o homem
> de todos os homens. Toda mulher é a mulher de todas as mul-
> heres, todo homem é o homem de todos os homens, e cada um
> deles poderia se apresentar onde quer que se julgue o homem.
> Mas apenas em imanência, porque só alguns atingem o ponto de,
> em nós se reconhecerem. E então, pela simples presença da
> existência deles, revelarem a nossa. (112)
>
> Depersonalization as the great objectification of one's self. The
> greatest exteriorization that one can achieve. Whoever attains
> depersonalization will recognize the other in any guise: the first
> step with relation to the other is to find in oneself the man of all
> men. Every woman is the woman of all women, every man is the
> man of all men, and each one of them could appear wherever
> man is judged. But only in immanence, because only some
> achieve the point where they recognize themselves in us. And so,
> by their simple presence, they reveal ours.

Finding others in oneself is the first step toward the other, to lose
oneself by knowing others' immanence in oneself. Our existence is
therefore revealed in theirs although they are not present. G.H.
necessarily arrives at this epiphany in Janair's absence and by way of
failure, by way of that inadequate language that constitutes the singular basis for human thought. "Minha voz é o modo como vou
buscar a realidade; a realidade, antes de minha linguagem, existe
como um pensamento que não se pensa, mas por fatalidade fui e

sou impelida a precisar saber o que o pensamento pensa. . . . A realidade é a matéria-prima, a linguagem é o modo como vou buscá-
la–e como não acho" ("My voice is the way I am going to seek reality; reality, before my language, exists as a thought that one does not
think, but I was and am fatally impelled to need to know what the
thought thinks. . . . Reality is raw material, language is the way I am
going to seek it out–and how I don't find it"; 112-13). The voice
that G.H. finds paradoxically yields silence; language cannot represent the essential reality of her experience. Language must therefore
lie (115). Yet this lie at least describes through negation what G.H.
saw; this lie does not constitute the *false* truth that Lispector condemns in the fragment "Mentir, Pensar" 'To Lie, To Think' from *A
Legião Estrangeira*: "O pior de mentir é que cria falsa verdade . . . se
a mentira fôsse apenas a negação da verdade, então êste seria um
dos modos (negativos) de dizer a verdade. Mas a mentira pior é a
mentira 'criadora'" ("The worst part of lying is that it creates false
truth . . . if a lie were only a negation of the truth, then this would
be one of the (negative) ways to say the truth. But the worst lie is
the 'creative' lie"; 143). G.H.'s lies signal language's inability to
express her revelation beyond that which her revelation is not.

Lispector expands and explores in this novel the delegitimating
"lies," contradictions, and paradoxes in Jesusa's, Menchú's, and
Carolina Maria de Jesus's *testimonios* when they are seen as manifestations of language's representational inadequacy. At the same
time, Lispector illuminates G.H.'s dependence on keeping what is
represented by the roach as *not* her, as distinctly separate. To find
her "ser" she must project her "não ser" onto the roach. Moreover,
G.H.'s depersonalization through exteriorization combines the
individual and the plural selves that interact somewhat paradoxically in testimonial texts, yet her conclusions contradict and threaten
to undermine the basis for testimonial texts of articulating another
reality, a true reality, through the person who lives it. If others can
reveal our existence, if the transcriber could just as well tell the
informant's story, the testimonial process would become unnecessary. While they indirectly describe a process of identification, as
we have seen, testimonial texts are based on differences and divisions that make any attempt by the transcriber to speak for the
informant an act of betrayal and appropriation. *A Paixão* problematizes linguistically mediated communication of an experience; however, where *A Paixão* portrays silence as an alternative (non-)lan-

guage, *A Hora da Estrela* exposes the fact that the difficulty of communicating another reality leaves one subject silent and the other with voice and privilege. Macabéa's silence exposes more violently the process of finding oneself through another at the expense of that reality so impossible to communicate. G.H. reaches out to the other and encounters herself even as she loses herself. Her interiorized encounter with passion in which she simultaneously compensates a lack and again loses herself through her identification with subaltern others still allows her self-expression and contrasts with Rodrigo S.M.'s version of passion: in *A Hora da Estrela* sadistic appropriation.

TESTIMONIO AS FRAMEWORK FOR LISPECTOR'S *A HORA DA ESTRELA*

Clarice Lispector's last novel before her premature death, *A Hora da Estrela*, is narrated through the male author Rodrigo S.M., a deliberately transparent mask for the real author, Lispector. This inserted figure should be taken as ironically as the tone of his narration. Throughout my discussion of *A Hora da Estrela* I will use "author" to refer to Rodrigo S.M. and Lispector's surname to distinguish her from the fictional author. I occasionally refer to Rodrigo as "transcriber"; although he never performs this role in the ethnographic, journalistic sense, I use this term in allusion to his suggestion that he is merely transferring to paper those facts imposed from without.

Rodrigo feels driven to tell the story of Macabéa, a hopelessly ugly, ignorant and poor young woman who migrated from the Northeast to Rio. Rodrigo alternately identifies himself with his "Maca" and distances himself from her, alternately perceiving her as a saint who embodies an essential, transcendental spark of life and as a demon who reminds him of his superfluous, empty, bourgeois existence. After subjecting Macabéa to a series of humiliating experiences, including a brief courtship, and a revelatory trip to a psychic, Rodrigo has her killed (watches her killed?) by the very car that Macabéa's supposed future husband drives. Macabéa's moment as a star occurs as a crowd gathers round her lifeless body and her blood forms a star pattern on the pavement. *A Hora da Estrela* consists of a philosophical exploration of being and creation that portrays attempts to translate and communicate another reality as monologues that leave one subject in silence and the other with voice and privilege. Macabéa's silence violently exposes the process of finding oneself through another at the expense of that other reality so urgent to communicate.

This text develops naturally from the issues that concerned Lispector throughout her work and that we have seen in *A Paixão*, most importantly those of alienation, faith, the almost mystic approximation to other beings and the search for life's most essential elements. It also enriches our examination of dialogue across lines of privilege through construction of that dialogue within the concerns common to her writing. Rodrigo S.M.'s approximation to, and creation of, Macabéa's existence emerges from his interiorization and investigation of his own existence, as does G.H.'s approximation to the roach. This paradox lies at the heart of both Lispector's writing and, ultimately, the mediated testimony.

Several central problems underlying the testimonial text's production as they appear in fictional form in *A Hora da Estrela* emerge from the "author" Rodrigo S.M.'s self-conscious writing process. First, his reflections exhibit the links between testimonial texts and fiction that contemplates its own production. Rodrigo legitimates himself through Macabéa's identity, an identity that both represents and fills a vacuum, and concurrently distances himself from Macabéa. He demonstrates acute sensitivity to writing as a mimetic act whose veracity or verisimilitude affects textual authority. Rodrigo also considers collective versus individual identity and the possibilities of ceding authority to a marginalized voice. The relationship between him and Macabéa therefore offers a fictional analogy to both the transcriber's dilemma in relating another's life story in a way that maintains its authenticity, and also to the testimonial reader's choices before the completed text. Furthermore, the novel confronts a situation impossible in a real testimonial text: how to write the story of those who are so completely bereft and anonymous that they would never come to the attention of a journalist or other writer? How to know that anonymous experience, that truly representative person, in a way that inspires solidarity and action? As Sommer rightfully corrects and redirects the implied responsibility in Spivak's question, can the subaltern speak?: who is listening? (*Proceed* 20). From the insulated space of his room Rodrigo S.M. feels compelled to tell the true, unembellished facts about the impoverished, anonymous object and, for him, singular being, Macabéa. Finally, *A Hora da Estrela* emphasizes the authorial (of the creator of texts) and authoritarian (of obedience to authority) possibilities of the testimonial process most critically through the intercalation of a male author who assumes a central role not seen in the male editor of *Quarto de Despejo* and also through the fact that Macabéa almost never has the opportunity to speak for herself.

The basic motive of the testimonial text, as we have seen, is to "hacer hablar," to cede textual control, to inspire activism, and to place authority in the hands of the silenced, although the silenced who represent an imposed notion of their truthful identity. In the *testimonios* examined in the first chapter this involves approximation of the power positions of transcriber and informant, thus increasing the identification between the two in such a way that in those specific texts the transcriber achieves a vicarious identity and self-legitimation as much as she alters relationships of power, a goal of the ideal *testimonio*. Gayatri Spivak has noted in *The Post-Colonial Critic* that focusing on the margins as "de-centered" in fact serves to valorize the center (156). The *testimonio* and the *novela testimonial* do aesthetically and morally valorize the margins over the center, attempting to bring the margins to the center in order to question dominant historical and literary discourses. Nevertheless, for many readers the margins must enter the center performing their marginal nature, and here the testimonial gesture's potential for "de-centering" those dominant discourses can falter on its own methodology. The manner in which testimonial texts emerge in part from self-legitimation returns focus to the center the transcriber represents. The transcriber's appropriation of or desire to be what the testimonial narrator represents functions to valorize the transcriber's own identity through a purer truth than one compromised by privilege.

The process of identification between transcriber and narrator, who in *Quarto de Despejo* meld into one, makes more difficult an answer to the question of whose testimony this is, or an answer to Spivak's well-known question, "can the subaltern speak?" An affirmative answer depends on linguistic transparency of the current medium and on if the *testimonio* informants are what one would define as the subaltern. The tension between individual and collective subjectivities lies behind Spivak's point that the subaltern whose voices enter dominant discourses consist of the "regional elite-subaltern" (285), meaning there exists an ideal subaltern subject, perhaps the one whom the transcriber chooses for reasons of identification and, in the end, legitimation. This is not to discount what *testimonio* can and does do, but because the testimonial process is drawn to or produces its own "subaltern elites" the current testimonial medium would lead us to agree with Spivak and Daphne Patai that the subaltern cannot in fact speak: "the fact remains that we cannot know those stories which genuinely silent people might disclose" (Patai, *Brazilian* 5). I interpret that conclusion not as meaning the subaltern do not know how to speak, but rather that they are not given the chance. To repeat Sommer, the problem is that we do not listen.

This is the answer that the novel *A Hora da Estrela* offers when examined within the framework of these issues, although the complexity of Lispector's novel extends far beyond the scope of the present study. Macabéa is the truly subaltern in a silent life (that we, and Rodrigo, do not listen to), that seems to be nothing more than subsistence; she cannot speak for herself because she is unaware of herself. It is her lack of self-awareness that particularly brings to light the presumptuous notion that the true subaltern are not self-conscious of their status. In the context of a critique of Deleuze and Guattari, Christopher L. Miller points out this gesture as "one of the most questionable tactics of colonial anthropology: that of attributing to natives preconscious thoughts that the Western interpreter makes explicit" (16), creating the intellectual division of labor that still plagues academic readings of *testimonio*. Miller later adds, when discussing one of Deleuze and Guattari's sources in *A Thousand Plateaus*, "Africans will thus *instinctively* and *unconsciously* lead European thinkers into the promised land of nonrepresentation; but only the Europeans will know what has happened and why" (31). Rodrigo takes it upon himself to make explicit what has happened to Macabéa and why, but with a wink to the reader from Lispector. Making Macabéa unconscious thus parodies the process by which we speak *for* the testimonial subject.

SELF-KNOWLEDGE IN *A HORA DA ESTRELA*

The fact that Rodrigo S.M. speaks in first person and not Macabéa, who is purportedly the "star" to which the title refers, constitutes the first inkling of how *A Hora da Estrela* reflects and plays ironically upon the potential usurpation of the testimonial narrator's subject status. The irony and cruelty of the word play behind the novel's title become clear with a critical reading and will be addressed more closely in the next chapter. Rodrigo's first-person narration contradicts *A Hora da Estrela*'s structure that teasingly promises a relationship where the author-transcriber is responsible for communicating the real story of the protagonist Macabéa to a privileged reading audience. His motives stem in part from personal impetus and in part from outside pressure that alternately takes the form of "as sociedades" 'society' and a "força maior" 'greater power.' The text is not based upon a simulated transcription of interviews, but upon the narrator's supposed first-hand knowledge of the "object of study." Here the reifying possibilities of the expression "object of study" become particularly highlighted, since Macabéa often seems to literally be an object: something that exists and is manipulated by others with little consciousness of self. [8] Hence the text's task is to purportedly expose this subaltern existence.

This artifice obscures, however, the manipulative dynamic between Rodrigo and Macabéa, a potentially exploitative dynamic. His narrative voice and identity, as he experiences them vicariously through Macabéa, steal the show from the star and he effectively silences the cry his narrative should lend her, appropriating it for himself: "Porque há direito ao grito. / Então eu grito" ("For one has a right to shout. / So, I am shouting"; 18, 13-14). [9] Rodrigo releases the cry of horror that is this text, changing the cry from a

---

[8] Debra Castillo identifies among the four essential elements of Lispector's work the "common object" (193). If this is so, the reification of Macabéa certainly places the protagonist in that category. (The other elements Castillo mentions are: the subject or placeholder for "that elusive position"; essential verbs; and the "operative element that sets these various elements in motion—the negative.") I will more closely analyze the sadistic repercussions of Macabéa's treatment as object in the third chapter.

[9] The quotations in English from *A Hora da Estrela* are from Ponteiro's translation where two page numbers are noted. Otherwise the translations are mine.

life or death scream for recognition into a cry of existential angst: "através dessa jovem dou o meu grito de horror à vida. À vida que tanto amo" ("through her I utter my cry of horror to existence. To this existence I love so dearly"; 41, 33).

Why must Rodrigo write through a poor, miserable other? What initiates this supposed true life of Macabéa? What brings him and Macabéa together? "Tudo no mundo começou com um sim. Uma molécula disse sim a outra molécula e nasceu a vida. Mas antes da pré-história havia a pré-história e havia o nunca e havia o sim. Sempre houve. Não sei o que, mas sei que o universo jamais começou" ("Everything in the world began with a yes. One molecule said yes to another molecule and life was born. But before prehistory there was the prehistory of prehistory and there was the never and there was the yes. There always was. I do not know what, but I do know the universe never began"; 15, 11). Thus begins *A Hora da Estrela*. This passage suggests a text of foundation, of creation, of origins, of religious origins, of imprecise origins. It also implies subjectivity and the free will to choose yes over no; therefore, it implies authority. At the same time, this beginning suggests the opposite: no beginning. Lispector continues: "Enquanto eu tiver perguntas e não houver resposta continuarei a escrever. Como começar pelo início, se as coisas acontecem antes de acontecer?" ("As long as I have questions and I don't have answers I will continue writing. How to start at the beginning if things happen before happening?"; 15). She writes in response to unanswered questions, in search of an answer to the paradox of simultaneous free will and predestiny, an answer that does not necessarily exist. This is only one of the myriad "texts and antitexts" underlying Lispector's writing, as Debra Castillo terms similar paradoxes (196), yet this specific contradiction regarding origins addresses Macabéa's identity and Rodrigo S.M.'s adoption of that identity in a fundamental way.

Typical of her sensory experience of reality, Macabéa at one point looks at herself in a discolored mirror and thinks, "tão jovem e já com ferrugem" ("so young and already tarnished"; 32). The narrator echoes this illusion of antiquity when he observes, "Embora a moça anônima da história seja tão antiga que podia ser uma figura bíblica. Ela era subterrânea e nunca tinha tido floração. Minto: ela era capim" ("Although the anonymous girl of this story could be so ancient that she could be a biblical figure. She was subterranean and had never flowered. I lie: she was grass"; 38). "The girl," Macabéa, is an anonymous one in a million (18), the artifact of a nameless collective as ancient as the Bible, as prehistoric, earthy, and unattractive as G.H.'s cockroach. Buried, unseen and silent, she is like a primitive, annoying weed that has survived to the present. In this way Rodrigo associates her with the "préhistória" that has no beginning and the two molecules that met with a yes to form life; she provides a link with the origins of that which is essential to being. Similarly, though perhaps with less philosophical consequences, Jesusa Palancares comes to represent the essence of what Poniatowska values in *lo mexicano* and Rigoberta Menchú represents customs predating the conquest. The anonymous, pitiful Macabéa therefore seems to predate the narrator and make impossible his creation of her and his authority over her, thus questioning his free will to decide the outcome of this text opposite Macabéa's predestined effect on him. Macabéa characterized in her transcendental essence as a bothersome weed mocks both her and the narrator's project, in addition to ironically reflecting how privileged classes may indeed see these anonymous, ever-present people.

In contrast, another reference to Macabéa's connection with ancient origins reveals the opposite view of her anonymous continuity through time: her enormous potential (for faith, for autonomy, for a rich inner life, for subversion), a potential that with Macabéa's ancient essence further threatens Rodrigo's privileged position and has facetiously slipped his mind despite its significance (impairing his dependability as narrator):

> Esqueci de dizer que era realmente de se espantar que para corpo quase murcho de Macabéa tão vasto fosse o seu sopro de vida quase ilimitado e tão rico como o de uma donzela grávida, engravidada por si mesma, por partenogênese: tinha sonhos esquisóides nos quais apareciam gigantescos animais antediluvianos como se ela tivesse vivido em épocas as mais remotas desta terra sangrenta. (72-3)

> I forgot to say that it was really frightening how, as shriveled as Macabéa's body was, her breath of life was so vast, almost limitless, and as rich as that of a pregnant virgin, self-impregnated, by parthenogenesis: she had schizoid dreams in which giant, antediluvian animals appeared, as if she had lived during the most remote ages of this violent earth.

Again, she represents an antediluvian biblical figure, although one who seems to dream of dinosaurs. Her "breath of life" is as rich as

that of a pregnant virgin, a religious allusion that lends Macabéa the
saintliness and purity the narrator frequently attributes to her. She
does not, though, receive the seed through a patriarchal authority
from without, but rather impregnates herself from within. Even her
withered body with shriveled ovaries (41) contains the germ to create this life–this is her powerful potential and her nagging attraction
for Rodrigo S.M.

Nevertheless, she does not know this–because Macabéa exists
in the pure, sensual sense of a living organism. Her subversive
potential stems from her perceptions of existence that in their simplicity touch on the complex essence of life: "não tinha conciência
de si e não reclamava nada, até pensava que era feliz" ("she was not
conscious of herself and did not demand anything, she even
thought she was happy"; 83). Since suicide necessitates a consciousness of life that could be ended, killing herself had never occurred
to her and she did not realize that she was a suicide case (71).
Macabéa thus possesses a great will to live, unconsciously. Rodrigo
lacks this essence, or does not comprehend it. "Só uma vez
[Macabéa] se fez uma trágica pergunta: quem sou eu? Assustou-se
tanto que parou completamente de pensar. Mas eu, que não chego
a ser ela, sinto que vivo para nada" ("[Macabéa] only once asked
herself a tragic question: who am I? She scared herself so much that
she completely stopped thinking. But I, who cannot manage to be
her, feel that I live for nothing"; 40). The question "'quem sou eu'
provoca necessidade. E como satisfazer a necessidade? Quem se
indaga é incompleto" ("'who am I' provokes needs. And how to
satisfy need? Whoever searches oneself is incomplete"; 20). Here
the author differentiates himself, distances himself, from Macabéa
in a moment that highlights their proximity; his project is indeed an
example of this self-investigation that leaves him incomplete. He
envies her ability to simply be, nothing more. She apparently lives
for nothing, but he has the luxury and curse of not being able to
lose awareness of his insignificance and consequently loses sense of
an essential "it." Macabéa signifies what Castillo calls an "uneradi-
cable 'is'" and Rodrigo amounts to a mere "placeholder" on the
verge of dissolution as he seeks the essence in "it" (194). Macabéa
is permanent; he is an unstable subject, imminently replaceable:
"também eu não faço a menor falta, e até o que escrevo um outro
escreveria" ("I also am not at all needed, and someone else could
even write what I am writing"; 18). This insignificance ties author

and protagonist together, yet by the end of the novel we realize that
Macabéa is in fact a great deal more significant than Rodrigo; she
possesses a sensitivity that belies her pathetic existence: "a grandeza
de cada um" 'the greatness in each one.' In fact, her capacity to
experience beauty in *Rádio Relógio*'s music and the otherwise
insipid or ugly demonstrates a contact with the world that exposes
Rodrigo's alienation as all the more profound in comparison. While
Macabéa contains "muita liberdade interior" ("a lot of inner freedom"; 86), Rodrigo fears liberty, the liberty that confronts him with
decisions.

Rodrigo's self-awareness and self-knowledge unveil an absence
that prohibits his truly being able to cross over and enter the other
person; his consciousness of self strengthens the divisions between
him and others and reinforces the alienation resulting from his inte-
gration into the privileges of class structure. Hélène Cixous dis-
cerns in Rodrigo the paradox of this appropriation when she
observes it is impossible to take a vow of poverty. Even those who
rid themselves of everything retain the memory of having: "Those
who have had, always will have left that memory and a trace of narcissism, be it ever so slight, of the effort made to impoverish themselves. There are always remains of having, even if one no longer
has. That is Clarice's dilemma in *The Hour of the Star*" (*Reading*
153), Clarice's dilemma as testified by Rodrigo. [10] Very pleased with
himself, the narrator describes those efforts to reduce his diet to
humble white wine, relegating his horses to a memory with which
he compares Macabéa. The gesture of metaphoric identification, of
vicarious identity to compensate a perceived lack, is revealed as
laughably absurd. "Limito-me a humildemente–mas sem fazer
estardalhaço de minha humildade que já não seria humildade–limito-me a contar as fracas aventuras de uma moça . . ." ("With
humility I confine myself–without making too much fuss about my
humility for then it would no longer be humility–I confine myself to
narrating the unremarkable adventures of a girl . . ."; 19, 15) and of
himself through his self-conscious authorial task, as he realizes the
limitations of isolation within one being: "Ninguém pode entrar no
coração de ninguém" ("No one can enter another's heart"; 78).

---

[10] In the next chapter I will discuss how Cixous in fact mimics what she
describes in Rodrigo by problematically appropriating Lispector's writing to compensate a lack of writers who fit her own concept of a nurturing *écriture féminine*.

Macabéa, however, possesses no self-knowledge until the end of the novel, at death, at the hour of the star: "A morte é um encontro consigo. Deitada, morta, era tão grande como um cavalo morto" ("Death is an encounter with oneself. Lying there, dead, she was as great as a dead horse"; 103). Her death will be the moment of birth into herself: "Hoje, pensou ela, hoje é o primeiro dia de minha vida: nasci" ("Today, she thought, today is the first day of my life: I have been born"; 96). As she dies we enter into Macabéa's thoughts, where she speaks in first person, where she indeed is allowed to speak at all for herself, in this story of her life. Yet death and the feeling of incompleteness mark her birth into self-knowledge, and Macabéa's consciousness of self signals Rodrigo's death because his significance depends on telling her life. With her self-consciousness his intervention becomes superfluous. She, the essence he seeks, has touched on her own essence as she simultaneously gains and loses it: "o âmago tocando no âmago: vitória!" ("essence touching essence: victory!"; 102). Her self-consciousness also removes her from her pristine, subaltern state, enabling her to testify to her own abjection, but also belying the idea of *testimonio* as that of typical representative of the silenced because the moment she speaks for herself she leaves that artificial category and she dies as who she is. Macabéa has touched on the truth of her reality in one of the epiphanies that mark the consciousness of Lispector's characters. In her discussion of the epiphany in Lispector, Olga de Sá refers to the Joycean epiphany to demonstrate its influence on Lispector. De Sá quotes Joyce's epiphany of the object in *Stephen Hero*:

> First we recognise that the object is one integral thing, then we recognise that it is an organized composite structure, a thing in fact: finally, when the relation of the parts is exquisite, when the parts are adjusted to the special point, we recognise that it is that thing which it is. Its soul, its whatness, leaps to us from the vestment of its appearance. The soul of the commonest object, the structure of which is so adjusted, seems to us radiant. (Sá 163 n. 29)

Macabéa as object (of study) at death seems to become "cada vez mais uma Macabéa, como se chegasse a si mesma" ("more and more a Macabéa, as if she came into herself"; 98). She arrives at her whatness, the truth.

PARADOXICAL TRUTH IN *A HORA DA ESTRELA*

This is not the truth of a defined set of events or personal experiences by which *testimonios* like Rigoberta Menchú's are judged. This truth is a consciousness of one's position in comparison to others, of one's marginal state, of what one lacks. Through the concept of truth, inappropriately equating their self-awareness, Rodrigo associates his approximation to Macabéa with his self-exploration; it is both a contact with the self and what Rodrigo sets out to transcribe. The two therefore merge through the truth which "é sempre um contato interior e inexplicável. A minha vida a mais verdadeira é irreconhecível, extremamente interior e não tem uma só palavra que a signifique" ("is always an inner and inexplicable contact. My truest life is unrecognizable, extremely intimate, and there is are no words to describe it"; 15). The nature of this "inner contact" makes impossible its expression, the expression of the truth that the narrator wishes to transcribe into writing, either his truth or Macabéa's, alternately identical and distinct. He repeats this interiority of the truth upon Macabéa's death and adds: "A verdade é irreconhecível. Portanto não existe? Não, para os homens não existe" ("Truth is unrecognizable. Does that mean it does not exist? No, for men it does not exist"; 96). What, then, is the truth he can hope to transcribe? Asking as she dies what the truth of "my Maca" was, he replies that it is enough to discover that she no longer is. "Pergunto: o que é? Resposta: não é" ("I ask: what is she? Answer: she is not"; 102). She had to exist in order to no longer exist; her existence is confirmed in the negative, in her death. Similarly, Rodrigo as writer of her story only exists in the negative: what he cannot express.

Recognizing his own lack of life's essence he desires to know the other and appropriates another's essence, which he cannot come to understand or express with words, although he writes through her and reaches her by entering into himself. Macabéa's truth is paradoxically within him and beyond him, both a safe diversion and a danger to his authority. His self-consciousness leads him to seek her and the only route by which he can touch her is through the filter of his consciousness and her unconsciousness, thus projecting himself onto her. He can only seek her through himself; she is only his mask or his creation, since she surges from something within him,

"na certa de algum modo escrito em mim" ("certainly in some way
written within me"; 26). Rodrigo and Macabéa's convergence
results both from the fact that she is within him and from his desire
to be identified with her since he alone is so little: "eu que quero
sentir o sopro do meu além. Para ser mais do que eu, pois tão
pouco sou" ("I who want to feel the breath of my hereafter. In
order to be more than I am, because I am so little"; 26). While this
statement must be understood in the context of Rodrigo's facetious-
ness, he will indeed transform himself into another: "A ação desta
história terá como resultado minha transfiguração em outrem e
minha materialização enfim em objeto" ("The action of this story
will produce my transformation into another and ultimately my
materialization into an object"; 26). His materialization into an
object signals his death into Macabéa. Similarly, his only significance is as author, so the only manner in which he can exist is
through writing Macabéa: "Escrevo porque sou um desesperado e
estou cansado, não suporto mais a rotina de me ser e se não fosse a
sempre novidade que é escrever, eu me morreria simbolicamente
todos os dias" ("I write because I am desperate and weary. I can no
longer bear the routine of my existence and, were it not for the constant novelty of writing, I should die symbolically each day"; 27,
21).
     Nonetheless, this quotation's reference to frivolity signals how
in the context of his privileged life, this desire becomes a mere
diversion—or danger. Divorced from reality and tired of his own life,
he wishes to have more than one: "Transgredir, porém, os meus
própios limites me fascinou de repente. E foi quando pensei em
escrever sobre a realidade, já que essa me ultrapassa" ("Transcending my own limits suddenly appealed to me, though. That is when I
decided to write about reality, since reality exceeds me"; 22). Apart
from this entertaining novelty as he seeks the essence of being, he
faces danger in assuming Macabéa's identity since her existence
reflects the truth of his own. In carving her out from the facts like
solid rocks in his writing he lets fly sparks and splinters: "Não, não
é fácil escrever. É duro como quebrar rochas. Mas voam faíscas e
lacas como aços espelhados" ("No, it is not easy to write. It is as
hard as breaking rocks. Sparks and splinters fly like shattered
steel"; 24, 19). The mirrored splinters reflect himself, as when
Rodrigo sees his own face when Macabéa looks in the mirror.
Macabéa reflects Rodrigo's inutility and her death ends his life.

"Macabéa me matou. Ela estava enfim livre de si e de nós. Não vos assusteis, morrer é um instante, passa logo, eu sei porque acabo de morrer com a moça. Desculpai-me esta morte" ("Macabéa murdered me. She was finally free of herself and of us. Do not be afraid, to die is instantaneous, it happens quickly, I know because I just died with the girl. Forgive me this death"; 103). He asks our pardon, we know not for which death, since they are so united that both deaths intertwine. Even though he ironically mimics Macabéa Rodrigo fears being her. He fears facing the truth she represents, which reflects himself, since the two are so closely linked. He experiences the reality outside his isolated room through Macabéa, and this reality horrifies him, both because of its misery and because of what it reveals about himself, the very person that leaves him feeling empty. Macabéa is the truth he did not want to know: "A moça é uma verdade da qual eu não queria saber" ("The girl is a truth I did not want to know about"; 48). He is horrified by the very street where Macabéa lives and where he would not set foot because of his terror of the "pardo pedaço de vida imunda" ("dark piece of filthy life"; 38), which reveals itself to be a terror of life as lived through Macabéa. Bordering on clichés, the narrator insists that the toothache that passes through this story "deu uma fisgada funda em plena boca nossa . . . é a minha própia dor" ("gave us a deep pain in the mouth . . . it is my own pain"; 15). The guise of commiseration dissimulates Rodrigo's annoyance with the persistence of Macabéa's story: it is an irritating pain in the mouth. If we consider the fact that the verb "fisgar" can also mean to mock, the toothache could also insinuate how Macabéa's being comes to actually belittle Rodrigo and diminish his authority.

Indicating his temptation to evade this unpleasant truth, Rodrigo wonders how he is going to manage with pure facts: "É que de repente o figurativo me fascinou: crio a ação humana e estremeço" ("It's that figurative language suddenly appealed to me: I create human actions and tremble"; 28). The figurative distances him from fearsome facts. He thus seems to separate himself from Macabéa, yet this fear of the truth emerges in Macabéa as well, becoming yet another aspect that fuses the two. She, like he, turns away from images of herself and becomes horrified upon finally confronting her reality as seen from the outside when the fortune teller makes her conscious of her suffering (91). The truth links the two, despite the vastly different realities that separate them.

Macabéa literally reflects Rodrigo in the mirror. She is the truth, as associated with purity and simplicity: "tinha medo de inventar" ("she was afraid of inventing"; 61). She is a truth almost impossible to describe.

Unfortunately, since Rodrigo legitimates himself before "as sociedades" and a vague higher power by telling the true story of the "nordestina" 'north easterner,' the appearance of truth becomes crucial despite the dangers of doing so and his temptation to fabricate: the text must be a document, must be simple, must contain facts. Constantly stressing the facts that like hard stones cannot be molded or ignored (21), Rodrigo insists that he does not lie when he writes (24), that he is tired of literature (84)–contradicting other moments in the novel and defining literature as the opposite of truth–and that this story imposed itself upon him: "O fato é que tenho nas minhas mãos um destino e no entanto não me sinto com o poder de livremente inventar: sigo uma oculta linha fatal. Sou obrigado a procurar uma verdade que me ultrapassa" ("The fact is that I have someone's fate in my hands and nevertheless I don't feel I have the power to freely create: I follow a hidden, fatal line. I am obliged to look for a truth that exceeds me"; 26). Literary embellishment would ruin the effect and even his lies should lead to the truth. Again, for Lispector the creative lie is the worst lie.

Just as paradox challenges Rodrigo's capacity to utilize language and just as fiction threatens his stance before "as sociedades," paradox subverts his efforts at authenticity and hence legitimation by not conforming to convincing, singular representations of truth. Rodrigo's ambivalence toward his task manifests itself most explicitly through his alternating activity and passivity, through his alternating identification with Macabéa and horror at her miserable condition, so different from his own. He flaunts his privileged life, he removes himself from the exterior world beyond the boundaries of his room, and exhibits inaccurate knowledge of Macabéa's situation. In effect, he undermines his authority as the narrator of another's life. Contradiction and denial characterize his position as pseudo-transcriber: "Como é que sei tudo o que vai se seguir e que ainda o desconheço, já que nunca o vivi?" ("How is it that I know everything that is going to happen and that I still don't know, since I never lived it?"; 16). This phrase refers on a deeper level to Lispector's question of what fundamental aspects of existence unite everyone, but its paradoxical articulation underscores Rodrigo's

futile and alienating experience of writing the "other." Any responsibility for the story is out of his hands: "não tenho culpa e que sai
como sair" ("I am not to blame and it will turn out however it turns
out"; 45). He lost three pages describing the encounter between
Macabéa and Olímpico when his cook discarded them (an indirect
reference to his social status) and therefore divorces himself from
responsibility for how that section of the book turns out (52). He
cannot accept responsibility because he is writing "aquém e além de
mim" ("beneath and beyond me"; 87). He is writing outside himself and nothing is certain out there. One cannot faithfully represent what one has not lived. At one point, he states that he did actually live with Macabéa (27), only to contradict himself again later
on. After asking himself whether or not he should jump ahead to
outline the end of the story, Rodrigo corrects himself: "Acontece
porém que eu mesmo ainda não sei bem como esse isto terminará"
("But it's that I myself still don't know how this is going to end";
21). How could he know how the story will end if he is simply taking down reality? He also denies having any particular knowledge
of this "girl" whose name he does not even discover, along with the
reader, until page fifty-three when she herself pronounces it to
Olímpico, her "almost" boyfriend (24). The book's multiple and
contradictory subtitles, each separated by "or" to designate them all
as simultaneous descriptions of the story, announce from the beginning the antithetical truths that constitute the novel.

    Thus, as Rodrigo describes his approximation to Macabéa he
paradoxically emphasizes their separation. Rodrigo experiences his
identification with Macabéa in the flesh: "Será que o meu ofício
doloroso é o de adivinhar na carne a verdade que ninguém quer
enxergar?" ("can it be that my painful task is to discover in the
flesh the truth that nobody wants to face?"; 69). Yet, he treats ironically his paradoxical identification with Macabéa. "Vejo a nordestina se olhando ao espelho e–um ruflar de tambor–no espelho
aparece o meu rosto cansado e barbudo. Tanto nós nos intertro-
camos" ("I see the Northeasterner looking at herself in the mirror
and–a drum roll–my face appears in the mirror, tired and unshaven.
That's how much we change places"; 28). The drum roll evokes
either the suspense of a cheap carnival show or the beat that brings
her closer to her inexorable end. Rodrigo also takes similarities
between him and Macabéa and adds allusions to his privileged
position to make ironic their identification and trivialize her miser-

able reality. For instance, the author wonders if "the girl" knows
that his joy also comes from "minha mais profunda tristeza e que
tristeza era uma alegria falhada" ("my deepest sadness and that sadness was a failed joy"; 44). While she exhibits her extraordinary
capacity to find joy in nothing, he indulges in melancholy. Macabéa,
a typist in charge of transcribing spoken words into written ones,
spells by ear so that "designar" becomes "desiguinar" (20), amusing
if seen as parody of the ethnographic attempt to maintain orality,
while Rodrigo determines that his uncertain, deficient writing
process emerges from the same process: "E a pergunta é: como
escrevo? Verifico que escrevo de ouvido assim como aprendi inglês
e francês de ouvido" ("And the question is: how do I write? I find
that I write by ear the way I learned English and French by ear";
24). This observation also signals his privilege: how else could he
learn English and French by ear if he had not traveled abroad? He
too, is alienated, outside every social class (24); however, his isolation is an aesthetic choice to bring himself closer to Macabéa, to
maintain himself on a simple diet of cold, white wine and fruit,
abstaining from sex and soccer matches (28-9). The irony lies not
only in his version of an abstemious lifestyle, but also in the fact
that he does not need all these superficialities and masks to
approach the object of his attention–he must only face himself.

The truth's persecution of Rodrigo drives him to write Macabéa's life, feeling not so much guilt as his own insignificance.
Macabéa's story is an exorcism, a defense, a tactic for self-legitimation before the accusation that she embodies toward the narrator of
empty privilege (as interpreted by the narrator), and her story converts his task into a singularly uncomfortable one. The text also
responds to a higher power, not only to the "nordestina." In fact,
the text responds to a "força de lei" ("The force of law"; 23). The
narrator finds himself before an imagined figure of authority, a figure of legal authority, where he is responsible for the truth and for
the crime of Macabéa's death. He is afraid because until this typist
entered his life he had been "até mesmo um pouco contente" 'even
a bit content' in spite of little literary success. "Ela me acusa e o
meio de me defender é escrever sobre ela" ("She accuses me and
the way to defend myself is writing about her"; 22). Despite the
safety of his room, he feels persecuted: he hears voices laughing at
him and feels a shiver of fear at the cadenced steps outside in the
street, in the unprotected world (26). Just as Carolina Maria de

Jesus took up the pen to defend herself against the *favelados* behind the original purpose of publicizing the *favelados'* plight, Rodrigo responds to what Macabéa's more innocent presence represents behind the artifice of commiserating with her suffering. She becomes a demon tormenting him, not the saintly, pure, virgin typist. Only ridding himself of this girl will he return to his peaceful existence–it is, after all, strawberry season (104). At the end of the novel, as if a Christ arisen from the death into which Macabéa has sent him, Rodrigo protests his innocence and sardonically begs that his hands and feet be cleansed of guilt, then asks that they be rubbed with perfumed oils, turning exculpation into a pleasurable massage.

Rodrigo feels pressure to provide a convincing story, yet he must fight with the inadequate instrument he possesses: "A palavra tem que se parecer com a palavra" ("The word must look like the word"; 25). The word cannot simulate the object, the signifier cannot be the signified, since it mediates reality, yet only through writing can he search for legitimation, defend himself, and exist:

> Quanto a mim, só me livro de ser apenas um acaso porque escrevo, o que é um ato que é um fato. É quando entro em contato com forças interiores minhas, encontro através de mim o vosso Deus. Para que escrevo? E eu sei? Sei não. Sim, é verdade, às vezes também penso que eu não sou eu, pareço pertencer a uma galáxia longínqua de tão estranho que sou de mim. Sou eu? Espanto-me com o meu encontro. (45)

> As for me, I only escape being an accident of fate because I write, which is an act that is a fact. And when I make contact with my inner forces, I find your God through myself. Why do I write? How do I know? I don't know. Yes, it's true, sometimes I think I am not myself. I am such a stranger to myself that I seem to belong to a faraway galaxy. Is it me? The encounter with myself frightens me.

Writing, authoring, authorizes Rodrigo. Writing is a fact that confirms his own existence, legitimizes him. Thus, simply telling Macabéa's story, regardless of the content, justifies his existence. Like John the Baptist who precedes Christ, Rodrigo precedes Macabéa and testifies to her deeds and her grace which fills him. Macabéa becomes the word made flesh, yet is never able to speak her own words. Rodrigo usurps Macabéa's cry, and represents her permanence as a bothersome weed. Writing brings Rodrigo into contact with his interior forces, Macabéa's grace, and confronts him with someone he does not know. Through himself he finds the reader's God: Macabéa, alternately demonic and saintly. The encounter frightens him, whether he encounters Macabéa, his own uselessness, or a reality that inverts and confuses knowledge's organization into the binary opposites of good and evil, beauty and ugliness.

Rodrigo's fear contrasts with Macabéa's faith. Macabéa believes. "Pois, por estranho que pareça, ela acreditava. Era apenas fina matéria orgânica. Existia. Só isto. E eu? De mim só se sabe que respiro" ("For, as strange as it may seem, she believed. She was only delicate organic matter. She existed. That and nothing more. And me? I only know that I am breathing"; 48). Life is a luxury taken for granted by the narrator; for Macabéa it is an act of faith similar to the leap of faith that perhaps produced that initial "sim." "Ela acreditava em anjo e, porque acreditava, eles existiam" ("She believed in angels and, because she believed, they existed"; 49). Her belief is creative and her almost purely spiritual being lends her a saintliness that Rodrigo perversely desires. Faith creates the truth: if she believes in angels, they are real. Belief makes the word flesh. She does not believe in death (45), since one must have a consciousness of one's life to believe in the absence of that life. As an involuntary saint, the "nordestina" practically does not exist; she uses nothing and produces nothing, living in an infinite almost. "A maior parte do tempo tinha sem o saber o vazio que enche a alma dos santos. Ela era santa? Ao que parece. Não sabia que meditava pois não sabia o que queria dizer a palavra. Mas parece-me que sua vida era uma longa meditação sobre o nada" ("Most of the time she possessed, without knowing it, the emptiness that fills the souls of saints. Was she a saint? It seems so. She didn't know she meditated since she didn't know what the word meant. But I feel her life was a long meditation on nothingness"; 47). Evoking images of mystic union with nothingness, as well as the existential encounter with nothingness, Rodrigo attempts to come closer to Macabéa. He must undergo abstinence, meditation and a closeness to his own being. In addition, he cannot embellish his writing for danger of destroying the simplicity of Macabéa's essence and his union with her. To fill an absence in himself, he finds himself in the position of having to replace it with the nothingness that is Macabéa, a nothingness that harbors rich potential for truth.

In her literal usage of language Macabéa subverts meaning and questions linguistic disguises such as those worn so transparently by Rodrigo–and Lispector. Her miserable condition and absolute lack of future render vacuous, and also cynical and violent, banal expressions that Rodrigo inserts into his narration, such as, "Mas nunca se sabe, quem espera sempre alcança" ("But you never know, success comes to those who wait"; 46). [11] The same occurs for the passivity in Macabéa's obedience to the pastor's recommendations: "O pastor também falava que a vingança é coisa infernal. Então ela não se vingava" ("The pastor also said that revenge is infernal. So she didn't avenge herself"; 46). Her obedience to the pastor contrasts laughingly with Carolina's outraged reaction to a priest's similar recommendation. The pastor's message becomes sinister–not the word of good, but of oppression. Macabéa's urge to eat the cold cream appearing in an advertisement simultaneously exposes the subtle commercial gimmick and a cold cream's wasteful superfluity for the vast majority of people (47). Also, Macabéa does not immediately interpret the product as something for the surface, for appearances; for her it is something substantial. Her conversation with Olímpico is filled with questions that have no answer, such as if one can buy a hole, valorizing something seemingly empty like herself, or questions that hit the irritating truth and even suggest philosophical problems, such as if Olímpico's dreams of riches are not just an illusion (60). She presses him to explain the trite phrases he spits out to complain about women, and since he cannot defend himself he becomes irritated. Olímpico scoffs at her interpretation of the giraffe as an elegant animal in the same way Pedro gave no value to Jesusa's interpretation of the book he read to her. Macabéa interprets beauty into homely, simple things similar to herself and sees beyond façades, reading the truth behind faces (77), since she is not integrated into the accepted social codes that mask other truths. If Rodrigo struggles with how to linguistically represent reality, Macabéa shows language's duplicity that masks reality. This is the language with which Rodrigo must describe reality: the paradox of simultaneous being and not being, being poor and being rich, being simple and being bewilderingly complex.

As is the case for the works examined in the first chapter, subverted codes, hidden meanings, and multiple interpretations have

---

[11] I address the violence in *A Hora da Estrela* in Chapter 3.

broad consequences for the text itself, for Rodrigo's representation of Macabéa. As Rodrigo warns early on, this story will consist of words grouped in phrases that vaporize into a secret meaning that goes beyond words and phrases (19). Hidden meanings and Rodrigo's need to limit or control the danger of other interpretations manifests itself in one of the many subtitles to the novel, ".Quanto ao futuro." '.As for the future.' The narrator explains that the exterior and explicit story of "the girl" contains secrets, beginning with this subtitle, "que é precedido por um ponto final e seguido de outro ponto final. Não se trata de capricho meu—no fim talvez se entenda a necessidade do delimitado" ("preceded and followed by a full stop. This is no caprice on my part—hopefully this need for confinement will ultimately become clear"; 17, 13). The future cannot extend without limit. He cannot cede her life to other interpretations, nor his text. He cannot cede control. Foretelling the conclusion, Macabéa's future is cut short, delimited, controlled. The periods belie Rodrigo's disclaimer immediately following the above quotation: "(Mal e mal vislumbro o final que, se minha pobreza permitir, quero que seja grandioso)" '(The ending is still so vague yet, were my poverty to permit, I should like it to be grandiose.)' The secret is that he does control the end and feigns his poverty.

TESTIMONIO AND FICTION IN DIALOGUE

In *testimonios* where the narrator is granted the chance to speak for herself, questions that arise include: What has the testimonial subject revealed and why? What has the transcriber understood from what she has heard? What has the testimonial subject hidden? How does the transcriber construct an alternate, legitimizing identity through a marginalized speaker? How must the speaker maneuver through power relationships and preconceived notions of her identity? In *A Hora da Estrela* these questions convert to: What has the narrator revealed about Macabéa and why? What has he hidden or altered? What does he perceive in Macabéa's pitiable existence that prompts his desire to be her, to absorb her and to discard her? How is Macabéa's identity constructed to epitomize the purity and danger offered by that pitiable existence? While *A Hora da Estrela* does not incorporate an explicit rewriting of history and official discourse, the novel's concern with social conditions and problematization of misleading appearances, questions of agency, and the incapacity of language to signify produce comparable questions. Macabéa's wretched body contains a creative spirit of great sensitivity as inscribed by a desiring, privileged gaze, and Rodrigo's poses as author (transcriber or creator) or fellow sufferer clearly constitute artifices. Can he write another's existence?

The ambiguous answer parallels the ambiguous relationship of identification-distancing between transcriber and informant in the testimonial texts where metaphorical relationships with the testimonial subject contrasts with construction of the informant's identity as distinctly marginal and different. Rodrigo's close identification with Macabéa may represent a motive and a goal for *testimonio* and a way of assuring a revealing and authentic account, yet Rodrigo's ambivalence toward his task challenges the authenticity of the result. His shifting between identification and distancing, between knowledge and ignorance, between fact and fiction, playfully erode the possibilities of transparent, stable communication (or of a transparent, stable reading of a life outside privilege). What these ambiguities come down to is the question of subjectivity or agency: who is authorized to author the text? While Poniatowska's and Burgos's motives to authorize their informants are sincere, if thwarted by misreadings, and Carolina's belief in both her roles is honest, if manipulated, Lispector creates a transcriber whose mask purposely slips to reveal a different face: a certain politics of association and manipulation much like that of the metaphor of Jesusa Palancares exploiting the woman she has put into trance. Lispector's novels make fictitious the gesture to cede authority and space to the voiceless: the author-narrator-transcriber himself becomes witness and informant. Fiction writing allows Lispector to concretize rhetorical dynamics obscured in testimonial texts. Janair's absence and Rodrigo's continual, self-absorbed postponement of facts about Macabéa discursively perform and carry through to its extreme the self-reflection involved in the transcribers' and critics' readings of *testimonio*. In this scenario, both for transcriber and reader crossing boundaries becomes an object of consumption, a commercial view of the relationship between educated transcriber and testimonial narrator.

Macabéa's identity as a disguise to explore Rodrigo's own identity, along with the fact that as a writer Rodrigo's occupation is obviously to create, literalizes the point in the previous chapter that some aspect of the transcriber's self draws her to the testimonial subject to compensate for some absence in herself. Rodrigo is drawn to his protagonist for similar reasons. Still, despite Macabéa's existence within Rodrigo and for Rodrigo, writing becomes a doubly uncomfortable experience since not just the text's content, but also the process itself of writing must prove its authenticity. Rodrigo must dabble superficially in Macabéa's lifestyle in order to place himself on her level (Lispector, *Hora* 25). Nevertheless, Rodrigo's trivial sacrifices that leave privilege intact seem a literary complement to Nance's assertion that readers of *testimonio* take various evasive actions to avoid the discomfort of *testimonio*'s demands while remaining sympathetic. His method places him in the position of listener, absorbing what is said to him as he learns from a source outside himself, as Burgos presents herself in the prologue to *Me llamo Rigoberta Menchú*. Rodrigo also frequently places himself in the position of reader and hence distances himself from creative intervention in Macabéa's life story; if anything, her history has been imposed upon him. That is, he has the pretension of relinquishing control of the text, and literary embellishment, to the truth.

The paradoxes inherent in Rodrigo's task and Clarice Lispector's work bear meaningful resemblance to the contradictions inherent in *testimonio* and in Barnet's essay. Rodrigo's characterization of his tale as "verdadeira embora inventada" 'true yet invented' well describes the *novela testimonial* and the narrative craft of the *testimonio*'s informant. Reflecting the genre he attempts to describe, Barnet incorporates contradictory elements into the *novela testimonial*'s characteristics: its description of reality and its creation of reality;[12] the informant who is both extraordinary individual and representative of a collective reality; the artificiality of recreating the "authentic" oral language of the informant and the necessity of basing the text on spoken language (292). John Beverley also utilizes paradoxes to describe testimonio: "el *testimonio* es

---

[12] This simultaneous description of reality and creation of reality corresponds to William Paulson's point in comparing *A Paixão Segundo G.H.* with M.C. Escher's "Print Gallery," which "reminds us that we are a part of the picture of the universe that we look at and that our culture . . . has created" (517). According to Paulson, G.H. "pursues reality through the constructions of language," but also understands "language to be a particular outgrowth of material and organic life" (525).

y no es una forma 'auténtica' de cultura subalterna; es y no es 'narrativa oral'; es y no es literatura; concuerda y no concuerda con el
humanismo ético que manejamos como nuestra ideología práctica
académica; afirma y a la vez desconstruye la categoría del 'sujeto'"
("*testimonio* is and is not an 'authentic' form of subaltern culture; it
is and is not 'oral narrative'; it is and is not literature; it corresponds
and does not correspond to the ethical humanism that we use as
our academic, ideological praxis; it affirms and at the same time
deconstructs the category of 'subject'"; Introducción 10).

A *Paixão* and *A Hora da Estrela* take this deconstruction of
individual subjectivity a step further in presenting us with two subjects whose representativity is unquestionable, but who are clearly
silenced by the narrative devices that valorize their identities. The
simultaneous representativity and individual subjectivity with which
the reader can identify, all without contradictions, is a fiction.
Macabéa does not tell her own story because she is unaware of it.
Rodrigo's purification of Macabéa suggests the simplified concept
of the testimonial informant's identity as typical representative of a
group without corrupting manipulations or privilege. Autobiographical and testimonial narration as self-representation necessi-
tate self-knowledge, self-conscious subjectivity, knowledge of the
self's position in the world. The testimonial narrator is not naive. If
readers desire an unquestionably representative testimonial informant unaware of herself and who does not understand concepts
that intellectuals do, that is fiction. Lispector presents us with that
testimonial subject the only way possible: in fiction. If this is what
the reader desires, here is Macabéa, albeit tongue-in-cheek. She
cannot speak for herself since she is not aware of the meaning of
her existence. Macabéa is a parody of the true subaltern who cannot speak, but who also threatens the privileging of that subjectivity
by the strength of her life force without it. She is wild grass–an
ever-present, bothersome weed that does not draw one's attention
by each blade's interest, but by its persistence in surviving. Lispector's text asks us to consider the extreme, cynical perspective that
highlights *testimonio*'s existence as object of consumption: why
should we listen to the weed's life? Will we listen? Who would transcribe the *testimonio* of the true subaltern, the unextraordinary
human weed? Lispector's ironic description of Macabéa displays
before us the specious notion that the testimonial informant's life
represents complete marginalization, interpreted in colonial think-

ing as cultural purity and innocence. The completely marginalized and subaltern would have the commercial appeal of a weed.

All of this does not address an important, pending question: why does Lispector insert Rodrigo S.M. between her and Macabéa? The fact that Lispector assumes the mask of a male narrator casts an ironic look at gender differences in the question of writing another's existence. The increased difference between Rodrigo and Macabéa as a result of gender emphasizes the general distance between transcriber and informant, thereby signaling the questionable nature of their identification that concerns these texts. *A Hora da Estrela* exhibits through fictional devices "the outrageous presumption that writing the other, especially the oppressed other, implies," as Marta Peixoto expresses the problem (92). Someone else could replace Rodrigo as author, "mas teria que ser homem porque escritora mulher pode lacrimejar piegas" ("but it would have to be a man for a woman would weep her heart out"; *A Hora* 18, 14). A woman would be stupidly sentimental, would identify too closely with the protagonist. Despite this obviously unfounded argument, the novel exposes our presumption that, indeed, a woman would cry her heart out. Deborah J. Archer reads from this presumption of female identification when she quotes Carol Armbruster to support her argument that "the female author [Lispector] and the male narrator [Rodrigo] create and offer the text 'without loss or repression being incurred in the process' . . . , by establishing a female relationship to the other" (256). On the one hand, Rodrigo's pose of objectivity without sentimentality does not entirely obscure his intimate, supposedly female, identification with, and dependence on, Macabéa. On the other hand, Rodrigo, as a man, carries out a violent appropriation of Macabéa that exaggerates the dynamic at work in mediated testimonial discourse and, as we shall see in the next chapter, in critical theory. The difference is that, between a man and woman, the unequal relationship is more easily portrayed as violent and perverse, more easily characterized as a power relationship. Through our own preconceptions his gender draws our attention to exploitation, creating an analogy between rape and the process of writing and appropriating another identity. The violation and penetration that the rape metaphor suggests and their subversion of the identification fostered by testimonial discourse and some feminist ethnography will occupy one of my central focuses in the next chapter. The transcriber's intrusion into another's life as textual rape particularly attacks notions of a non-exploitative dialogue between women as an alternative to aggressive, "male" tactics. Lispector takes advantage of unequal gender relationships and the readers' assumptions about gender to undermine not only the possibility of understanding and communicating another's existence, but also the idea that a woman would escape an exploitative mode: we are fully aware of the female author behind Rodrigo's mask.

Thus, Rodrigo's disguises and appropriations point to the novel's self-reflective meditation on the act of writing, on engaging reality, and on constructing other identities. Writing is the disguise through which one dons certain identities, and, like G.H.'s life as bourgeois ectoplasm, there seems to be no content behind the artifice of being someone else. Without his characters Rodrigo becomes alienated from himself to the point of disappearing altogether: "Nestes últimos três dias, sozinho, sem personagens, despersonalizo-me e tiro-me de mim como quem tira uma roupa. Despersonalizo-me a ponto de adormecer" ("In these last three days, alone, without characters, I depersonalize myself and remove me from myself like someone removes clothes. I depersonalize myself to the point of nodding off"; 85). [13] The fortune teller who deals in appearances of truth, or one could say ironic truths, recommends makeup to Macabéa, a kind of mask: "Quem não se enfeita, por si mesma se enjeita" ("Without a touch of glamour, you don't stand a chance"; 89, 74). Macabéa's inability to mask herself, to be anything but what she is, unsettles Rodrigo and the hierarchy on which his existence depends. This forms one of the challenges to the testimonial transcriber and reader, explaining why the testimonial subject sometimes negotiates her authority to speak through rhetorical masks. Nevertheless, on gaining consciousness of the hierarchy she is crushed–no longer Macabéa, no longer what he seeks. The testimonial speaker who shows expertise in manipulating those hierarchies is sometimes no longer what the reader seeks. That testimonial speaker no longer embodies archaic essence, but rather dynamic agency.

The texts studied in this chapter exhibit some or all of the issues raised in the previous chapter, including relationships of authority that incorporate disguises and the appearance of truth,

---

[13] This passage is curiously absent from Ponteiro's translation.

self-legitimation through the appropriation of a stable, subaltern identity, paradox, silence and linguistic control. While the *testimonios* and *novela testimonial* studied in the first chapter offer a frame for an enriched analysis of Lispector's novels, these works of fiction compose a critical commentary on the testimonial and discursive relationships they reflect. *A Paixão Segundo G.H.* and *A Hora da Estrela* reflect through their protagonists' encounters with another the shifting, constructed, and discursive relationship in testimonial texts between privilege and margins. These narratives represent that encounter in very distinct linguistic and structural contexts, yet both share the effort to compensate some lack through another who seems characterized by just that: lack. Lack, however, is in the eyes of the privileged beholder. Material lack comes to need its own "breve rótulo" to explain that not having does not mean not knowing. Significantly, G.H. and Rodrigo come to adopt the testimonial mode of narration, even though the text and the narrator's identity continue to depend upon Janair/the roach and Macabéa. The subject of attention is subject to change. As represented in these works, the gesture of ceding voice is rendered especially transparent and the possibility of writing another's existence especially uncertain or even exploitative. In other words, these novels carry to their potential extreme the narrative situations underlying testimonial texts and articulate them in gendered terms that take advantage of and question our assumptions about "male" and "female" approaches to the testimonial process. The next chapter returns to the testimonial texts and Lispector's work from the first two chapters and examines the violent sacrifices, splits, and displacements involved in the subaltern subject's division, as either contradictory expectations of veracity or the privileged subject's identification with a marginalized position that displaces the other's voice. As the works of fiction carry to their extreme the self's fulfillment through another, so they carry to their extreme the violent undercurrents of the constructed identity and vicarious identity behind all the texts studied here.

CHAPTER 3

READING *TESTIMONIO* WITH THEORY: VIOLENCE, SACRIFICE, DISPLACEMENT

> The truth is, however, that the oppressed are not "marginals," are not men living "outside" society. They have always been "inside"–inside the structure which made them "beings for others."
>
> Paulo Freire, *Pedagogy of the Oppressed*

> . . . yo me afirmé a base de gentes que todo el tiempo me quisieron destruir.
> . . . I affirmed myself through people who the whole time wanted to destroy me.
>
> Rosario Castellanos

U NTIL this point we have seen how two of Clarice Lispector's novels provide examples of how certain works of fiction elaborate metaphors, tropes, and narrative structures similar to those of mediated testimonial discourse, showing exaggerations of the obstacles to "true" self-representation for the testimonial subject. Rarely do the marginalized women comprising the fiction texts' raison d'être, internal tensions, and objects of obsession speak for themselves in the first person. This critical distinction from testimonial texts cannot be overlooked, but nor should it be overestimated as justification for ruling out an intertextual reading from one corpus to the other. Obviously the first-person testimonial narrative reminds us of the real contact between speaker and transcriber preceding transcription, or of the fact that the informant herself is writing, and of *testimonio*'s significant continuation of Latin American narrative written through the voice of the disenfranchised. Reflecting revolutionary discursive change to complement political resistance or revolutionary political ideals, testimonial texts under-score salient questions of privilege in writing, as have certain critical theories contemporary with the most prolific decades of testimonial production. Nevertheless, I have shown in the previous chapters how *testimonio*'s ideals are partially thwarted by its linguistic medium, its methodology, and patterns of interpretation, points demonstrated in the present chapter for those theoretical positions seeking to undermine traditional authority in writing.

Testimonio's struggle with linguistic and ideological roadblocks to translating the truth of oppression or poverty and with representations of personal and collective identity do not allow us to read its unusual contribution to writing's democratization to blindly preserve a false purity. We must acknowledge *testimonio*'s kinship with other discursive expressions of power relationships and subalternity since the testimonial narrator must create an identity, a rhetorical persona, that lends her authority before her various audiences according to the identity they seek. Meanwhile, the transcriber legitimates herself by experiencing through the informant a fulfillment of the identity she would prefer insofar as its epistemological associations; the fictional author(ity) figures of G.H. and Rodrigo S.M. similarly find identities in their marginalized "others" with which to compensate a lack. In the works of fiction, these overlapping subjectivities constitute the texts' central concern, while this self-reflective compensatory act remains obscured in testimonial discourse, or its supplementary texts written by transcribers, in language that strains to perform its transparency, and in a testimonial narrator who cannot afford to explicitly deviate from transparent testimony. All the texts studied so far thus signify as much a reflection of the author as of the advertised subject of the life story. This result of the transcriber-informant interaction contradicts the constructed intention of the *testimonio* and *novela testimonial* of opening a space of articulation for the silenced, as we have seen, and suggests betrayal. Significantly, feminist theorists have signaled feminist theories' equally partial success in opening discursive space, to the point that such is common knowledge: much feminist theory has produced hegemonic tendencies stemming from its white, middle-class roots, highlighting through exclusions the differences among women. This fact serves to reiterate one of the principle reasons for this study's focus on women authors and also links *testimonio*'s "gesto ficticio" and the prescriptive consequences of a com-

mon women's experience to violence in its broadest sense. Derrida
has written, "If it is true, as I in fact believe, that writing cannot be
thought outside of the horizon of intersubjective violence, is there
anything . . . that radically escapes it?" ("Violence" 127). Considering Derrida perceives writing at the origin of everything (without
asserting origins), does this include even the politically conscious
testimonio that seeks to undo violence? Although Derrida's theories
on alterity are problematic for feminist theory, for reasons I will discuss further ahead, his concept of writing that establishes difference, that forms the "other," can contribute to a feminist discussion
of violence in testimonial texts.

   Discursive violence in the mediated *testimonio* and *novela testimonial* arises from the contradictions inherent in their representational methods and from the consequent textual tensions, imposi-
tions and violations. For example, testimonial texts produce an
internal tension by both pointing out that which makes the speaker
different, thus reinforcing distance, and also eliciting solidarity that
implies some sort of identification with the narrator and encourages
equal valorization of her experience, thus closing the distance. The
dialogue, or encounter, between speaker and transcriber, or between
protagonist and author figure, may manifest an exchange or meld-
ing of two points of view, even of two identities, but also a clash of
discourses. These texts work to cross and blur boundaries between
speaking subjects, between women of different classes, between narrative genres, yet the texts also work to construct the boundaries
they cross, an assertion in line with Levinson's essay on Latinamericanist orientalism and "de-orientalism," as I shall elaborate further
ahead. Thus, those crossings can create certain violences through
just the process that seeks to avenge unjust violences and silences,
as the works of fiction make especially explicit. In the novels examined in Chapter 2 the clash is emphasized and the conflict laid bare
to a greater extent than in *Hasta no verte, Jesús mío, Me llamo
Rigoberta Menchú* and *Quarto de Despejo*. Furthermore, the works
of fiction exaggerate through literary devices the displacement that
takes place in all the texts: the displacement of the transcriber or
author's voice onto the body of the testimonial subject or fictional
character, plus the multiple displacements of the testimonial subject
or fictional character, including the displacements that allow her to
give her testimony to the transcriber in the first place. Jesusa Palancares leads a life of constant movement, eventually migrating from

the country to the city, as does Carolina Maria de Jesus, and Rigoberta Menchú recounts her story in exile. Janair has left a room that
was not her own space in any case, and Macabéa also migrates to
Rio from the interior. The term displacement summarizes well the
marginalized figure's situation on all levels both literal and figurative, and summarizes the means by which both transcriber and
informant, author figure and named character, exist in a matrix of
shifting positions resulting from a search for authority and voice.
Moreover, from the physical displacement of Guatemalan Indians,
including Rigoberta Menchú's exile, and the movement of poor
North Easterners to Rio, represented by Macabéa, to the appropriation of another's voice, displacement involves violence. Representation, in its displacement and potential betrayal through *traduc-
ción/traición* 'translation/betrayal,' can cause violence to what the
informant herself has characterized as her weapon: words.

Borders and displacements occupy central sections of this chapter, but I begin with the question of violence. Concepts of violence
and sacrifice leading to the marginalized's disappearance, where I
rely on the work of René Girard among others, relate to authority
and the law, to the judicial court's institutionalized vengeance, and
to religious sacrifice. Pseudo-sacrificial rites, particularly apparent
in Lispector's texts, lead to the search for self-knowledge that motivates crossing the boundaries of the self to seek the self in others
and also crossing borders between center and margin, inside and
outside. In examining borders' formation, crossing, and blurring I
integrate several critics' thinking, but particularly Brett Levinson's
observations on Latinamericanism. After outlining displacements at
work in sacrificial violence and border crossings this chapter turns
to those elements in theorists' writings that repeat the vicarious
identities and essentializing tendencies evident in mediated testimonial discourse and played out in fiction. Cixous's reading of Clarice
Lispector, Derrida's reading of woman, and Deleuze and Guattari's
reading of the "Third World" in "minor" literature and nomadology provide instances of theories intent on undermining dominant
ideologies but unable to escape those ideologies' presence in the
critics' methodology and medium. Their writings overlook their
own discursive displacements in attempts to take on a subversive
rhetorical position that benefits their theoretical strategies while
fortifying traditional relationships of privilege and authority, thus
expropriating and in effect neutralizing the alternative voice present in texts like the *testimonio*.

PHYSICAL VIOLENCE, DISCURSIVE VIOLENCE

Violence lies inherent in the textual relationships described thus far in terms of *testimonio*, vicarious identity, disguise, and legitimation. One could assert, as does Derrida, that violence underlies all narratives through textual reflections of power struggles and the nature of writing, and while that assertion does constitute part of my argument, I wish to also point out the particular repercussions of violence on the corpus of texts I study here. Most *testimonios* recount a story of concrete, traumatic, political, psychological and physical violence from the victim's perspective in order to reverse that violence, directing it toward the authorities and discourses that oppress the speaker, and that may in fact also oppress the transcriber, for example as a woman. Readers could also be implicated in oppressive structures, however, especially from the testimonial subject's point of view. Testimonial writing articulates a statement against violence while transcribers and readers do not necessarily reflect on the text's and their own potential participation in certain forms of discursive violence, such as disappearance of the speaker's subjectivity through a preconceived notion of her cultural identity and representative identity that compensates the lack the transcriber perceives in her self. Sommer observes violence not just in gestures to appropriate others, but also in maintaining distance that respects both subjects' autonomy across difference. In other words, violence seems inevitable, even when productive, in the space where differences encounter each other, on the border: "Yet the gap that allows for enough autonomy to make mutuality possible also risks misrecognition and violence. The risk is worth taking, because without it we allow the violence of forcing sameness on others: either they are forced to fit in or they are forced out" (*Proceed* 3). The greater the text's confessed fictional content, the more acute the text's self-reflection on its mediated nature and its intrusion on another's intimacy and self-representation, entailing more explicit problematization of the violent possibilities contained in testimonial discourse and its related discourses of privileged solidarity with marginalized causes. This fictional content runs the gamut from Jesusa's directly challenging her supposed testimony to the brutal deaths of the cockroach and Macabéa. As the violence in the text–not just the given violence preceding or outside the text–intensifies, the pose of neutral transcription or narration becomes more visible as a mechanism compromised in its stated opposite.[1]

The violences dissected in the next pages are of a mainly rhetorical nature, yet the object is not to trivialize the real traumas recounted in testimonial texts nor to diminish the possibilities for real political action effectuated by texts that on one level do serve as propaganda in a positive sense. At the same time, *testimonio*'s ideal complements liberation movements in a rhetorical medium; thus we are also dealing with violence in language and figures of speech. Again, one of Menchú's weapons is her narrative. Beyond the physical violence suffered by the informant or protagonist, other violences directed toward the narrator center on the construction and adoption of her voice and identity. Who defines that voice and identity? How does vengeance emerge in testimonial texts and how is it related to the testimonial subject's sacrifice? How do displacements lead to the subject's disappearance? What are the consequences of crossing the boundaries of one's subjectivity? What does the violence behind women's testimonial texts mean for feminist theory? Rape as metaphor for the penetration of one subject into another in the testimonial process ties together the last two questions. If woman constitutes a victim of rape, somewhat explicit in *A Hora da Estrela*, how does such a metaphor of violent domination and humiliation comment on the female transcriber's role? On the other hand, how do these texts aim violence against hegemonic repression, representations and genres?

The *testimonio* emerges from an antecedent violation, aggression, injustice or inequality. It recounts a tale of survival, of witnessing violence. Jesusa experiences physical and emotional violence and witnesses the Mexican Revolution. Carolina Maria de Jesus witnesses the *favelados'* premature deaths after a meager existence. Rigoberta Menchú's testimony is most clearly constructed as a trauma account in the vivid descriptions of her brother and mother's torture and deaths, as well as in Menchú's own hardships and pain. (I describe her testimony as "constructed" to recall her narrative

---

[1] In the context of *decadentismo*, in "La política de la pose" Sylvia Molloy has explored the pose's effect of reinscribing and making visible that which is not mentioned. Her observation dovetails nicely with the concept of the many poses, or disguises, involved in the *testimonio* and then highlighted by the *testimonio* and works of fiction.

agency and the question of veracity in relation to reader and listener expectation.) Jesusa, Menchú and Carolina tailor their narratives to the audience whom they must convince and simultaneously criticize as part of the system that brings upon them the violence they undergo. Their narrations mark the relationship between authority and violence, a relationship that links this chapter to the first: with the convincing representation of violence the narrator gains authority, as does the transcriber who furthers her cause through the narrator. As in a court of law, their testimonies describe violence. The brutality of Rigoberta Menchú's description must shock the reader's complacency and evoke a response that brings sympathy to, and belief in, her cause in the written testimony. Physical violence's presence becomes fundamental to veracity and the translation of experience into testimony.

While Menchú stresses the superior pacifism of her people, who do not harm a soldier captured by them, Jesusa enacts violence as a positive method of survival given her circumstances. Her fighting personality breaks stereotypes and sparks Poniatowska's attention, and hence, sparks the text. As noted earlier, Poniatowska describes the behavior that caught her attention: "cuando le dan un trancazo es porque [Jesusa] ya dio dos" ("when they give her a blow it's because [Jesusa] gave them two"; "La literatura" 27). Jesusa likes a good fight and successfully justifies herself before the listener and reader so that we cheer her on as she defends herself or gives it to those who deserve it. Her mixture of moralist and pugilist authorizes her and endears her to the reader. In the case of *Quarto de Despejo*, the act of testifying as a victim of violence becomes a method of survival. Carolina embeds her individual history within a testimony of *favela* life, leaving any personal motives hidden behind or mixed with a message meant to heighten political awareness of a collective reality and to attract the publisher's support. Her survival story's publication becomes her tool for survival by allowing her to escape the *favela*, albeit temporarily. A constant stream of domestic fights, suicides, accidents and other tragedies populate her pages:

> **29 de abril** Hoje eu estou disposta. O que me entristece é o suicidio do senhor Tomás. Coitado. Suicidou-se porque cansou de sofrer com o custo da vida.
>
> Quando eu encontro algo no lixo que eu posso comer, eu como. Eu não tenho coragem de suicidar-me. E não posso morrer de fome. (136)

April 29 Today I feel alright. What makes me sad is Senhor Tomás's suicide. Poor man. He killed himself because he got tired of suffering with the cost of living.

When I find something in the garbage I can eat, I eat it. I don't have the courage to commit suicide. And I can't die of hunger.

This passage typifies Carolina's descriptions of the violence poverty inflicts on her everyday life. Among so many entries that begin with her feeling ill, her feeling well merits first mention. Disease and pain, other violences on the body, appear as frequently as do anger and despair. Yet, her survival instinct prohibits her from committing violence on herself to escape her poverty. Like Menchú, Carolina's testimony disavows any violence on her part.

Violence falls into the hands of the narrator or authority figure in Lispector's *A Paixão* and *A Hora da Estrela*, where the search for a connection with another being in whom one sees oneself reflected leads to the destruction of that other. Thus, the creation of that entity in language effects its destruction. Appropriation results in the disappearance of the object of fascination, or "study." As represented in these works, self-authorization takes place over a dead body. While violence in *A Paixão Segundo G.H.* remains chiefly metaphysical except for the sacrifice of the cockroach (who *does*, however, represent the maid), violence erupts powerfully in *A Hora da Estrela*. The toothache throughout Rodrigo S.M.'s meditations does not compare to the humiliations and bruising Macabéa receives on the path to her final, bloody end. The irony of the novel's title reminds us of the culminating insult against Macabéa: her hour as a star is the grand moment when her blood pools on the pavement in a star-shape, the moment when she has been given a glimpse of her own misery, only to have her growing concept of future crushed in an amusing play on Madame Carlota's prediction that she will marry the rich man who probably drives the car that hits her. The articulation of violence, even in its most common meaning, engenders the texts I examine. Later I will assert that violence en-genders them as well.

Testimonial genres and selected works of fiction not only represent the "articulation of violence," the personal history of a victim of violence, but also the "violence of articulation" (Brink 6). With a slightly different emphasis, Teresa de Lauretis utilizes a similar *retruécano*[2] in her study of women and violence: the rhetoric of violence and the violence of rhetoric. For De Lauretis the adoption of rhetorical positions for reasons of style can cause consequences such as rendering the sign of woman as a vacant space. The violence of rhetoric may also emerge from the performative function of language, particularly in legal discourse. The judge is of course one figure in whom such authority manifests itself, and this connection with legal authority clearly pertains to questions of testimony and testimonial literature, both through the latter's literary genealogy and its contemporary circumstances. Here I am referring to the *Lazarillo de Tormes* as literary precursor of testimonial literature and of the novel, as discussed in the introduction. The judge to whom Lazarillo tells his story, and before whom he defends himself, remains present in the transcriber and the imagined reader of testimonial texts. Unlike Lazarillo, the narrator of testimonial literature does not necessarily face accusations of wrong-doing; on the contrary, these narratives suggest perpetration of a crime against the narrator. Nonetheless, the testimonial narrator must defend her accusation of injustice and her right to be heard from the margins. In the same vein, Rodrigo S.M. interprets Macabéa's existence as an accusation, an implicit disdain like the maid's unannounced departure and her drawing on the wall that initiate G.H.'s existential search. In these works of fiction, the marginalized woman's presence upsets in a violent fashion the privileged woman's authority and sense of self. In Lispector's texts the accusation directed at the privileged figure inspires simultaneous desires to absorb the other's essence and to exact revenge for this violence committed against privilege's comfort. Thus the other becomes sacred and dangerous. We do and do not want to be this other. As we shall see in the next section, Andrew J. McKenna's description of the sacrificial victim in his intertextual reading of René Girard and Derrida aptly applies to the testimonial and fictional other: "Any word designating this object will be double, self-contradictory, antithetical. Sacred words differ from all others in that they differ from themselves from within themselves, designating what is attractive and repulsive, holy and accursed" (71).

---

[2] *Retruécano* is a word with no equivalent in English that describes the figure of speech where a play on words is based on an inversion of word order.

VENGEANCE AND SACRIFICE

Where there are crimes and accusations, particularly in testimonial language, there follows an urge for rectification, for a vengeance through recognition of the testimonial subject's predicament and version of historical events and through punishment for perpetrators of violence. The accusation calls for the judge's (the transcriber's? the reader's?) textual interpretation, to legitimate that vengeance and its own violent potential. As Robert M. Cover puts it, "we must understand in what way the judge's interpretive act authorizes and legitimates [a violent deed]" in the form of justified punishment (1614). Interpretation becomes practice (1611), upon a body and an individual's identity, not only in law but also in the readings testimonial discourse elicits. The judicial institution links language and text to practice, or rhetoric to violence, through interpretation. As we shall see, literary criticism can also link rhetoric to violence through acts of interpretation. Cover points out that interpretation "suggests a social construction of an interpersonal reality through language," yet the pain and death that can result from a judge's "interpretation" of a text, and testimony, destroys that social construction, since pain is unshareable and "destroys, among other things, language itself" and meaning (1602). Although the testimonial transcriber and reader of course do not hand down institutional punishment for a crime–they might be implicated in the offending structures–and although testimonial literature usually stems from political motivations that seek to undermine structures of authority in which the official court participates, the judicial setting and the *proceso*[3] of testimonial literature share a situation in which the informant must either defend her testimony's truth and importance, or effectively disappear from the text. Cover's observations on the relationship between law, text and violence that portray interpretation as possibly destructive to the personal interaction on which it depends offer an analogy that would carry to an extreme some aspects of the appropriation and contradictory methodology present in testimonial texts I have examined. Lispector's novels also carry these aspects to an extreme. Such an act of interpretation

---

[3] The Spanish word appropriately signifies the double meaning of "process" and "trial."

entails the possible destruction of the individual who stands before the judge. Also, judicial interpretation serves as an example of the "agentic" state in which one acts through another. In the case of a court of law, the judge depends on others to enact the chosen punishment (Cover 1614). In the case of the testimonial texts and works of fiction, the transcriber or author figure speaks or acts through another to level an accusation against oppressive institutions, and the testimonial subject publicizes her story through another. Following Nance's observations on testimonial readers' defense strategies to disarm *testimonio*'s accusations toward them, resistant readers rely on others to act on the situations the narrator presents to them.

Indeed, the testimonial subject risks disappearing through a kind of discursive sacrifice, either through vicarious identity and criteria of veracity that "freeze" her in a prescribed identity, or her fictional analogy is sacrificed through an obsessive ritual in Lispector's two texts. Both evoke what Moreiras calls the "postauratic" in *testimonio*: the sacrifice and disappearance of the informant through the auratic self-legitimation of the transcriber. The auratic, in turn, is "the constitution of a self-legitimizing locus of enunciation through the simultaneous positing of two radically heterogeneous fields of experience" (201). As René Girard sustains in *Violence and the Sacred*, religious sacrifice simply amounts to another version of the law, a form of controlled violence and vengeance. Girard explains sacrifice in what he calls "primitive" societies as the equivalent of a legal system wherein violence is carried out in such a way as to allow retribution without provoking an unending cycle of vengeance and violence. The sacrifice essentially functions as substitute for the real culprit when killing the guilty one entails the danger of further retaliation and escalating violence. The sacrificial victim must therefore be removed enough from the situation of the original violence in order to be untainted and pure and to not spark mimetic desires for vengeance (27). On the other hand, the sacrifice must be similar enough to the real object of violence in order to appease the urge for retribution. Girard places the origins of human social structures in this violent substitution that obscures the community's own complicity in the violence. The ritual accompanying sacrifice functions, like the sacrifice itself, to establish order but also to hide the move from one object to another, the move from object of anger to sacrificial substitute (8, 19). "The sacrifice serves to protect the entire community from *its own* violence; it prompts the entire community to choose victims outside itself" (8). Also, "between these victims and the community a crucial social link is missing, so they can be exposed to violence without fear of reprisal" (13). The victim construed as an outside entity that saves the community is then sacralized in the forgetting of the originary violence. "Sacrifice restores order by restoring difference" (McKenna 30), so the sacred is always outside, always not us. In our presumably less "primitive" society, the judicial system limits vengeance to a single act governed by a sovereign authority, while it conceals its resemblance to vengeance (Girard 15, 22). In addition, just as a sanctioning authority underlies violence and the law, behind the ritual of sacrifice lies a deity who must be appeased, thus displacing the vengeful nature of the killing (Girard 7).

Although vengeance always lies present in the sacrificial process, the *testimonio* and *novela testimonial* function as vengeance by setting the record straight and attempting to give voice to dissenting versions of history and truth by recording injustices in order to avenge the narrator. *Hasta no verte, Rigoberta Menchú* and *Quarto de Despejo*, through their public accusations before the transcriber and reader, correct erroneous stereotypes and violent oppressions and exclusions. The sacrifices offered are those made by Jesusa, Menchú and Carolina, in the non-religious sense, in order to survive among those oppressions and exclusions. As we have seen, their sacrifices allow them to adopt a moral superiority that becomes a useful tool for convincing the reader of their versions of the events they recount. Moreover, even though the testimonial narrator's identity per se remains crucial to the transcriber's identification with, and adoption of, that identity, the narrator becomes lost, sacrificed to another's self-knowledge. In *A Paixão* and *A Hora* that appropriation becomes more violently vengeful and sacrificial.

McKenna offers interesting observations on the identity of Girard's sacrificial victim that correlate well with the self-reflective character of vicarious identity and the concomitant rigidity of the subaltern's relegation to the margins. "The victim is not desired for its own sake; all its value emanates from the desires it animates and magnetizes" (71). A marginal identity appeals to desires to leave one's own boundaries, as Rodrigo S.M. muses, to leave behind corrupting complicity in structures of power. McKenna later writes: "The victim has no value; all values derive from its expulsion in the same way that, though the letter has no value, all linguistic value, all meaning as representation, derives from its entombment or what its entombment represents: ob-literation of originary violence" (95). Here McKenna's intertextual reading of Girard and Derrida is evident with reference to the letter. I return to McKenna's ideas when I focus on Derrida later in this chapter, but, briefly, the comparison is based on Derrida's concept of philosophy's systematic exclusion of writing from its own origins in order to generate and stabilize concepts in philosophy from a position outside the phenomena philosophy describes (McKenna 27 and passim). For now the foremost point of this quotation is the victim's value in its expulsion. The subaltern figure's expulsion from dominant authority previous to the testimonial process and her potential expulsion from discursive space through the testimonial process are central to her importance to *testimonio* and to the people and mechanisms that write her identity. An idealistic reading of testimonial discourse and the patently ironic insistence by Rodrigo S.M. on his concern for his "love" object's interests carry out an "ob-literation" of the other's disappearance, of her expulsion from the written word, and of that expulsion's process. [4] Charles Merewether begins his essay "Zones of Marked Instability" with a passage from Franz Fanon that Merewether glosses with a phrase suggestive of the way the marginalized's representation evolves into disappearance. Fanon demands we attend to figures of emergence (a term that allows those figures mobility and presence on a global scene) rather than focusing on the past from which they have emerged. That past signifies origins that, according to Merewether, "fix identity in some distant vanishing point" (101). The nostalgic desire to fix the testimonial informant's identity in the past rather than in that identity's transformative, present reality "others" her until what she is vanishes.

The novels more clearly frame the tension between authority figure and protagonist that perpetuates that vanishing. In *A Hora da Estrela*, Rodrigo S.M. reflects with pleasure on his authorial power over Macabéa's life and death in mystical terms. The reli-

---

[4] In this discussion of sacrifice my use of the term "victim" does not mean a slip back to framing the testimonial speaker as victim rather than subject, against which Rogachevsky and others warn. "Victim" is the role assigned the scapegoat in sacrificial ritual and in my arguments signals a *problematic* disenfranchisement in certain approaches to testimonial writing.

gious connotations in Rodrigo's narration are clearly ironic, in keeping with his tone throughout, but they lend an air of ritual to Rodrigo's sadistic treatment of his object of love and hate. His initials are, after all, "S" and "M." He creates Macabéa as pure, virgin, truly innocent, almost sacred: a perfect object for violent sacrifice. Girard writes of the paradoxical nature of sacrifice that "because the victim is sacred, it is criminal to kill him–but the victim is sacred only because he is to be killed" (1). As discussed in the previous chapter, Rodrigo marks his distance from Macabéa at the same time he gestures to approach her more closely, seeing himself reflected in her. His sacrificial object must resemble that which it substitutes while remaining distinct. Macabéa must not represent Rodrigo too exactly, for, despite his ploy of self-effacement, he would risk his own demise in more than a casual, recreational manner; he experiences death only vicariously. After all, it is strawberry season, as he points out in the novel's last line, and he would not want to miss that. Rodrigo must maintain Macabéa as other and simple in his search for the essential meaning of existence, and in so doing, deny her any luxury. Not only the narrator's pose of investigating the simple, unadulterated facts, but also Macabéa's purity through impoverishment necessitates that he deny her, and the text, any embellishment:

> como todo escritor, tenho a tentação de usar termos suculentos: conheço adjetivos esplendorosos, carnudos substantivos e verbos tão esguios que atravessam agudos o ar em vias de ação, já que palavra é ação, concordais? Mas não vou enfeitar a palavra pois se eu tocar no pão da moça esse pão se tornará em ouro–e a jovem (ela tem dezenove anos) e a jovem não poderia mordê-lo, morrendo de fome. (19)

> like any author, I am tempted to use succulent terms: I know splendorous adjectives, meaty nouns, and verbs so fit they pierce the air in lines of action, since words are actions, remember? But I'm not going to adorn my words because if I touch the girl's bread that bread will turn into gold–and the girl (she is nineteen years old) and the girl wouldn't be able to bite into it, dying of hunger.

He cruelly forsakes succulent, mouth-watering, luxurious words which would overwhelm the deprived senses of his "Maca." As he flaunts his power to transform Macabéa's meager food into gold (his writing could inspire action), he cynically deprives her of her

own means (he forsakes action) in order to keep her his "Maca."
Rodrigo deprives her to such an extent that she becomes titillated
by a soldier and his gun, wondering if he is going to shoot her, min-
gling sexual connotations of rape with death and pain as pleasure:
"Devo dizer que ela era doida por soldado? Pois era. Quando via
um, pensava com estremecimento de prazer: será que ele vai me
matar?" ("Should I say she was crazy about soldiers? Because she
was. Whenever she saw one, she thought, trembling with pleasure:
could he be going to kill me?"; 44). She could ask the same of the
author who, despite his protestations that Macabéa forced her way
into his life, suggestively intrudes on the intimacy of Macabéa's
body.

In the block quotation above, Lispector plays with the relationship between actions and words, the subject of Cover's essay on violence and the word. As an author, Rodrigo S.M. plays with this connection through Macabéa's creation and representationality. She is
just as alive as he (24). He later uses double meanings to make ironic his assertion of her concrete existence: "Não há dúvida que ela é
uma pessoa física" ("There is no doubt she is a physical person";
28). She is physical in her acute awareness of physical sensations. Yet, Rodrigo utilizes his position of creative power to seek
vengeance. His desire for vengeance emerges from his urge to compensate himself and compensate *for* himself. She enrages him when
she leaves him empty, and the less she demands, the more discomfort she causes him: "Estou com raiva. Uma cólera de derrubar
copos e pratos e quebrar vidraças. Como me vingar? Ou melhor,
como me compensar?" ("I am enraged. The kind of anger that
makes you smash cups and plates and break windows. How am I
going to avenge myself? Or, better yet, how am I going to be compensated?"; 33). Later, he feels himself mutilated and insecure at
Macabéa's hour as a star and struggles with a desire for vengeance
against a metaphorical suffocation from his incompleteness: "E
minha vida, mais forte do que eu, responde que quer porque quer
vingança e responde que devo lutar como quem se afoga, mesmo
que eu mora depois" ("And my life, stronger than I, responds that
it really wants vengeance and tells me I should struggle like someone drowning, even if I die in the end"; 98). Incomplete without
Macabéa, incomplete with her presence that justifies his authorial
existence and reminds him of his inutility, Rodrigo desires revenge.

As sacrifice, Macabéa's innocence transforms itself into an evil to expulse and exorcize. Macabéa, on the other hand, lacks "jeito" 'aptitude' (31); she does not seek vengeance, and this gives Rodrigo the pretext to disdain and belittle her even more. Rodrigo needs her in order to exorcize her, to exorcize all that she signifies and of which she accuses him by his perception of her presence. His recognition of his own insignificance leads him to compensate through Macabéa, yet this compensation is completed by killing her: he can eliminate both a part of himself through their identification, and also that which exposes his inadequacies and meaninglessness in the first place. Killing her thus combines expiation with expulsion. In her study of Lispector's work, Marta Peixoto has pointed out the ritualistic process "that culminates in the killing off of the protagonist," as well as the betrayal that the sacrifice of Macabéa entails (98). Peixoto also notes that the death of the narrator's double comprises one of the essential acts that motivate Lispector's narratives in general, and that *A Hora da Estrela* offers a representation of the violence permeating the narrative act, including the guilt stemming from the impossibility of innocent narrative (99). Lispector's representation of the narrative act as violent thus provides an interesting reflection and illumination of the potential for violence in testimonial texts, the guilt involved in the transcription process, and the ways *A Hora da Estrela* parodies the transcription process, even if unintentionally. Peixoto's observations also indicate issues of authority that implicate narrative in general and fundamentally tie mediated testimonial genres to works of fiction in a manner that, apart from the key aspect of the originating interview in testimonial texts, seems to question any profound distinctions between their *writing* processes beyond the position that the text adopts as document or fiction, liberational or aesthetic.

Rodrigo S.M.'s poorly-acted self-effacement in a narrative that ultimately purges the marginal echoes the profound elaboration of a similar loss of self in which the other must die or disappear in *A Paixão Segundo G.H.* This novel contains especially provocative religious, ritual elements, as the title already intimates. G.H. addresses the reader throughout *A Paixão*, imagining someone holding her hand while she narrates her dangerous excursion into a world that demands her losing, or sacrificing, the contained, ordered self she has known. G.H.'s previous self depended on the law's reinforcement of boundaries and order: "Os regulamentos e as leis, era preciso não esquecê-los, é preciso não esquecer que sem os regulamentos e as leis também não haverá a ordem, era preciso não esquecê-los e defendê-los para me defender" ("It was important not to forget the regulations and the laws. It's important not to forget that without the regulations and laws there wouldn't be order. It was important not to forget them and to defend them to defend myself"; 39). G.H.'s identity, no more than an image reflected onto her by others, depended on enforced hierarchies reflecting the authority of law. She receives her new identity, however, through identification with the roach, implicitly linked to Janair who represents countless maids moving unseen behind the walls of countless homes (46). Yet, G.H.'s self-discovery is made possible only by Janair's sacrifice, by her disappearance, and by various forms of violence underlying the narration. Janair must disappear to elicit the crisis beginning when G.H. enters the maid's space, the room that inverts prescripted hierarchies. The text reflects G.H.'s own mediated experience of the "others," not the others' experience, even though G.H. undergoes a metamorphosis through her realization of other realities and subaltern truths. Despite the fact G.H. loses her previous identity as she had constructed it, her narration depends on other absences and violences in order to reconstruct her new self. The cockroach's sacrifice on the "altar" of the closet, and G.H.'s consequent assimilation of its matter by eating it, as she would the host, compose the ritual necessary for G.H.'s self-knowledge. The sacrifice, however, assumes images of the demoniacal, thus confusing holy communion and the painful ecstasy of hell in appropriation of the subaltern identity. This perverse Eucharist reveals a metaphor in extreme terms for the sacred value that the testimonial subject and her story acquire for the transcriber. Identification with the testimonial subject's position, however, endangers the transcriber's privilege and knowledge, casting her into the infernal reality of having nothing. The testimonial subject's testimony thus becomes both sacred and taboo, as does the sacrificial victim according to Girard. If we approach the sacred victim too closely, the community's violence may indeed turn upon us. McKenna explains, "identification with the victim is not reducible to moral sympathy. . . . It is the logic of 'there but for the grace of God go I'" (63).

Only in the other's death does G.H. understand its life and therefore her own. The ritual involves at the same time an inner process of self-mortification, of devouring oneself just as one arrives at an essential nucleus of existence and meaning, since one's previous existence is devoured by the new "truth":

> Mas tens medo, sei que sempre tiveste medo do ritual. Mas quando se foi torturada até se chegar a ser um núcleo, então se passa demoniacamente a querer servir ao ritual, mesmo que o ritual seja o ato de consumição própria–assim como para se ter o incenso o único meio é o de queimar o incenso. (75)
>
> But you are afraid, I know you were always afraid of the ritual. But when one was tortured to the point of being a nucleus, then one demoniacally comes to want to serve the ritual, even if the ritual is the act of self-mortification–just as the only way of having incense is to burn the incense.

If ritual is the act of consuming oneself, or being consumed into oneself, G.H.'s ritual consumption of the roach's substance signals their union and G.H.'s appropriation of a subaltern identity. Instead of mystical union up to God, this union leads G.H. down to the infernal subversion of hierarchy. The paradoxes of existing and not existing, of losing oneself and finding oneself, of loving and hating the other, and one could say of speaking as oneself and as another, appear in G.H.'s concept of ritual. In fact, the ritual forms the basis for existence itself. G.H. states, "o ritual é o próprio processar-se da vida do núcleo, o ritual não é exterior dele" ("the ritual is the process itself of the nucleus's life, the ritual is not outside of it"; 75). The nucleus's inner life relates to a self-centered, self-consuming, instinctual process. Ritual as a term linking G.H.'s approximation to the roach and an uncontained, natural life force leads to a connection between the fear of ritual that G.H. projects onto "you" in the quotation above and her fear expressed from the beginning of entering into a new, "non-human" world. The roach (Janair) already carries out the ritual in her cells, and ritual forms the common thread among all living beings. Despite its interiority, however, this ritual still involves masks, changing the meaning of "mask" from "lie" to "essencial máscara da solenidade" 'essential mask of solemnity.' Further: "Teríamos de pôr máscaras de ritual para nos amarmos. Os escaravelhos já nascem com a máscara com que se cumprirão. Pelo pecado original, nós perdemos a nossa máscara" ("We would have to don ritual masks to love each other. The scarabs are already born with the mask that will complete them. We lost our mask through original sin"; 75). G.H.'s approximation to subaltern others incorporates an attempt to regain ritual symbolized by a mask that humans have lost because of the original sin, a mask the roach retains with her carapace. What G.H. had hidden, the insect exposes: her fundamental identity. The roach, like the immortal scarab, always wears a mask, yet does anything but dissimulate. She wears a mask of herself, a ritual mask necessary to love, necessary to G.H.'s approximation to another. Here, original sin does not initiate communion, but prohibits communion with others, alienates. Thus, as in the rest of the texts I examine, *A Paixão* mirrors the importance of the mask to identity and its indispensability to approaching the other, to experiencing through an other. Nevertheless, this text redefines the mask as fundamental to unembellished existence and truth. Identity, linked to the inherent ritual, is prohibited to G.H. in her former life (65), yet she dares don her mask by entering the nakedness of an essential identity through the cockroach. Loss of the mask marks guilt, the fall from grace and expulsion from paradise (75).

Yet, G.H.'s plunge into the abyss of deconstructed hierarchy through identification with a representation of pure existence confuses the divine and the infernal, the sacred and the accursed. Her confrontation with the roach is a painful torture to which she succumbs and confesses (74), transforming the novel into a confession of guilt, before the reader and before the roach and what it represents. This transformation suggests a radical analogy for the manner in which the *testimonio* can become as much the transcriber's testimony as the informant's. Violence underlies sacrifice of the cockroach, but also G.H.'s painful confrontation with that cockroach. The text responds to the accusation implicit in Janair's scratched drawing containing repressed violence: "Carvão e unha se juntando, carvão e unha, tranqüila e compacta raiva daquela mulher que era a representante de um silêncio como se representasse um país estrangeiro, a rainha africana" ("Charcoal and fingernail joining, charcoal and fingernail, calm and compact rage of that woman who represented silence as if she represented a foreign country, an African queen"; 29). Both violences appear in this drawing that comprises Janair's only first-person testimony; Janair's silence, rage and pride determine the lines made by pressing the finger nails hard into the charcoal, but she remains a foreign entity, queen from a strange, African land. Tellingly, the maid's testimony displays her

own rage, yet describes G.H.'s figure to direct violence toward
G.H.: the room "era uma violentação das minhas aspas, das aspas
que faziam de mim uma citação de mim. O quarto era o retrato de
um estômago vazio" ("was a violation of my quotation marks, the
marks that made me a quotation of myself. The room was the por-
trait of an empty stomach"; 29). The room functions as an accusation that breaks the ironic quotation marks neatly containing G.H.'s
identity, forcing aperture and the solemnity of life and death which
she learns from the roach. There has been a sin, a crime, because
she feels pardoned when she cedes to the roach and all the things
around her. The eighth chapter ends and the ninth begins, "Perdão
é atributo da matéria viva" ("Forgiveness is an attribute of living
matter"; 43-4). Her quotation marks' violation has opened G.H.'s
eyes in the bright maid's room to another world she had ignored,
and the violation opens G.H. to guilt. Her identification with the
roach saves her. There is no punishment (78).

"Mas esta não é a eternidade, é a danação" ("But this isn't eter-
nity, this is damnation"; 43). There is no punishment in hell because
what would be punishment is transformed into pleasure (78). The
love she discovers in the epiphanic moment results from her
descent into filth and disorder: "Ah, o amor pré-humano me invade.
Eu entendo, eu entendo!" ("Ah, prehuman love floods me. I understand! I understand!"; 75). Eating from this tree of knowledge, the
inverted Eucharist of the roach's substance, Janair's inscription
made flesh, will be the death of her human soul (12), yet this constitutes her passion: filth and knowledge. She has touched the impure,
foreshadowing Rodrigo S.M.'s desire to degrade himself and roll in
the mud: "Eu fizera o ato proibido de tocar no que é imundo" ("I
had committed the forbidden act of touching the filthy"; 46).
Reaching across boundaries, across hierarchical levels, across classes, is prohibited. The "we" that G.H. directs toward the reader
refers on one level to humans as opposed to the creature facing her;
on another level she refers to people of her social class who live
swimming in the humidity of plants and the sheltered interiors of
homes as opposed to the dry, desert life of others represented by
the roach and Janair.

She has violated the law on which she depended for her identity: "a lei manda que só se fique como o que é disfarçadamente vivo.
E a lei manda que, quem comer do imundo, que o coma sem saber"
("the law mandates that one be like something half alive. And the

law mandates that whoever eats filth do it without knowing"; 47).
Her violation of the law will result in her expulsion from paradise.
G.H. will discover the hidden truth by knowingly tasting the
roach's substance, by crossing dividing lines of privilege and she
will thus commit sin, damning her soul. In this way her approximation to divine essence assumes images of demonic rituals. Referring
back to the earlier block quotation, the ritual of returning to the
nucleus involves a sort of torture, indeed a sort of vengeance, since
life avenged itself of her, "e a vingança consistia apenas em voltar,
nada mais" ("and the revenge consisted in simply going back, nothing more"; 46). Life violently returns her to the origins she had lost;
in the process her self, her privilege, her sense of superior and organized humanity are sacrificed. Hell combines the torture of losing
the security of her previous identity and the joy of understanding
and uniting with the life force in the other: "o inferno não é a tortura da dor! é a tortura de uma alegria" ("hell is not the torture of
pain, it is the torture of joy"; 66). Tell this to the cockroach. Her
love for the roach is infernal and the violence of her hell exults her
(75, 81). In the violence of her newly found passion, death brings
pleasure and G.H. simultaneously feels love and hate. This passionate hatred leads her to the inebriating desire to kill, to strike out
against that which has sparked her passion (35). G.H.'s attraction
to the other and her search for knowledge stem as much from
hatred as from love, inflict as much pain as pleasure, and accentuate the violence inherent in fulfillment through another. She depends
on the other's impurity. The impure forms the unembellished root
of meaning, and thus the dry, impure existence of the roach and
Janair must remain so for G.H. to carry out her perverse communion. The other must remain representative of the dry desert of
essential existence; G.H. may cross into the desert, but the other
cannot swim through the humidity of G.H.'s privilege.

This one-way border between a constructed, stable, subaltern
identity and a shifting, privileged identity seeking self-fulfillment
establishes yet one more advantage for the privileged subject at the
same time the move articulates, publishes, and values the marginalized subject for her knowledge. This outlines in stark terms the border at work in mediated *testimonio*, in the fiction studied here, and
at the heart of critical displacements that shift the aura [5] of the testi-

---

[5] See mention of Moreiras's "aura of *testimonio*" in Chapter 1.

monial subject's representative knowledge (as represented by the readers) onto the transcriber and reader's ideas. This is the direction the next sections of this chapter take. Rhetorical violence leading to a sacrificial act à la Girard that risks the marginalized subject's disappearance, obscures the process where the sacrifice originates, and glorifies the marginalized precisely because of her disappearance, sets the stage for the rhetorical blurring of boundaries based on the rhetoric that forms them in the first place. Rodrigo desires to possess the spark of life enclosed in Macabéa's scrawny body, but destroys her. Janair violates the neat quotation marks containing G.H.'s orderly, superficial existence and G.H. *knowingly* traverses corporal boundaries when she eats of the unclean, yet Janair remains an exoticized African queen, the roach is split in two, and the novel is G.H.'s self-discovery. Returning to the testimonial texts, in less violent terms Poniatowska discovers her self in Jesusa, in Jesusa's voice. Menchú's American identity softens Burgos's feelings of being an outsider.

I do not imply that in testimonial texts the transcriber also obscures a wish to carry out revenge on the informant, yet it is worth noting that the sacrifice acted out in works of fiction that suggest a critical reading of testimonial texts are driven by a desire for vengeance when the testimonial texts themselves seek vengeance through a critical reading. The sacrifices ritualized in fiction nonetheless suggest the violent potential of the informant's disappearance behind the transcriber's disguised voice. Levinson contrasts the colonizer's achievement of the "Other's" silence "through murder, violence, and annihilation" with the "de-orientalist's" achievement of the "Other's" silence "by simulating violence through rhetoric, through a poetics. [De-orientalism] 'silences' the Other through a turn of a phrase. It kills the Other's voice in order to bring back that voice, to redeem it through 'poetry,' through a trope" (181). Testimonial discourse, *read through privilege*, does sacrifice legitimation of the informant's free representation because the medium describes the borders of veracity, authority, and representativity even as the *testimonio* breaks the limits of official histories with alternative experiences.

SELF-KNOWLEDGE AND THE BORDER CROSSING

The disguised search for meaning of the self associates these testimonial texts and fiction with the paradoxical nature of textual violence and sacrificial mechanisms: creative and destructive. Elizabeth Burgos comes to better understand herself as a Latin American through a woman disenfranchised by Latin America. Carolina Maria de Jesus alternately condemns and defends the *favelados* in order to better her situation. Rodrigo S.M. desires to understand the essence of existence through Macabéa, whose existence he terminates. In an epiphanic encounter with the previously unknown G.H. is reborn by means of her old self's destruction and the construction of outsider identities for Janair and the cockroach. Pursuit of broader meaning and knowledge of the other in the textual relationships studied bring the author or protagonist to the self and problematize that other's self-representation. Crossing the boundary between the two may thus strengthen the other's boundaries.

Violence can arise from a search for meaning, and from the ambiguity of that search's outcome. Andre Brink utilizes a quotation from Robert Musil to begin his comments on this aspect of violence: "We all want to discover what we're alive for: it's one of the main sources of all the violence in the world" (5). Violence asserts the individual or the collective's agency. Brink adds that

> When violence becomes the expression of the search for meaning, the concept loses the one-dimensionality of its general usage, i.e. to denote exclusively the negative and destructive use of force, the misuse of power. It demands the exploration of its interface with a set of positive meanings. And indeed, how closely related are destruction and creation, how thin the membrane that separates our different kinds of violence. (5)

And indeed, how closely related in the texts studied here are the violence toward hegemonic authority to create space for marginalized voices and the violence that delimits the possibilities of those voices as a condition of their publication. Identity achieved through another in this context bears the danger of erasing those other voices. Both Musil's and Brink's statements incorporate the notion of individual agency into violence's role in meaning, insinuating self-exploration's integral part in the violence they outline. Similar to Brink, who calls violence a prerequisite for our existence, Ariel Dorfman perceives violence as the very structure in which one finds oneself; it is inside one and proves one exists (14). Writing in 1970, Dorfman considers violence a given of Latin American life and analyzes changing representations of agency in literature in reaction to that condition: until the narrative of the 1940s "man" was passive victim of injustices; through the 1960s the subject takes an active role before the state of violence (9-10). One could see the *testimonio* as contemporary to the later pattern in its aperture to new voices as active subjects, to survivors of various violences. In addition, the change Dorfman notes may have been accelerated by the Cuban Revolution, as was testimonial discourse's success and institutionalization as a mode of textual production in itself. Nevertheless, lending agency to the testimonial subject becomes tangled in rhetorical violence that may sacrifice the subject's self-representation to the necessity of eliciting a privileged readership's activism before the state of violence.

Yet, Dorfman characterizes the subject's active role as *implication* in the violence. Describing the active subject's thoughts in response to his violent reality, Dorfman melodramatically writes: "Me convierto en afluente del caudaloso río de lo real, siento que estoy interpretando el sentido oculto de las cosas, que con un rito individual estoy imitando la estructura de una realidad exterior que me parece casi divina por su omnipresencia" ("I become a tributary of reality's fast-flowing river, I feel I am interpreting the hidden meaning of things, that with an individual ritual I am imitating the structure of an outside reality that seems almost divine by its omnipresence"; 13). Despite Dorfman's exaggerated mystification, perhaps an ironic commentary, of interest here is that the religious vocabulary he chooses to explain participation in a reality structured by a violence so omnipresent it appears divine recalls the religious overtones of sacrifice discussed above. Through violent ritual the subject approaches a divine scheme that brings with it an understanding of hidden meanings.

Nevertheless, the liberating violence that permits self-affirmation of course requires the presence of others. This chapter's epigraph by Freire once again bears relevance in the way in which those "others" are not outside the dominant system but inside it, crucial in their role as marginal. Along Dorfman's lines, this vio-

lence comprises a fundamental characteristic of the border where
an individual meets others. Dorfman writes that in Latin America
violence establishes a connection with others as well as establishing
a source of intimate being: "ha sabido buscar en la violencia su ser
más íntimo, su vínculo ambiguo o inmediato con los demás" ("he
has known how to seek his most intimate being in violence, his
ambiguous or immediate connection with others"; 9). Yet, the rest
threaten the self with the same structural violence in which one participates, recalling the danger of associating too closely with the
Girardean sacrificial victim whereby one may become the community's next victim: "[¿]qué significa que frente a mí esté un otro que
es mi esperanza, es mi mirada hablándome desde otros rostros,
pero que me amenaza con la muerte; qué hago con mi violencia, esa
solución que puede también destruirme?" ("What does it mean
that before me stands another who is my hope, who is my own gaze
looking at me from other faces, but who threatens me with death?
What do I do with my violence, that solution that can also destroy
me?"; Dorfman 11). Other faces reflecting one's own gaze evokes
the scene in *A Hora da Estrela* where Rodrigo's face appears in
Macabéa's mirror reflection. While the transcriber, authority figure
or narrator may come to depend on the interlocutor or mirror
image for the discovery or understanding of her own identity, that
which the other represents threatens to undermine her precisely
because the other signifies absence for dominant ideology. Adoption of the threatening identity thus neutralizes the threat at the
same time it menaces the self's integrity.

The mirror image in which the transcriber or authority figure
sees him or herself reflected comes to embody something sacred in
that it represents a subversive cause or identity, individual or collective, meaningful to the transcriber. The *testimonio* and *novela testimonial* interject that voice into a public sphere as something of value that acquires a special purpose, something to be heard, and
something to be protected. Certainly, Rigoberta Menchú's receiving
the Nobel Prize indicates recognition of that value. The testimonial
subject is someone in danger or threatened whose further violation
testimonial discourse seeks to avert. When the informant is constructed as a valuable authority to be protected, that which the
informant represents and that of which she speaks may not be questioned without the sensation of a violation, of a crime, hence the
natural perspective that questioning the transparent veracity of the

testimonio commits another violence. Does that sense of violation include, however, sacrificing the sacred? That act involves a ritual reinforcing the paradoxical nature of the sacrifice: it does not profane, but rather strengthens the sacred status of the victim; it augments the desire to approach the victim, but reinforces her position *outside*. Again, in Girard's words, "the victim is sacred only because he is to be killed" (1), or rhetorically constructed to remain limited to self-representations conforming to the borders defining her identity as representative of difference.

Rodrigo S.M.'s narration, for instance, establishes limits and divisions, then breaks them. He maintains his distance through Macabéa's humiliation and sacrifice, then breaks the boundaries he sadistically establishes, since entrance into another who is pure in her difference must be made to gain legitimation, to gain greater self-understanding. Thus the boundary between subjects must be crossed, the split in some way reconciled. Rodrigo S.M. desires to transgress the limits of his identity and adopt another identity as a diversion, part of Lispector's commentary on the writing process in general: "Vejo que escrevo aquém e além de mim" ("I see I am writing beneath and beyond me"; 87). Also: "Transgredir, porém os meus próprios limites me fascinou de repente. E foi quando pensei em escrever sobre a realidade, já que essa me ultrapassa" ("Transcending my own limits suddenly appealed to me, though. That is when I decided to write about reality, since reality exceeds me"; 22). Alienated from reality, but self-consciously desiring transcendence, Rodrigo reaches out for another identity to transgress boundaries of self, of gender, of social class, with violent consequences for the protagonist with whom he strives for a facetiously mystical union to compensate, to avenge, his lack: "É paixão minha ser o outro" ("It is my passion to be the other"; 37). Similar to G.H.'s passion, "transgression" characterizes the action of entering another in *A Hora da Estrela* and with Rodrigo's drive for revenge suggests rape. "Meter a faca na carne" 'to stick his knife in meat' excites Olímpico, Macabéa's brief boyfriend whom the author praises for his capacity for vengeance (70), as opposed to Macabéa who lacks the necessary "jeito" 'aptitude.' Vengeance and images of violent rape merge in this sleazy character who murdered someone in the Northeast, and whom Rodrigo admires. Olímpico literalizes with a knife the act of transgression, boundary crossing and murder that Rodrigo commits more complexly through ritual, writing and appropriation. Suggestions of rape, including Rodrigo's occasional mention of his desire for his humiliated protagonist, supply a key to one reason for Lispector's male mask: just as Lispector sarcastically asserts through Rodrigo that a woman could not have written this story for she would be too sensitive, in order to write Macabéa's humiliations and figurative rape, Lispector must don the disguise of rapist, of victimizer, of male. However, she knows we know who stands behind Rodrigo. While Olímpico seeks penetration, not only into raw meat, but also into Macabéa's co-worker Glória, in contrast, Macabéa wishes to be nothing more than herself (40), to not be deprived of the only thing she possesses. She does not desire to transgress her boundaries, to enter into others, yet in her intense experience of her own sensations she paradoxically transcends herself, entering into Rodrigo's guilt and sense of lack and alienation.

Through an unspecified question implicitly posed in the dedication and missing an answer, the novel initiates the process of crossing in its embodiment of an unanswered question. Without an answer, the text remains unfinished. Lispector writes: "Resposta esta que espero que alguém no mundo me dê. Vós?" ("An answer I hope someone somewhere in the world may be able to provide. You perhaps?"; 8, 8). She reaches out to the reader foreshadowing the same gesture by her author mask, Rodrigo, who will seek his own answer to meaning in the sacrificial appropriation of Macabéa. The text's status as a question is crucial to the idea of boundaries since a question's location at the limits evokes both repression and transgression. "What can be more violent than a question?" asks Brink. "Questions determine our limits, define the periphery of what is permissible, of what has so far been thinkable. And it is our search for answers to those questions which prompt us to transcend limits" (5-6). Brink might also say that questions, by eliciting answers, determine limits. The answers define and classify. Yet, Lispector provides no answer, but a chain of paradoxes. The answer, if it exists, is left to the reader, Rodrigo's accomplice.

David Avalos writes in dialogue with John C. Welchman a series of observations on the Mexican-US border region entitled "Border/Place/Practice." In one section of the essay he relates an incident in December 1986 where uniformed police officers went with one dressed as Santa Claus to an area within US territory where undocumented Mexicans prepare for night-time crossings. There they gave out presents to the children with a public announcement.

Avalos asks why these officers did not do the same across the border in civilian clothes and answers that "this side of the border has the power to give and to take away the border, and it must be shown, it must be related publicly, it must be staged" (190). Two weeks later a patrol shot a man in the back in the border zone, calling him a bandit. Avalos asserts the two incidents demonstrate "the official border is maintained by the exercise of a power that says, hey, we can erase it when we want to hand out candies and Christmas sugar canes; but we can assert it in a flash where we sight a bandit, and we can summarily execute the bandit" (190). With a similar lesson, Menchú describes her difficulty crossing borders, even after winning the Nobel Prize, with an indigenous face (181, 184). At the same time the author declares there is no border; it is staged to distract us from the permeability of the border, of the border's extension far into US territory (passim). The border between economic and ideological differences, here between what are conceived of us the "First" and "Third" Worlds, is controlled by the dominant party. The border is violent; "the border is the visibility of power in discourse" (Welchman 167). Yet the possibility exists that the border does not even exist at all. We may be permeated by aspects of the other side or the other side may not be as "other" as we predict. Levinson contends Latin American "de-orientalists" expect the heretofore silenced to "speak differently, as 'Other'" (177), and that this prescriptive condition of breaking their silence in essence reproduces silencing by not permitting the unheard a certain freedom of self-representation and of fluid borders, a certain influence from the dominant discourses accompanying globalization. [6] The sacrificial victim's disappearance (silence) reaffirms the border between self and difference and expels the originary violence before construction of that border. "Sacrifice restores order by restoring difference: between the sacralized victim . . . and the rest of the community" (McKenna 30). The border enforces order and can be opened or closed at will, or crossed at will, from one side but not the other. In other words, the border is not *a priori* but of our own construction.

Therefore, when the transcriber or fictional character representing privilege rhetorically crosses a border of subjectivity, economic

---

[6] See discussion in Chapter 1 of the controversy over revelations about aspects of Rigoberta Menchú's *testimonio*.

status, or culture to find him or herself in another, the border either offers little resistance or is in fact illusory. The border crossed is either one constructed by dominant ideology for a one-way crossing or it is a false border that distracts from real boundaries that a privileged subject cannot or does not want to cross, boundaries established by the testimonial informant such as those Doris Sommer analyzes in *Me llamo Rigoberta Menchú*. Is crossing limits then either transgression (challenging a law or command) or personal violation, or is it a staged subversion of nonexistent borders or those open to the authorized? Does crossing constitute an act of solidarity or perpetuation of restrictions? Does traversing boundaries reinforce boundaries? Borders delimit, but invite transgression; transgression and subversion depend on pre-existing borders. Borders protect, systematize the chaotic, and restrict. Borders are geographical, somatic, and discursive, imposed and self-made. Borders create hybrid blurrings and binary oppositions. Borders lie on the margins, yet are controlled by a central authority. Borders witness and produce violence, yet are established to maintain peace. The contradictions among the uses and constructions of borders, boundaries, or limits, like the contradictions among the uses and constructions of identity and truth evident in testimonial texts, must be interpreted in a shifting context. For Welchman the border should be thought of as "a kind of holographic projection" or a mobile "texture" that facilitates "re-articulation of discursive formations" (177). The violent tears, ruptures, and conflicts of the border "are not fetishized as a final cut: they are instead, or they may be, re-sutured, re-circulated or re-bonded" (178). Such a concept of borders resists rigid binary oppositions where truth, for example, becomes divorced from the forces acting on the informant in a particular context.

Outside the shifting context of lived violence, *testimonio* as expression of power relationships' potential violence along borders risks becoming normalized like the border itself and like the informant's preconceived cultural identity. Welchman perceives a recent philosophic tendency to "re-stabilize the conflicted border, to channel and divert the institutional empowerments around which a border is always constructed, always implemented and always maintained" (171). *Testimonio*'s intended audience is the privileged reader, yet its discursive violence against dominant ideology is embraced by an academy that normalizes the transgressive border

as another intellectual tool. As an intellectual tool, anthropology
creates the borders it sets out to traverse, as Christopher L. Miller
notes (12), and according to Levinson "de-orientalism" creates
silence like a border it then works to break (180). In *testimonio* the
boundary between inside and outside has been set up by repressive
regimes or economic inequality and is then taken as ontological.
Moreover, sacrificial violence maintains order by creating the border between inside and outside, then sacralizes that which is taken
as ontologically outside the community. These parallel processes
illuminate *testimonio*'s place among a series of discourses that
attempt to bring to public consciousness that which lies over the
border, a limit ultimately perpetuated or normalized by those discourses. Further ahead similar continuities evident in postmodern
theorists' critical expressions of vicarious identity will come to light.
Binary contrasts incorporating borders like modernism/postmod-
ernism, orientalism/de-orientalism, and non-nomadic/nomadic are
set up by the latter term to form a contrast, but the latter term
repeats moves made by the first through its methodology. *Testimonio* seeks to free the marginalized voice in a process that undoes
appropriation, creating a contrast with those appropriations through
the speaker's direct discourse, but its methodology and our reading
sets up antithetical tendencies. It is a methodology that like the
process explained in Girard's theory of sacrifice camouflages a disappearance at its origins, camouflages a process that makes sacred
what was violently eliminated, sacred in an essentialized form
imposed by the system *testimonio* attempts to undermine.

Vicarious identity, compensating one's lack with another's desirable authenticity, evokes the idea of the violation of the boundaries
of something whole and integral. The sacred is whole and complete, obscuring the previous violence that crossed the boundaries
of the victim's body. The creation of a contained, integral, representative, "sacred" subjectivity for the informant or other marginalized
figure can reinforce a disenfranchised position whose continuing
existence legitimizes those on the other side of those boundaries
and can constitute another type of repression. A contained being or
identity is constructed for the sacrificial victim and for the testimonial subject; violation then becomes "an action through which this
body or space is broken into, opened up, defiled, profaned, interrupted, interfered with, perverted, its integrity invaded, its freedom
challenged" (Brink 5). Yet the imposed creation of a contained,
uninterrupted, integral identity may challenge its freedom as well.

Boundary crossings open the door to the desecration of the sacred by violation of his or her integrity as contained subject, by misrepresentation, by interference in his or her discourse.

Limits created or crossed by the testimonial subject of course open the door to her resistence, however, as well as to the writing subject's disintegration as cultural token. Thus, crossings and blurrings suggest a site for violence toward the testimonial narrator, but also for violence toward that which oppresses her. Opening meaning becomes one of the dangers resulting from identifying with the other, since crossing the boundaries of the self risks exposure and exteriorization, a tearing aside of the disguise. The periods on either end of *A Hora da Estrela*'s subtitle ".As for the future." and the quotation marks surrounding G.H.'s name serve similar functions: to contain meaning and establish the subject's boundaries. Both narrators expose themselves to the dissolution of those boundaries through their attempts to compensate their limit(ation)s through another, although ultimately dissolving the boundaries for themselves, not for Janair or for Macabéa. Reading testimonial discourse without limits on the informant's narrative strategies allows her to wield words as weapons against dominant assumptions about her and about hegemonic construction of meaning within the self-erected boundaries of truth. Readings that limit the testimonial subject's self-representation constitute the periods or quotation marks.

Lispector's aperture of the text through *A Hora da Estrela*'s open-ended questions and *A Paixão*'s punctuation and circularity, returns us to how the transgression of set boundaries and limits forms the most subversive quality of these novels. Lispector's texts break boundaries by experimenting with new forms of representation and language. Even those aspects of the texts that leave intact power relationships between characters problematize those relationships through their interference with the texts' explicit purposes. Breaking boundaries creates a violence as much against hegemonic structures that hold differences in place as against the oppressed. The *testimonio* and *novela testimonial*'s break with previously established genres, their evasion of easy classification, the alternative histories they contain, and their forum for collaboration across class and racial lines question existing cultural and disciplinary boundaries. Simultaneous with the continuing struggles for authority, legitimation and identity that I have been describing, testimonial texts do open a dialogue that Brink views as the creative violence that parallels socio-political, democratic processes: "the provocative and creative violence which, in the meeting of text and reader, allows each party (including Spivak's erstwhile 'subaltern' . . .) to 'talk back' to the other" (12). In dialogue, the written word may be questioned as sole authority. The oral testimonies depend on their transcription into writing for authority, yet the transcribers' written texts depend on the legitimizing authority of the oral testimonies, and the testimonies' contents accuse not only the transcriber, but also the reader. Dorfman calls "violencia narrativa" 'narrative violence' the "barroquismo" 'baroque style' and "retorcimiento" 'convolutedness' that attempt to destroy the reader's cosmovision: "Es la violencia contra las formas establecidas, los modos de ver tradicionales, la gran violación de las reglas del juego social-literario" ("It is violence against established forms, traditional ways of seeing, the grand violation of the socio-literary game rules"; 36). This textual violation mirrors the testimonial speakers' and the sympathetic transcribers' desired vengeance on dominant discourses. Dorfman imagines the protagonist asking himself, "¿cómo me libero, cómo uso esta violencia en vez de que ella me utilice a mí?" ("how do I free myself, how do I use this violence instead of its using me?"; 10).

The Castellanos quotation in the epigraph to this chapter links this question, the counterhegemonic potential of testimonial genres, their concurrent participation in the informant's discursive disappearance, and women's situation. "[Y]o me afirmé a base de gentes que todo el tiempo me quisieron destruir" ("I affirmed myself through people who the whole time wanted to destroy me"; Poniatowska, "Rosario Castellanos" 119). The irony of Castellanos's statement strikingly reflects Dorfman's portrayal of violence as connection between self and other. Those in whom Castellanos saw herself, such as her family–"another who is my hope, who is my own gaze looking at me"–in fact worked to destroy her since she was female–"threatens me with death." How does she overcome this violence directed toward her, how does she use it "instead of its using me?" With some variation: How does the testimonial informant affirm herself in a medium and before an array of roles projected upon her that want to destroy part of her self-determination? How does she use that discourse instead of its using her? Furthermore: How does the transcriber utilize the testimonial subject's voice as the subject utilizes her as conduit? How can the transcriber affirm her identity in those whose testimonies want to destroy the position of privilege the transcriber occupies? The answers begin to define the discursive violence of the *testimonio*'s unique border region where a hard-to-define hybrid of document and fiction articulates not just a monologic life story, but also a dialogue of differences and a dialogue in language that struggles to undermine those differences' definitions while defining them. Translations, *traslaciones* 'movements or shifts,' occur in this border region, but by means of deviations and displacements that belie the stable locations *testimonio* readers strive to define. The discursive conflicts or incongruities examined in the next section will then logically lead us to the last section where critical displacements by theorists offer further instances of dependence on essentializing representations that in the end sacrifice the very identities whose subversive agency is valorized, sacralized.

TRANSLATIONS AND DISPLACEMENTS

Because of its concern for truth, aside from the complications discussed in the preceding pages, *testimonio* shares with much literature a preoccupation with the limitations of its linguistic medium to describe being, more so a being conceived of as quite distinct. This other experience of being is represented as so distinct that it requires a difficult translation (and thus lends itself to exoticization). As G.H. expresses it, the task is "traduzir o desconhecido para uma língua que desconheço" ("to translate the unknown into an unknown language"; 15). Not only does she not know the new language she has encountered, but she no longer knows her old language, since her new experience has defamiliarized it, or transformed her only possible language into a new hybrid. Crossing over the boundary to the mirror image, to the other who reflects the self, or whom the self represents as a reflection, necessitates translations and the confrontation of different languages, of different discourses. For this reason, the testimonial process, its ironic or critical treatment in certain works of fiction, and the tendency to compensate through others a lack in oneself all deal with translations of one sort or another. The confrontation of different discourses can generate betrayals and erasures along with the vicarious identities and self-reflective border crossings seen thus far. The neutral, scientific pose or the rhetoric of subversion through an affected and marginalized speaking position constitute transcribers and other readers' possible translations that threaten the pro-activist testimonial project or allied attempts to undermine existing hierarchies. Translation as used here denotes a moment when displacements can take place.

Displacement's many meanings all bear at least some relevance to the violences inherent in the testimonial process. With displacement, meaning opens, and power relationships manifest themselves in a language of spaces and movement appropriate to the physical shifts the informants and protagonists undergo. According to Mark Krupnick's overview of the term, in Freud's dream theories displacement refers to the dream differently centered from the dream thoughts (7). The concept in this sense refers to parallel relationships, although moved to a different center of attention. Krupnick maintains that the shifting of the center of the dream thoughts preludes deconstruction's "reversing the terms of a philosophical opposition, that is, reversing a hierarchy or structure of domination, and then displacing or dislodging the system" (1). In the next section I discuss the extent to which that dislodging is successful. Displacement defamiliarizes the familiar and thus produces an underlying incertitude toward accepted concepts. Displacement also creates distortion and disguise. The act of fulfilling one identity through another clearly constitutes a fundamental example of the speaking subject's displacement, of the narrative voice's shift. A split, displaced subject becomes a natural outgrowth of the clash between self-representation and representation through another in the texts at hand and reflects the divisions that feminist theories of women's identity have signaled: divisions arising from the conflicts between imposed limits and a woman's own desires, from the contradictions inherent in the roles imposed on her, and from the conflict felt by Castellanos, affirming herself in those who sought to destroy her. *Testimonio* may offer a welcome space for women's participation partly because of its aperture to marginalized voices and its splits and displacements relevant to the expression of female identities. Fulfilling one's identity through another and that act's paradoxical nature traces part of a long series of divisions and displacements characterizing these texts at various thematic and discursive levels.

In this chapter's introduction I mentioned how testimonial genres bear witness to displacements closely related to violence with the hope of turning displacement's object into its subject, while the texts eventually depend on other displacements the process creates and the fiction mirrors. These women do not possess a stable location, emphasizing their outsider status. Jesusa and Macabéa, to use examples from a testimonial and a fictional text, undergo the displacement of internal immigration to the city, where they each become "one among millions," as Rodrigo S.M. states. Seen thus, they come to occupy an authoritative representativity. Macabéa's alienation is exacerbated by her seemingly absolute disconnection from her surroundings while Jesusa shifts locations in a picaresque search for work to survive. Shaw insightfully analyzes how Jesusa's socio-economic reality then requires constant displacements of her identity and character as Jesusa represents them. Rigoberta Menchú gives her testimony in exile, on a visit to Paris where she lives as a guest in a virtual stranger's house so that her testimony issues from that uncertain ground. Menchú does not speak from a space of her own, but as a guest in Europe. Burgos herself describes her sensation of displacement as an expatriate Venezuelan in France, yet Poniatowska seeks not to recuperate her origins on the other side of the ocean, but to establish new roots in Mexico through Jesusa. Rodrigo's alienation plays on sensations of being uprooted like those of Poniatowska and Burgos, but reveals them as displacements themselves of privilege when confronted with the experiences of their informants.

The back room in *A Paixão* provides a variation on these dislodgings as the space Janair could not call her own while she occupied it and the space that G.H. no longer possesses once she steps into it and sees Janair's drawing. In the back room G.H. gains her own consciousness of displacement: her old self is the familiar defamiliarized in the new context of the exterior perspective she acquires. Physical displacements alter meanings and perspectives and leave the displaced on uncertain terrain. The testimonial transcribers' dislocations stimulate their associations with the testimonial subject to compensate the uncertain grounds on which they perceive the foundations of their identities, but without due attention to the uncertain grounds where the testimonial subjects' displacements have left *them*. The testimonial subjects and fictional characters' displacements result in new associations and meanings imposed from outside so that speaking from a different location alters the meaning and reception of the shifted voice and demands the illusion of stability.

Krupnick links displacement to the transformation of structuralist concepts (through its undermining the hierarchies described by those concepts) and he initially contrasts transformation with translation (4). In such a contrast his understanding of translation approximates the sense of a conventional literary translation, where the same meanings and relationships are preserved in a new language, where the center of signification remains the center. Later, however, he uses translation with a transformative meaning: "there is no translation without difference" (6), in effect stating there is no transgression without a border defining difference. Here translation becomes a method of displacement through defamiliarization or differences arising from the new language or context. To a certain point, all dialogue or other communication involves transformative translation as preparation of a message for the particular audience to which it is directed, incorporating techniques of persuasion and self-representation. Translation in the context of *testimonio* and *novela testimonial*, however, acquires special significance, first because their purpose consists of bridging a division between radically different life experiences for political reasons, secondly because multiple layers of translation work simultaneously or sometimes at odds with each other (oral to written, Quiché to Spanish), and finally because testimonial texts strive to obscure the effects of the transformative translations on which they in fact depend to retain a pure truth. In accordance with Lispector's clear preoccupation with textual transformations, G.H., on the contrary, does not at all obscure the transformative aspect of translation when she struggles with the need to shift the witnessed dissolution of her comfortable organization of the world into the written language that is still subject to the old hierarchy: "O que vi não é organizável. Mas se eu realmente quiser, agora mesmo, ainda poderei traduzir o que soube em termos mais nossos . . . . Se eu ainda quiser poderei, dentro de nossa linguagem, me perguntar de outro modo o que me aconteceu" ("What I saw is not organizable. But if I really want to, right now, I will be able to translate what I learned into terms more our own. If I still want to, I can ask myself in our language what happened to me"; 44). Lispector's transformed protagonist consciously confronts the difficulty of the transcriber's work and, as the quotation hints, G.H. contemplates whether or not she still wishes to translate her experience into writing, which would reverse the hierarchical dissolution she confesses to witnessing.

G.H.'s struggle disproves the irony of literary devices in testimonial texts since if *testimonio*'s outward logic advertises a transparent translation of a representative otherness, how can conventional language "transparently" describe what it itself has placed outside its methods of representation?

According to Castillo, "Lispector's own language [is] typically characterized by a constant structural antagonism between component parts of the sentence, which creates the appearance of a violent convulsion of language, torn against itself, and, alternatively, sets up a paradoxical incantation of strophe and antistrophe which is, for Lispector, the only guarantor of existence" (195-96). Dialogue between coexisting and seemingly irreconcilable meanings and linguistic elements generate the discursive violence behind her writing, and this clash guarantees existence, explaining in another fashion why Macabéa's death is Rodrigo the writer's death. Violence lends the subject agency that reconfirms existence, as Dorfman notes. Castillo's speaks of language's tearing "against itself," an inner conflict within the same entity, reflecting the manner in which Macabéa and the cockroach seem to emerge from within Lispector's protagonists. The "other within" is displaced onto an invading yet victimized figure, like the sacrificial victim. Rodrigo S.M.'s "translation" of Macabéa's reality marks the moment when two discourses sharing a certain vocabulary–alienation, hunger–but with radically distinct connotations based on context, meet and disrupt the other, displace the other through opening meaning and exposing the power relationship behind the meeting.

The heteroglossia of political or rhetorical positions contributes to the struggle for textual authority and forms the seams–the translations–where textual disguises and displacements reveal themselves. The seam between discourses in the testimonial texts becomes particularly evident in the shifting between individual and collective identity. In *Quarto de Despejo* Carolina Maria de Jesus's narration manifests her continual displacement between ethnographic and testimonial discourses in the alternation between her role as quasi-ethnographer and her role as *favelada* exposing the misery and exploitation of her fellow *favelados* through the example of her own experience. Carolina separates herself a few times from her own voice: "Como é horrível ouvir um pobre lamentando-se! A voz do pobre não tem poesia" ("How horrible it is to hear a poor person's lamenting! A poor person's voice has no poetry"; 119).

This posits a comment on misery's ugliness, and Carolina also distances herself from the indeed often poetic way she describes her own poverty's emotional fallout. The occasional incongruity of her two narrative modes threatens to violate her sympathetic representation of the *favelado* through her distancing and any contradictions emerging from the two agendas. The fact that this conflict of motives, of discourses, takes place within one person solicits a comparison of *Quarto de Despejo* with the fictional *A Hora da Estrela* and *A Paixão*, where not only do Rodrigo and G.H. identify with Macabéa and the cockroach, but also the representation of the other suggests that she in fact surfaces from within the protagonist's self. Whereas Carolina crafts a role for herself, the works of fiction poeticize this split where the protagonist arrives at self-confrontation, at a proverbial "other within." Poniatowska creates through her own love of *lo mexicano* a split in Jesusa between her mexicanness and her denial of belonging to Mexico. The narrative underscores a discourse of mexicanness, while Jesusa would deny any sensation or sense of being Mexican. This denial strengthens the text's apparent veracity by negating any contrived effort on Jesusa's part to portray *lo mexicano*. At the same time, Jesusa's denial highlights the imposition of Poniatowska's rhetoric upon her testimony.

Menchú's testimony also demonstrates a translation split between her personal story and her descriptions of Quiché culture: she distances herself through Spanish while she must remain representative and obscure the ways in which she stands out from her community. Menchú's need to publicize the Guatemalan genocide forces a new language upon her, including the outside perspective that Spanish implicates. Yet, for Quiché culture's collective concept of identity, translations of identity do not necessarily pose a threat to the individual's integrity, whose importance lies in relation to others. For Menchú, what western cultures perceive as fragmentation of individual identity means connections with others through her people's belief system: "Todo niño nace con su nahual. Su nahual es como su sombra. . . . Es como una persona paralela al hombre" ("Every child is born with his *nahual*. His *nahual* is like his shadow. . . . It is like a person parallel to the human"; 39). The *nahual* functions as a metaphor for the textual disguises in testimonial texts and also presumes the multiplicity of a being's representations, thereby questioning the possibility of a singular speaking position. In order to present an authoritative singular "truth" or speaking position the divisions must appear to be reconciled, but in traditional Quiché culture those divisions are not antithetical to coherent identity.

While translation signals a moment of displacement it also implies reconciliation. In testimonial discourse, translation as reconciliation seeks to smooth over the displacements the translations bring to the surface. Translation works to reconcile different positions or locations, even though as a result of those translations, the informants and transcribers become individual subjects or objects, or both, of displacements symptomatic of the testimonial process's inconsistencies. In other words, translation as an effort to reconcile different languages and to create an unproblematic space for alternative voices *requires* the displacements that challenge that reconciliation. For instance, in order for testimonial informants to give testimony, they must already find themselves displaced–Menchú in Paris, Carolina distanced from the *favela*, Jesusa in Mexico City–and must negotiate the discursive encounter that subverts fixed meaning. Translations in this sense both attempt to reconcile discursive differences and depend upon the shifting positions from which the testimonial project originates. Displacements dispute the legitimacy of the transcriber's identification with the informant; translation seen as reconciliation allows the possibility of knowing a fixed truth. As Walter Benjamin asserted, translation is dialogic, where displacement is mutual and both languages are altered in an approach toward a purer truth (73, 74, 77, 81).

Reconciliation reminds us of the differences between recreational or rhetorical border crossings and displacements by choice, and those made to survive. Caren Kaplan states at the very beginning of her book *Questions of Travel*, and develops throughout her arguments, the idea that "displacement is not universally available or desirable for many subjects, nor is it evenly experienced" (1). Merewether affirms Rosalind O'Hanlon's similar observation of the "chasm between intellectual mobility and mass dislocations" (110). The informant's physical displacements cause a violence not to be romanticized by visions of travel and intellectual exile. Such a distinction should not, however, reinforce the fixation of the informant's identity as the quintessential displaced who has been forced away from where she "really" belongs and who depends on others' lending her voice to get her back there. Involuntary displacements irrevocably alter that "native" subject who consequently participates in culture's globalization. Just as the concept of "border" must be contextualized to avoid essentialist tendencies and self-constructed boundaries, so must the other geographical vocabulary used by critics: "sites, borders, maps, and diasporas as well as exile, nomadism, and migrancy. To historicize the use of these terms in critical instances rather than simply assuming their value and currency can politicize our critical practices and make them sharper, more meaningful" (Kaplan 26). "Assuming their value and currency" perpetuates binary oppositions like those that certain critical theories establish between their ideologies and those of their precursors. Earlier I signaled the parallelisms between appropriation and those binary contrasts in theory: modernism/postmodernism, orientalism/de-orientalism, non-nomadism/nomadism. The latter terms emphasize their subversion of the term on the other side of the binary border, but in fact repeat moves made by the first through their methodologies akin to *testimonio*'s efforts to subvert the informant's marginalization through a methodology that depends on the informant's marginalized identity on the previous ideology's terms. Burgos may reconcile her American self with a traditional indigenous culture whose traditional form has been violently and permanently altered, as especially driven home in Menchú's second book, *Rigoberta: la nieta de los mayas*. When Krupnick links displacement, clearly associated with poststructuralist theory, with the transformation of structuralist concepts of hierarchy, he also reflects the acceptance of these critical binary contrasts. The following section outlines similar poststructuralist displacements of the critic's speaking position to the margins, displacements that mirror the vicarious identities that contradict efforts to lend agency to the testimonial subject. In addition, the "translations" of Lispector's writing, of the notion of "woman," or of the "Third World" into these theorists' critical language produce discursive clashes reminiscent of those studied above in works of *testimonio* and fiction.

CRITICAL DISPLACEMENTS

The following examination of theories that exhibit the same paradoxes as mediated Latin American *testimonio* does not intend to reproduce a colonial dynamic where Latin American texts provide primary material for the manufactured product of Euro-Amer-

ican theory. On the contrary, a critical reading of Latin American
testimonial discourse offers as many lessons for reading theory as
those theories contribute to awareness of language's role in constructing power relations and borders. *Testimonio* comprises a complex, self-conscious commentary reflecting back on the methodology of certain theories. In the process, Latin American testimonial
discourse, a participant but on the margins of Euro-American poststructuralist thinking, resists the appropriative dynamics revealed in
some Euro-American theories precisely by mirroring them through
an engaged praxis in *testimonio* or a critical reflection in both *testimonio* and fiction. *Testimonio's* contradictions ultimately place it as
a Latin American interlocutor that claims its place as subject in discussions of identity and representation, a place that disappears in
the rhetorical devices of the theories upon which *testimonio* indirectly comments. Beyond exhibiting the same dilemmas, *testimonio*
does involve a praxis beyond the discursive, an important difference addressed in the next chapter.

Just as testimonial discourse has opened a space for at least discussion of privilege, identity formation, appropriation, and official
language, while coming against the limitations of its very medium,
the theoretical texts covered here have extended tools with which
to attack privilege without being able to deconstruct their own
involvement in the processes of exclusion.

Hélène Cixous's (mis)reading of Clarice Lispector's work creates the most romanticized and intimate mirroring of the vicarious
identities testimonial transcribers gain through the voice of the other woman. The desire for sisterhood with Lispector communicated
in the lavish praise and mystification of the Brazilian author makes
especially frustrating Cixous's careful scrutiny of paradox and
poverty's presence in Lispector, without attention to the latter's
irony and paradox's context. Cixous has ignored Kaplan's warning
to not assume the value and currency of particular terms. Cixous's
desire for a writing that justifies her own work and theory of feminine writing, one that creates a pacific encounter with an other and
with an earthy voice at the source, one that circles gently around
meaning instead of overpowering it, to use Cixous's language, leads
Cixous to ignore the violence and acts of humiliation underlying *A
Hora da Estrela* and other texts by Lispector (Cixous, *Vivre* 8-16).
She in fact ignores her own gentle circling in interpretations of
Lispector that threaten the Brazilian's disappearance from the criti-

cal text. Marta Peixoto writes that in *To Live the Orange* another woman's "otherness is entirely disallowed and effaced to the extent that it does not coincide with the feminine libidinal economy that Cixous charges her with representing" (45). Cixous's self-fulfillment depends on a preconceived notion of Lispector (as poor) and of Brazil (as marginal). In addition, Cixous's appropriation of Lispector ironically replicates the dynamic of self-legitimation and fulfillment Rodrigo carries out on Macabéa in one of the very texts Cixous analyzes.

Lispector's "gleaming hands in the darkness" and her apparition before Cixous, described as a mystical revelation, seem to signal Cixous as the chosen one. In *To Live the Orange* Cixous describes a lack, an insecurity, in her writing that Lispector dissipates. "I felt guilty that my writing was aside from reality" (12). Lispector's writing somehow links Cixous's concerns to reality and to sources, even though Lispector comes from "far away, from outside of my history" (15). Cixous's association of a Brazilian's writing with reality more "real" than her own adds another example to Spivak's critique of Foucault's and Deleuze's valorization of the oppressed's concrete experience while overlooking the intellectual's historical role. Their blind spot in glorifying the real reinforces an international division of labor. Exhibiting a simultaneous identification and distancing seen in mediated testimonies, Cixous insists on Lispector's difference at the same time she appropriates her. Cixous correctly observes in relation to *A Paixão* the "other must remain in all its extreme strangeness within the greatest possible proximity" ("Extreme" 29). The Frenchwoman gains greater legitimacy, a closer contact with reality to combat criticism, by emphasizing upper middle-class Lispector's origins in a stark, poverty-stricken land and by dubbing her "my angel of poverty" (34, 42). The sacrifice is complete when Cixous writes, "I feel women writing in *my* writing" (34; emphasis added).

Practically speaking, dialogue between Lispector and Cixous is impossible, since Cixous "discovers" Lispector's writing after the latter's death: Lispector's voice "reached" Cixous on precisely October 12, 1978 (*Vivre* 10), significantly a date that recalls America's colonization. Nevertheless, Cixous suggests the illusion of dialogue since Lispector's "gleaming hands" seem to reach out in Cixous's direction. Lispector's writing seems to beckon to Cixous. In fact, Cixous relishes an author's final insights on the edge of the abyss of death: "On the last day before death, the author sits on the edge of the earth, feet light in the infinite air, and looks at the stars. Tomorrow the author will be a star among the stars . . ." ("Extreme" 9). Lispector's imminent death when she wrote *A Hora da Estrela* augments the sacredness and mystery Cixous finds in her writing and evokes Girard's claim that the sacred acquire that status because they are to be killed. Cixous mystifies Lispector's effective disappearance from her analysis through inattention to the violence in the moral dilemmas so central to the paradoxes Lispector finds in existence. Moreover, Cixous's reference to the novel's title glosses over the context in which Macabéa becomes a star and in making Lispector a star also she confirms the Brazilian's disappearance through the comparison with Macabéa and through a misreading.

Cixous does touch on key aspects of Lispector's work, yet misses the violent undercurrents in *A Hora da Estrela* in her enthusiasm for a writer whose work seems to embody the love and breakdown of binary opposites that Cixous seeks. Indeed, Lispector's exploration of paradox does subvert such divisions but, with a wink to the reader, the novel differentiates between recreational border crossings and the involuntary. Lispector explores the abstract, philosophical limit, but conscious of socio-economic disparities that beg the troubling questions of how do those deprived of almost all comforts and dignity survive, and what comes of contemplating such while sipping cold white wine in one's living room. Although Cixous mimics Rodrigo by problematically appropriating Lispector's writing to compensate a lack of writers who fit her own concept of a nurturing female libidinal economy, the French critic is able to perceive in Rodrigo the paradox of this appropriation. Cixous observes it is impossible to take a vow of poverty. Even those who rid themselves of everything retain the memory: "Those who have had, always will have left that memory and a trace of narcissism, be it ever so slight, of the effort made to impoverish themselves. There are always remains of having, even if one no longer has. That is Clarice's dilemma in *The Hour of the Star*" (*Reading* 153), Clarice's dilemma as testified by Rodrigo. Yet, by assuming Rodrigo's honest empathy for Macabéa the theorist also is able to privilege female identity:[7]

---

[7] Tellingly, Cixous states further on that "what is at stake for *me* in these stories is the fate of the *so-called 'feminine' economy*" ("Extreme" 15, first emphasis added).

She goes into the masculine, and this particular masculinity impoverishes her. To go into the masculine is, she suggests, an impoverishment, and like every process of impoverishment with Clarice Lispector, it is a positive movement, a form of asceticism, presented in a thoroughly legible way, a way of bridling a part of pleasure. Moreover in his turn this man "monasterizes" himself, deprives himself, bows down. ("Extreme" 12)

Very pleased with his monastic self-privations, Rodrigo describes those efforts to reduce his diet to humble white wine, relegating his horses to a memory with which he compares Macabéa. He sarcastically ruminates how he humbly–without great attention to his humility, mind you–humbly limits himself to Macabéa's emaciated adventures (19) and to himself through his self-conscious authorial task, as he realizes the limitations of isolation within one being. Cixous also appears to take Rodrigo's humility at face value when she states, "Macabea needs a very special author. Clarice Lispector creates the necessary author out of love for Macabea" ("Extreme" 10).

The French theorist describes in earnest her encounter with the Brazilian novelist, but with language reminiscent of Rodrigo's sarcastic pseudo-union with the sacred Macabéa (48). Rodrigo's gentle circling indeed enables the ironic language he utilizes to toy with Macabéa. Although Cixous speaks of Lispector's "violent patience" and of the dangers she risks, including complicity in murder, such references become sublimated into crossing the self's borders, finding ourselves in others, or more specifically, women finding themselves in other women. Leaving the borders of the self assumes sinister possibilities, however, in *A Hora da Estrela*. Cixous approaches my central point of appropriating another identity from the opposite perspective: she does not speak in terms of appropriation and authority, but of nurturing and common origins. Cixous suggests the "intervention of the other" is necessary for the novel's ending since Lispector in the dedication appeals to the reader to perhaps provide the answer the book does not provide (*Reading* 152). What she says about a necessary intervention is true, yet a concrete one and Cixous's reading implies the reader as the so-called other, leaving one to wonder where Macabéa is left, for the reader is Rodrigo's accomplice. He expects the reader to identify with him, producing yet another level of violence directed against the protagonist: our complicity and amusement at the humorously pathetic things that happen to Macabéa.

In *Spurs*, Jacques Derrida reacts to the singular unity of women in seventies feminism (Gallop 9), of which Cixous's reading of Lispector could provide an example, and advocates an anti-essentialist concept of women through a reading of Nietzsche. As several critics have underscored, Derrida's rhetorical, plural women fade into a repetition of essentialist stereotypes. In "The Violence of Rhetoric," Teresa de Laureates addresses Derrida's appropriation in *Spurs* of the place of woman as a rhetorical device, as does Gayatri Spivak in "Displacement and the Discourse of Woman." Skeptical of truth claims, a subject constantly shifting through disguise and even faked disguise, "woman" appeals to Derrida as a position from which to deconstruct. When Derrida hypothesizes, "if woman *is* truth *she* at least knows that there is no truth" (*Spurs* 53), in other words, that the truth is there is no truth, she becomes for Derrida a vehicle to contradict concepts of originary presence. She will not be misled by appearances of truth, as will not the testimonial subject before official truths. Just as woman is the truth of non-truth, the absence of one truth, woman disconnected from regulated femininity breaks the duality of sexual categories that perpetuate violent appropriations, as Feder and Zakin assert in their essay "Flirting with the Truth" (23). One might say woman is reterritorialized onto shifting ground that destabilizes centers of power, or in testimonial discourse, centers producing official versions of truth. Derrida's strategy clearly makes ironic the stereotypical association of woman with lies, versus the real story in *testimonio*, yet allows Derrida's woman to stereotypically and mischievously play with man's insistence on truths behind his back (*Spurs* 61). Taking this gendered metaphor to its extreme, the subversive, "female" role of the testimonial informant would be a manipulator of the transcriber's "male" desires, with no desires or agency of her own. Protection of the informant's authenticity can enforce dualisms that like Derrida's leave the informant/woman not quite there. While the aim of both discourses is to empower, subtle rhetorical structures within them work against them. In addition, linking the violence of appropriation to the duality of sexual categories recalls the idealized feminist ethnography that supposedly eliminates that violence.

Testimonio and its readings thus dialogues with Derrida, both reflecting his deconstruction and his participation in the processes he wishes to undermine. Derrida's deconstruction depends on the constant inessentiality of woman, of her becoming a position open to all. Her power comes about through "a non-identity, a non-figure, a simulacrum" (49), and woman becomes an absence. Derrida's appropriation of woman undermines its own subversive potential by keeping woman as marginal, as prone to artifice, and as an empty space to be occupied, similar to the prostitute's constantly shifting identity determined by others. His appropriation shakes the old order of originary hierarchies, yet he displaces woman as a subject of her own actions, repeating the hierarchies. De Lauretis reads his displacements in the context of scientific discourses that adopt a rhetorical position of (impossible) neutrality that in fact disguises the researcher or theorist's participation in structures that commit violence (13-4). Similarly, in *Violence and Difference*, when Andrew J. McKenna describes philosophy according to Derrida's deconstruction, he could be describing Derrida's construction: "Philosophy presumes to speak from outside a difference within which it is compromised; it is but a mark within what it claims to demarcate" (5). Like the legitimated, subaltern testimonial narrator who compensates the transcriber's perceived inauthenticity, Derrida's rhetorical position as woman centers on his own discourse, even if with the purpose of empowering marginal discourses.

In "What is a Minor Literature?" and *A Thousand Plateaus* Deleuze and Guattari's concepts of "deterritorialization" and "reterritorialization" also helpfully express the displacements and rewritings at work in the testimonial process, yet only *appear* to integrate the subversive potential of marginalized voices. Instead of completely empowering complex, subaltern identities, the authors' own territories, their own "politics of location," risk silencing the alternative voices to which they refer. Thus it is crucial to distinguish between *who* is deterritorialized, and whether or not one is the subject or object of deterritorialization. On one level, Deleuze and Guattari would probably define Latin American *testimonio* as deterritorialized. "Deterritorialization" refers to that–in this case, language–which no longer exists or functions in its original territory, to that which is exiled, to that which is excluded, to that which is in process or movement, to that which is in a state of "becoming," to that which approaches limits or extremes. Deterritorialization thus describes the circumstances of testimonial production where the informant can only recount her story after physical and political displacement, and then the linguistic displacement of transcription. *Reterritorialization* refers to new, subversive functions or locations resulting from deterritorializations. Here we may see testimonial discourse's ideal end, shaking accepted interpretations of history and deterritorializing the complacent reader. Yet, the greatest relevance of de- and reterritorialization to displacements, and the discursive boundary crossings and appropriations that accompany them, arises not from the content of the authors' terminology, but from the authors' own displacements, boundary crossings and appropriations. The heart of Deleuze and Guattari's displacements lies with the concepts of a "minor" literature and "becoming-woman."

Deleuze and Guattari summarize a minor literature as "that which a minority constructs within a major language" ("What" 59); the "minor" does not only refer to specific literatures, but to "revolutionary conditions for every literature within the heart of what is called great (or established) literature" (61). The idea of a minor literature brings together three central qualities significant to Latin American testimonial genres: a high coefficient of "deterritorialization," political relevance and collective value. When Deleuze and Guattari write that "everything in [minor literatures] is political [. . . and that] the individual concern thus becomes all the more necessary, indispensable, magnified, because a whole other story is vibrating within it" (59), their phrasing recalls Barnet's idea of the protagonist's double importance as extraordinary individual and representative of a transcendental historical moment in the *novela testimonial*. As a result of the "minor" literature's political nature, according to the authors, what is of passing interest in other literature becomes a matter of life and death (60). Certainly the critical states in which testimonial narrators find themselves, and even G.H.'s fictional encounter with the roach, correspond to this observation. Deleuze and Guattari's, as well as Barnet's, connection between the protagonist and the historical moment, and the authoritative representativity of the testimonial informant, indicate how the collective value of a "minor" literature results logically from its political relevance. Like the creation of that representative identity, however, the collective value of a "minor" literature constructs a misleadingly homogenous collective identity that risks essentializing, simplifying and further suppressing the revolutionary aspects of the "minor" that the authors advocate. Deleuze and Guattari's concept of collectivity stems in part from their thought that "talent isn't abundant in a minor literature" (60), but that the collective compensates the scarcity of talent because a "minor" literature "allows the conception of something other than a literature of masters" (60), although the authors do not seem prepared to sacrifice their own positions as masters who decide who constitutes the "minor" or what talent is. Collectivity in this form overlooks the contentious value of individual voices as they emerge, for example, in the tension between individual and collective that characterizes Rigoberta Menchú's testimony. Deterritorialization and the sequence of intensive states that it produces, the "becoming" that replaces proper names, could serve to characterize Lispector's novelistic work, yet she deals at least on one level with what Deleuze and Guattari do not: the real poverty of their abstracted, revolutionary "Third World."

In *A Thousand Plateaus* Deleuze and Guattari emphasize that minoritarian means for them a process and series of connections, not an actual "aggregate or a state" (291); that is, it constitutes a challenge to hegemonic standards and states of power and domination (105), without addressing the real confrontations that occur in situations like those producing testimonial discourse. Furthermore, a minor literature's characteristics include its problematic association with the "Third World" or the creation of "linguistic Third World zones" that according to Deleuze and Guattari are based on a revolutionary, but abstract, poverty in a language marked by a "lack of talent" that makes important the collective enunciation. Their concept of "Third World" oddly becomes associated with a minority, which it is not, except as represented in the dominant literary discourses from which Deleuze and Guattari write. In effect, Deleuze and Guattari maintain their concept of "Third World" as "minor," with all the connotations of that word. One must ask, would Rigoberta Menchú or the women on which Poniatowska based Jesusa Palancares consider "minor" a place of empowerment? Such a position does not characterize their rhetorical strategy, nor the interests of Burgos and Poniatowska as transcribers. The theory of deterritorialization does not completely question accepted hierarchies or the privileging of a certain literary language, even though it articulates the dislocated nature of testimonial discourse, both in its historical reality and in its contradictory adoption of a subaltern voice for the transcriber and the critic's self-legitimation. Like Derrida's woman, and as Caren Kaplan notes, Deleuze and Guattari's "advocacy of a process of 'becoming minor' depends upon the erasure of the site of their own subject positions" (86).

In addition, minor literature tends to depend upon the erasure of the subaltern because in order to legitimize a subversive speaking position, one can occupy the position of "Third World" or create his or her own "linguistic Third World zones." The marginal's subjectivity remains repressed since only the privileged can "travel" to these zones (Kaplan 88, 93). Is becoming minor not a strategy meant for those who would by choice cross over from the major to the minor in what Kaplan calls "theoretical 'tourism'"? A similar disappearance marks the position of woman in Deleuze and Guattari's nomadology, a concept both critiqued and adopted in modified form by some feminist theorists. Intending to describe a mode of thought that does not rely upon or reproduce fixed truths or notions of identity, and thus does not engage in exclusionary practices of hierarchy and order, Deleuze and Guattari use the figure of the nomad as "the Deterritorialized par excellence" since "there is no reterritorialization *afterward* as with the migrant, or upon *something else* as with the sedentary". In fact the nomad "reterritorializes on deterritorialization itself" (*A Thousand* 381). The unlimited, desert spaces in which the nomad moves allow the constant movement, process, and connections that characterize "becoming," a state that does not lead to a destination of definite subjectivity because the "only way to get outside the dualisms [on which order and philosophy are based] is to be-between, to pass between, the intermezzo" (277).

Becoming-woman occupies a privileged position in nomadology and becoming–already an indication that the concept is based on hierarchical thinking–since all becomings must first pass through becoming-woman (277). Men also must pass through becoming-woman, after woman. In her essay on *A Thousand Plateaus*, Alice Jardine points out that if woman is the first to "become woman," for men to follow her example, then she must be the first to disappear (54). Although meant to support an anti-essentialist concept of woman and a non-imitative state of thought, becoming woman comes to imitate the dualisms Deleuze and Guattari wish to undermine, repeating their failed empowerment of "Third World zones" and Derrida's disappearance of woman. In order to form liberating, rhizomic alliances among different beings becoming-woman uses woman's already familiar role: distant, unknowable, absent. She possesses the three virtues Deleuze and Guattari value in becoming: imperceptibility, indiscernability, and impersonality (280). Even though the authors carefully distinguish becoming-woman from

biological woman, they state that in writing one "should produce a
becoming-woman as atoms of womanhood" that can "impregnate
an entire social field" (276). While the figure of becoming-woman
facilitates a concept of identity as non-gendered, non-dualistic, fluid, connected, and constantly changing, in nomadology the figure
of woman finds some difficulty in gaining subjectivity outside of
dualisms and biological essentialism. Like the body without organs,
whose reconstruction is inseparable from a becoming woman (276),
woman seems to be "made in such a way it can be occupied" (153),
recalling the open position of woman's location in Derrida. [8]

The incomplete separation of essentialized woman denied subjectivity from a non-hierarchical, limitless, interstitial nomadology
that nevertheless seems meant for privileged wandering therefore
constitutes a problematic tool for feminists. Rosi Braidotti's *Nomadic
Subjects* attempts to rewrite Deleuze and Guattari's nomadism to
reconcile textual essentialism and political practices that recognize
difference and the fight for women's subjectivity. While she clearly
dissects woman's loss of subjectivity and ultimate disappearance in
the Deleuze and Guattari dependent on dualistic structures and the
"icon function" of woman (Braidotti 115), she does not adequately
address how to shake nomadism's origins other than to simply use
the term differently. Her definition of feminist nomadism stresses
the different situations from which women speak: "sexual difference as providing shifting locations for multiple feminist embodied
voices" (172); yet she repeats the very paradoxes she describes in
Deleuze and Guattari. The rhizomic network of shifts, alliances,
"emphatic proximity and intensive connectedness" in feminist
nomadism mysticize a relationship accessible only to the privileged
feminist. Nomadic writing "longs for" the desert, "in a flirt with radical nonbelonging and outsidedness" (16). This feminist nomadism
is a flirtation with a romanticized otherness, not an investigation of
radical nonbelonging as state of being imposed, which constitutes
the "nomadism" of the testimonial subject. Braidotti emphasizes

---

[8] Jardine differentiates Derrida's and Deleuze and Guattari's "women" in a
broader context: Derrida's "woman," with Lacan's, is "intrinsic to their minute
analyses of the potentialities for the pre- and inter-significations of modernity,"
while that of Deleuze and Guattari is "endemic to an era of *post*-signification"
("Woman in Limbo" 48). Jardine also clarifies that the body without organs does
not yet exist for Deleuze and Guattari, but is there as a "limit of desire," while for
Irigaray the body without organs is precisely the "historical condition of woman"
(50). Braidotti also critiques nomadism along Irigaray's lines (116).

the need to *embody* the woman denied subjectivity in Deleuze and
Guattari, but she does not appear to recognize its own implication
in the disappearance of *disembodied* female voices: as opposed to
the migrant and exile, the nomad "is usually beyond classification, a
sort of classless unit" (22). Braidotti, like Derrida and Deleuze and
Guattari, erases herself from a structure that undermines her representation of nomadism. In fact, Braidotti so much as states that
nomadism cannot escape appropriative tendencies when she explains:
"Avoiding romanticizing or appropriating the exotic, the 'other,' I
want to practice a set of narrations of my own embodied genealogy" (6). Although Braidotti's aim is to include all experiences and to
undo dualisms, including self/other, her theory commits some of
Deleuze and Guattari's errors when one considers the possibility of
reciprocal "nomadisms" between women of disparate privilege.

Does critiquing Derrida's and Deleuze and Guattari's appropriation of the space left by a distanced and skeptical becoming-
woman of imperceptibility mean indulging in a new essentialism, in
reaffirming borders between fixed identities? Does linking Deleuze
and Guattari's empowering reterritorializations to their questionable
creation of rhetorical Third Worlds based on "minor" literature
mean essentializing a Third World identity as something we cannot
hope to know? On the contrary, questioning these theoretical
constructs exposes the essentialisms and stereotypes never left
behind and the difficulty of attempts to forsake privileged subjectivity. While Derrida's deconstruction of truth as absolute corresponds to *testimonio*'s representation of alternative and subversive
truths (in the plural), his displacement mirrors the potential disappearance of the testimonial informant's discourse. While Deleuze
and Guattari's deterritorialization opens alternative, shifting reterritorializations, the authors' Third Worlds risk stagnation of the very
"linguistic zones" that inspire them. While Braidotti wishes to articulate a politically viable recognition of differences among women,
her own nomadism allows feminist intellectuals to cross boundaries
but leaves other women without a nomadic passport. While Lispector's writing allows Cixous to extend her *écriture fémenine* beyond
herself, she causes the disappearance of her sacralized, Brazilian
other within. She seeks to empower Lispector but silences a voice
that has already read through Cixous's appropriative gesture. This
fact emphasizes the reader's self-centered construction of a comfortable other that reaffirms the self, and it portrays the reader as

significantly more naive than the narrator who has already figured this out. The reader of *testimonio* who simplifies or empties the testimonial subject's speaking position can also appear naive, at best. Yet, at the same time, these constructs originated in intellectuals' desire in the sixties and beyond to work outside of exploitative systems of thought, to open discursive space to multiple voices. Like *testimonio*, the concepts of deterritorialization, nomadism, and becoming-woman are among those that have contributed to current concerns about intellectual production's participation in hegemonic structures. Problematically, *testimonio*'s seeming dependence on authenticity and the transparency of the transcriber advocate the formation of a singular, essentialized, identifiably marginalized subject that facilitates appropriation and falls short of truly lending agency to the testimonial subject. Nevertheless, *testimonio* is more than that, precisely through its failures, paradoxes and self-legitimating processes. Testimonial discourse resists through paradox an easy gesture of subaltern empowerment that oversimplifies the context of subaltern self-representation.

In "The Violence of the Letter," Derrida analyzes the violence of appellations in Levi-Strauss, yet the violence of absence, of no name, of not being recognized as a subject, is the violence from which testimonial texts emerge. One of Carolina Maria de Jesus's diary entries reads: "No outro dia encontraram o pretinho morto. Os dedos do seu pé abriram . . . Ele aumentou-se como se fosse de borracha . . . Não trazia documentos. Foi sepultado como um Zé qualquer. Ninguem procurou saber seu nome. Marginal não tem nome" ("The other day they found the poor black man dead. His toes were spread out . . . He expanded as if he were made of rubber . . . He carried no identification. He was buried as a John Doe. No one tried to find out his name. The marginal have no name"; *Quarto* 32). According to Deleuze and Guattari, writing comes to compete with food through the deterritorialization of the mouth meant for eating; writing transforms words into things capable of competing with food. In the case of *testimonio*, writing becomes a means to obtain food. The *testimonio*'s purpose consists of allowing the silenced to name themselves, to avenge their absence. Violence erupts from the conflict between the mediated *testimonio*'s (pur)pose and displacements produced by the testimonial process, jeopardizing the informant's presence in the text.

A drive for vengeance underlying the texts of fiction motivates the violent sacrifice of the informants or marginalized protagonists, ultimately leading to their disappearance from the texts that gesture to cede space to their voices. While women have traditionally played the role of victim, here they command the role of victimizer as well. These sacrifices with ritual overtones reflect the contexts of judicial authority and vengeance from which testimonial texts arise. The paradox and ambiguity that accompany the narrator's disguised search, in the informant's life history, for meaning of the self also accompany the simultaneously creative and destructive nature of textual violence. In order to search for the other person that allows one to understand the self, boundaries must be transgressed and limits violated even as they are created through struggles for authority and differences in privilege. Through the narrator's identification with the other, vengeful violence toward the other threatens the self, while at the same time, boundary crossings provoke apertures that also threaten hegemonic structures, such as literary genre or official versions of history. Boundary crossings lead us to the penetration of one discourse into another, such as ethnographic discourse into the informant's testimony, and to the many functions of translation in the *testimonio, novela testimonial* and fiction. The penetration of a pose of neutrality threatens a particular violence by overlooking the transcriber, narrator's, or critic's participation in maintaining the marginalized on the margin, such as Derrida's adoption of the rhetorical position of woman. Persistently unstable speaking positions arise from the multiple physical and linguistic displacements and "deterritorializations" that characterize these texts. The divisions must appear to be reconciled to maintain the text's authority, yet this reconciliation remains elusive and the unresolved displacements and clashes describe the paradoxical nature of testimonial texts and the fiction that reflects them.

The next chapter will examine Eltit's *El Padre Mío* and *Lumpérica* as two texts that do not seek reconciliation, that do not seek to mitigate violence as testimony to authoritarian violence. In the present chapter, the testimonial subject or marginalized protagonist's potential disappearance underlies the violence, sacrifices, boundary crossings, translations and displacements discussed in this chapter. Absence occurs at the time of translation or reading, by displacement, a term that ties together the violent sacrifices and border crossings of testimonial texts and the fiction that reflects them. In Eltit's two texts the absence is displayed, is performed, and perhaps reversed through its exposure, yet literarily.

CHAPTER 4

BEYOND *TESTIMONIO* IN TWO WORKS
BY DIAMELA ELTIT

> On a particular morning when the artifactuality of law
> (or any artifact) becomes suddenly and insistently visi-
> ble, what should be striking is not the fact that the law
> is not real, or the sense that its reality was a fraud, or
> that there is no difference between the real and the
> artifactual, but rather that x (the particular law) *is* arti-
> fice and that the artifice of x entailed at its center, up
> until last night, the appearance and force and responsi-
> bilities of "the real."
>
> Elaine Scarry, "The Made-Up and the Made-Real"

CLARICE Lispector's novels *A Paixão Segundo G.H.* and *A Hora
da Estrela*, read within the framework of testimonial discourse's contradictory construction of marginalized subjectivity and
its engagement with socio-political reality, reveal the fictionality of a
testimonial subject that conforms to many testimonial readers'
desires. The truth of a testimonial informant who is unproblemati-
cally representative and who does not conscientiously negotiate the
circumstances of her narration is fiction. Testimonial texts do move
to democratize authorship and do carry Latin American intellectuals' concern with the region's realities to a new level of engagement.
Nevertheless, the texts emerge from a process that does not allow a
neat, pure product from outside that very process. This highlights
the shortfalls of poststructuralist theories evolving simultaneously,
or subsequent to, the testimonial "boom" in Latin America. In
Lispector's two novels tropes of violence, vengeance, ritual sacrifice, and identitarian displacement create other ways of talking
about testimonial writing's outcomes in terms of what it materially
is: writing and dialogue, a cultural product, a political tool, and not
a seamless communion.

The Chilean author Diamela Eltit's work eliminates pretenses of
sympathetic mediation and self-affirming, satisfying life stories.
Eltit's work moves beyond *testimonio* in that her representations of
the completely disenfranchised under Pinochet's dictatorship highlight and exaggerate unstable speaking positions and the multiple
physical and linguistic displacements and "deterritorializations"
seen in the previous three chapters. Like Lispector, Eltit weaves
paradox into the language and the nature of her project, yet she
does not even tease us with reconciliation, and the experimentalism
characteristic of her work emphasizes multiple interpretations,
thereby discarding the visibility of transparent truth. Reconciliation
is hampered by the discomfort of these texts where the testimonial
speaker or fictional protagonist performs contradictions and accusations with disturbing distress or violence. While displacement is
suggested by inconsistencies in *testimonio*, in Eltit it becomes structurally important and pointedly disconcerting. The schizophrenic
speaker of the testimonial *El Padre Mío* 'Father of Mine' (1989),
who never utters a coherent sentence, and the protagonist L. Iluminada of the novel *Lumpérica* 'E. Luminata' (1983),[1] whose testimony exists in movements, sounds, chalk on pavement, blood, cuts,
and burns, seem to seek to bypass the written medium that in *testimonio* represses contradictions in order to achieve reconciliation in
a coherent text. *El Padre Mío* and L. Iluminada, the protagonist of
Lumpérica, signal writing's inadequacy for transparent representation of experience (a poetic gesture), and Eltit's emphasis on writing's presence "translates" that experience by leaving unaltered *El
Padre Mío*'s language and fragmenting *Lumpérica*'s representation.
Eltit ultimately offers another type of solidarity that underscores
and undoes her/our interpretive privilege or interpretive powerless-
ness, and does not provide a packageable narration of marginal
identity. At the same time, we are of course still dealing with texts
signed by Diamela Eltit, a question to which I return at the end of
this chapter. The "beyond" in this chapter's title refers to the way
testimonial discourse has constructed identity. Eltit represents marginal subjects who do not negotiate, who problematize their disappearances while they announce their absence from the recognized
social body. In contrast with Lispector's interiorized examinations

---

[1] All translations of quotations from *Lumpérica* are from Ronald Christ's translation, *E. Luminata*.

of self and other, el Padre Mío and L. Iluminada bear witness in public spaces. These are not *testimonios* taken down in intimate conversations in someone's home or in a diary. The flesh and blood homeless man of *El Padre Mío* and the fictional homeless woman of *Lumpérica* do not enjoy the luxury of privacy, nor do Eltit's texts enclose their language between walls of intimacy.

Both texts testify to the terror, violence, economic devastation, and distortion of the family under Pinochet. Moreover, *Lumpérica* uses the sexualized female body as testimony. The texts incorporate the weight women and the family carried in Pinochet's rhetoric and also in the grassroots resistance to the dictatorship. Mary Louise Pratt notes how the regime took advantage of the relative absence of women in political discourse and party structures, "not because the regime particularly cared about them, but because it saw patriarchal values as the key to the one thing it could not dictate for itself: legitimacy" (22). Women alternatively worked on the front lines to compensate for the economic havoc the dictatorship wreaked on much of the population; hence their public activism testified to authoritarian rhetoric's failure. With Spivak's observations in mind about the subaltern elite that is granted the chance to speak, as opposed to the "true subaltern," the principal figures of these two works embody the true subaltern and Eltit's text creates the transcription. The physical violence and disappearance under Pinochet play a major role in Eltit's work, but the economic hardships of the early 1980s exacerbate these figures' marginalization. Millions were pushed into poverty as the Pinochet government limited workers' wages to fuel the economic growth and export economy that came to be called the "economic miracle" (Neuhouser FN 5). While food consumption by the poorest 20% was down 20% between 1976 and 1981 (Neuhouser 13-4), huge private borrowing from foreign banks during those same years financed the conspicuous consumption of a spending boom. When in 1982 interest rates rose and the financial sector collapsed, the state assumed the private debt, leaving the entire population responsible for paying the elite's consumer debt. Harsh austerity measures then brought unemployment to between 20% and 40%. *Lumpérica* was published in 1983. The three "hablas" forming *El Padre Mío* were recorded in 1983, 1984, and 1985.

El Padre Mío brings together three recordings of a schizophrenic homeless man. This is not a text transcribed in the sense of

translated into a coherent, easily consumable product. The logic of
cause and effect, or even of grammar, does not exist. *El Padre Mío*
questions or undermines much of the testimonial process, incorporating commercial language into the confusion of discourses that
ultimately reveals the repressive structure underlying their rhetoric.
In the narrator's schizophrenic non sequiturs we begin to perceive
certain repetitions that form an omnipresent web of vigilance and
repression under the dictatorship. The economic discourse of buying and selling melds with usurpation, games of chance, the com-
merce in human rights, and the liquidation of human bodies. Truth
here is not bound to the order and consistency that legitimates the
mediated *testimonios* we have seen. The truth lies in the perverse
character of that order associated with authoritarianism, and thus
the perverse nature of that order becomes its "truthful" representation. This is not a text that asks for legitimation.

In *Lumpérica*, Diamela Eltit's interwoven critiques of authoritarian violence, class structure, exploitative commercialism, patriarchy,
and the discourses through which they operate emerge from the
simple image of the homeless woman L. Iluminada moving under
the nocturnal light cast on an urban plaza by a flashing advertisement. She is joined by other homeless, collectively the *pálidos* 'pale
ones.' At various points during this night she hits her head against a
tree and the ground until it bleeds, burns her hand, cuts herself,
rubs against the *pálidos*, rubs herself, writhes under the attention of
the lit advertisement, and writes in chalk. The scene is meanwhile
being filmed from a camera near the flashing light. The text at times
repeats itself with variations in the form of film takes; two chapters
narrate an interrogation scene involving a passerby; others adopt an
explicitly poetic form, though one could describe all of the text as
poetic, as does Idelber Avelar in "Overcodification of the Margins"
(173-4). L. Iluminada acts out layered representations that belie the
simplicity of her image. Guillermo García-Corales has stated that
much of *Lumpérica* comes down to the "verbo nuclear exponerse"
("nuclear verb to expose, to exhibit"; 114). In this sense I use Scarry's words as epigraph for this chapter. By mimicking and reflecting
back the dictatorship's authoritarian discourse (law) that presented
itself as real (authentic, true, right, really the way things are)
through a baroquely distorted mirror Eltit's texts make "insistently
visible" the law's invisible mechanisms of repression and distortion
of the nation. We should be struck by the processes that determine

for us what is real and what is not. Eltit's postmodern experimentation denotes literature, not the "real," yet hers is the language that describes real, personal, and social disintegration. Hers is language that is no more fragmented than the authentic delusions of el Padre Mío, a language which "strive[s] for . . . a solidarity through the aesthetic" (Tierney-Tello, "Testimony" 84).[2]

This chapter does not attempt to cover all the rich layers of Eltit's work; it describes how *El Padre Mío* and *Lumpérica* concretize the dilemmas of testimonial writing, fiction, and theory in ways that bring the dilemma forward without self-legitimation but rather with self-questioning, without reconciliation but rather with an approximation to the unstable foundation on which the marginalized must survive. At first blush *El Padre Mío* may not seem to fit with the rest of the testimonial writing studied in this volume; however, I have otherwise selected texts with female narrators not to arbitrarily exclude men but to consciously highlight gender and power relationships that play on gender discourse. *El Padre Mío* includes subversion of the patriarchal discourse of the family, abused by the dictatorship and participant in processes of essentialized identity construction. At the same time, more space is dedicated to *Lumpérica* in this chapter because in so many additional ways it supports this book's arguments.

ANTI-*TESTIMONIO* AND ANTI-NOVEL

Eltit's resistance to the written medium on which she depends and her baroque attention to form as source of innovation create a *testimonio* that undermines the possibility of metaphoric identification and a novel that Eltit has said "es una manera de atentar contra la novela como una forma monolítica y lineal de contar historias" ("it is a way of making an attempt to kill the novel as a monolithic and linear form of telling stories"; Garabano and García-Corales 66-7): anti-*testimonio* and anti-novel.

As explained in previous chapters, the aesthetic austerity of much testimonial writing reflects the emphasis on representational

---

[2] See Mary Beth Tierney-Tello's article for an examination of the aesthetic and the ethical in *El Padre Mío* and *El infarto del alma*, the latter written in collaboration with Paz Errázuriz.

transparency. Representational language can impose the effect of unity, or simply impose unity, where consistency may not best characterize the collective mode of testifying to trauma or social marginality. In effect, consistency facilitates a privileged reader's solidarity with a not-so-unfamiliar "other," one of testimonial writing's goals. Considering *testimonio*'s collective significance, consistency also tends toward homogenization, essentialization, or fetishization –depending on the circumstances and the views of the particular reader–of the group represented by the informant. Such a process threatens the agency of self-determination promoted through testimonial texts. Essentialization also emphasizes *testimonio* as commodity in that a well-delimited speaking subject does become less threatening to the privileged reader. Seeing the need for readers' sympathy as a prerequisite for a politically effective text therefore leads to the paradox of a less challenging and more easily consumed text.

El Padre Mío flaunts its absences, the utter lack that constitutes el Padre Mío's only stable characteristic. Most fundamentally he lacks a consumable life story ending in redemptive escape or defiance of the institutions repressing him. To use Nelly Richard's words, "El cuerpo del vagabundo, un cuerpo sin residencia ni pertenencia . . . no ha sido retocado compensatoriamente por una representación-de-identidad plena de contenidos de salvación" ("The homeless man's body, a body without a home or possessions . . . has not been retouched, in order to compensate for his condition, through a representation-of-identity full of promises of salvation"; "Bordes" 247). He also lacks any conventional identity with which to identify, and he lacks clearly-defined persecutors since they are as multiple as his own voices (a more devastating accusation than that found in *testimonio* because just as we cannot easily identify with the narrator, we cannot easily separate ourselves from systems of persecution that seem to emerge from everywhere). He cannot articulate a truth the reader can adopt and take home as his or her own truth. Richard has shown in "Bordes, diseminación, postmodernismo" how *El Padre Mío*'s speech also challenges institutional absorption of the *testimonio*. Like Jesusa's survival strategies in *Hasta no verte, Jesús mío* (see Shaw) and the necessary shifts Menchú and Carolina Maria de Jesus carry out, this *testimonio*, as Richard puts it, places testimonial narration "en una situación fluctuante: de ambivalencia enunciativa y de incertidumbre representativa" ("in a fluctuating position: of enunciative ambiguity and representational uncertainty"; "Bordes" 246). While other testimonial writing has used truth to recuperate the perverted meanings dictatorships construct as their own repressive truths, we have seen how those alternative truths can become prescriptive and hierarchical in such a way as to again question the narrator's authority. Testimonial discourse risks repeating the dynamic whereby empowerment is contingent upon the informant's remaining on the margins to maintain his or her otherness, hence limiting the informant's self-representation. Julio Ortega points out how Eltit's narrative is not about the polarities between truth and fiction, the literal and the symbolic, the empirical and the transcendent, and the object and the name, on which hierarchies of exclusionary power depend ("Diamela Eltit" 54). *El Padre Mío* does not achieve its authority through an alternative story, through the duality truth/fiction, but rather through the unquestionable wreckage left behind when reinforcement of that duality serves authoritarianism.

Eltit's avant-garde dissolution of the facile ownership of definitions of truth and fiction–not of the truth of state terror–has been criticized along with the artists and writers of the Colectivo de Acciones de Arte (CADA), founded in 1979, of which she was a member. To protect those whose experiences had already been omitted or dismissed by the State or reduced to anecdotal, individual accounts by the permanent disappearance of others submitted to the same traumas, the division between *testimonio* and aestheticized production has been morally charged. In *La insubordinación de los signos*, Richard states the political strategy of *testimonio*'s proponents in geographical terms: "No se quería seguir fragmentando una territorialidad de voces ya históricamente dislocadas por tantas violaciones de identidad, ni debilitar aún más su trama solidaria ya suficientemente fragilizada por la adversidad del contexto" ("They did not want to continue fragmenting a territoriality of voices that historically had already been dislocated by so many violations of identity, nor weaken any further their solidarity made fragile by adverse circumstances"; 56). Tierney-Tello's article "Testimony, Ethics, and the Aesthetic in Diamela Eltit" also discusses this split in Chile at length. Thus, artists and writers of the avant-garde *avanzada* in Chile, including Eltit, were suspect within the Left. The "derroche exhibicionista" 'exhibitionist waste' of the aestheticized artifice of poverty and deterioration could only mark a perversion for "creyentes en la moral del *testimonio* y en su referencialismo social de la denuncia política" ("believers in *testimonio*'s morality and in its political denunciation through reference to social reality"; 30). Yet, Richard asserts the loosening of repression under the dictatorship in Chile fomented a more visible creation of new forms that did not base critique of the military regime on linguistic or identitarian coherence (57). According to Richard *testimonio* has questioned canonical genres and the superior position of the author's voice in social narration, but the *avanzada* work altered *testimonio*'s "documentalizing language": the discourse of dominant identity was submitted to fragmentation and blackmail by "[v]oces *retocadas* que hiperficcionalizaron la 'verdad' representacional del *testimonio* mediante torsiones y contorsiones genérico-sexuales" ("*retouched* voices that hyperfictionalized *testimonio*'s representational 'truth' through generic and sexual torsions and contortions"; 30). In this way, fixed, mandated truths, although tools to combat the definitions and erasures imposed by the dictatorship, came to represent symptoms of repressive order, separations, and limits. The alternative truths of the Left did not attack boundaries themselves. As I will explain further ahead, the dissolution of the boundaries themselves, rather than development of identity on one side of a binary distinction, links L. Iluminada's performance of political violence to performance of gender.

As I asserted for the fictional texts studied in Chapter 2, the novel *Lumpérica* does not constitute testimonial literature in that it does not originate from an interview process, nor do I assert that the novel explicitly responds to the corpus of Latin American *testimonio*. Nonetheless, Eltit's writing clearly responds to the same situations from which testimonial writing arises, and of course she began the recordings for *El Padre Mío* in 1983. *Lumpérica*'s denunciations expressed through a subaltern protagonist follow through in a sense on Mary Louise Pratt's description of *testimonios* in Chile: "*Testimonios* lay bare the regime's practice of concealment, represented what was concealed, and reasserted the languages of evidence, bodily experience, and truth and falsehood, as well as the values of truth and falsehood" (24). *Lumpérica* centers on the visual, on the previously concealed, on the body, and on the truth. The truth is the complete lack of stability, of anything dependable, of anything safe, and of self-expression on the margins. The repression, disappearances and torture constitute truth. What happens to the self, to agency in the aftermath of that truth? What is the communication of that experience that resists reabsorption into the center? As fiction, *Lumpérica* is not mediated in the sense of *testimonios* where oral history is transcribed, but rather as a scene watched and interrogated by experimental language and a surveillance camera that suggests a torturer's presence. The performing body and performative identity in Eltit's text suggest a writing of marginalization that possibly navigates around and beyond the contradictions in mediated testimonial discourse and criticism on *testimonio*. *Lumpérica* enacts an unmitigated version of the testimonial process that emphasizes the visual over the oral and maintains its power as an accusation.

Through L. Iluminada's fragmentation in the film takes, the flashing light, and the incisions into her body, *Lumpérica* displays several characteristics and internal inconsistencies that testimonial texts manifest and usually sublimate or smooth over for the purpose of solidarity with the testimonial informant. Eltit's novel makes literal and literary the testimonial scene where marginal individuals representative of collective experiences occupy the center as agents of their own life histories, yet the excesses, the exaggerations, acted out by the *pálidos* who surround and watch L. Iluminada overflow the limits of testimonial representation even as they act out their own status as social excess.[3] As Tierney-Tello states with reference to *El Padre Mío*, here the aesthetic is not "a luxury reserved for elites" ("Testimony" 83). In addition to elements central to testimonial writing–violence, collectivity, and concepts of the truth–Eltit places on center stage certain problems left only implicit in mediated testimonial writing and on the margins of past readings of *testimonio*: the insistence on *testimonio*'s stable truth value as producing an appropriative process that risks fetishization of the informant's identity; the consequent, partial disappearance of the informant; and the body as not only the site of previous violences, but also as actor in testifying to those violations.

The internal inconsistencies in *Lumpérica* emerge most clearly in the repetitions that seem to insistently seek a truth that each rep-

---

[3] Eugenia Brito relates the excesses and overflows in *Lumpérica* with the "apertura hacia el límite" provoked by the question "Dónde vas" that begins the fifth section of the text (Brito 125). For Brito "Dónde vas" marks the novel's significance for Latin America as "peripheral" and "mobile" and also makes appear the surveillance of the Inquisition (124).

etition's variations make more impossible. Silvia Tafra also points out the desire for truth in *Lumpérica*'s repetitions (41), and yet they clearly also open interpretation beyond singular, unified truth as do the shifts in testimonial subjects' narratives. The film takes of the same moment and the reiterative flashes of the ad capture the shifting truth and identity that the *pálidos* collectively experience. Moreover, the interrogation scenes conflate the authoritarian regime and efforts to smooth over the internal inconsistencies of those testimonies to marginalization. As the questioner in the first interrogation demands an "ordered and coherent" description of what the witness saw in the film takes in the plaza, a patently ridiculous task, the interrogated notes how the passerby who at one point kept L. Iluminada from falling only half heard what she said in his ear and filled in the rest: "Él escuchó a medias y completó con sus pensamientos y con sus deseos lo que quería oír. Cambió palabras, suprimió frases enteras, obvió parlamentos importantes por creerlos secundarios. No pudo extenderse a totalidades. Ni siquiera reparó en sus gestos, ansioso como estaba por consumirse en los contenidos" ("He half listened and completed with his thoughts and desires what he wanted to hear. He changed words, suppressed whole phrases, cut important speeches, thinking them secondary. He could not extend himself to totalities. Not even heed her gestures, eager as he was to be consumed in their contents"; 54, 58). That is, he performed the role of editor. The viewer's and listener's desires homogenize the text's and L. Iluminada's options. In the second interrogation the interrogated questions the reading imposed by the questioner's script: "–Que mi guión era malo ¿eso quieres decir? / –Era impropio más bien, anacrónico, burdo. Sin recursos técnicos no había sino una unívoca interpretación" ("–That my script was bad, that's what you mean? / –It was unsuitable rather, anachronistic, rough. Without technical effects only a univocal interpretation was possible"; 146, 144). A singular interpretation inappropriately represents the experience testified.

   El Padre Mío's schizophrenia plays on the collective representativity necessary to testimonial authority and constitutes one of the many compulsive repetitions structurally crucial to both of these texts and to Eltit's resistance to the anecdotal. In *El Padre Mío* not only do the string of associated names repeat overlapping identities, but also el Padre Mío reiterates the list of names itself, mixing new but similar combinations. The entire book creates a collage of the same elements combined in different patterns, relentlessly torment-ing the narrator: "Porque yo no quise admitir que ahora, última-mente, me fuera a pasar lo mismo que anteriormente" ("Because I didn't want to admit that now, recently, the same was going to hap-pen to me as before"; 24). The desert of open signification, dis-cussed earlier regarding my introduction's epigraph, Lispector's *A Paixão Segundo G.H.*, and Deleuze and Guattari's nomads, emerges from these reiterations and could also geographically represent the lack so fundamental to el Padre Mío and L. Iluminada's realities.

    El Padre Mío is an accusation and a defense. No coherent artic-ulation exists in the text, but the repetition of certain phrases and certain fears bear uncanny resemblance to common elements of other testimonial narrative. *El Padre Mío* is an accusation and defense founded on privileged knowledge and the narrator's con-sciousness of the need to communicate this threatened truth. The first lines of this man's testimony draw us into his accusation: "Us-ted me lleva con el plan de eso. –¿Cómo no voy a saberlo yo?" ("You're taking me along as part of that plan. –How could I not know?"; 23). Some variation of "a mí me tienen planeado" 'they have plans for me' appears several times throughout, plans to silence him appear twice, and he describes his family's disappear-ance in these words: "esta persona frecuentaba antes a mi familia, que ahora no están en esta existencia, porque esta persona se deshi-zo de ellos" ("before, this person frequently visited my family, which doesn't exist anymore, because this person got rid of them"; 61). He assures the listener he is telling the truth and of his exclu-sive ownership of that truth: "pero eso ustedes no lo saben. . . . Eso lo sé yo no más" ("but you don't know about that. . . . I only know about that"; 25). His desire to communicate, constantly frustrated, is unambiguous: "y volví a ser planeado por lo que le estoy conver-sando a usted yo. Pero debería servir de testimonio yo" ("and they had plans for me again because of what I am talking to you about now. But I should serve as a testimony"; 57). One page later he says, "me tienen que conseguir un locutor y un periodista para que el hecho se dé a conocer en la misma propiedad donde estoy al cabo" ("you have to get me a newscaster and a journalist so that the fact is publicized on the same property I know all about"; 58). Nev-ertheless, he manifests the confusion between the desire to speak and the fear of exposure in illogical self-contradiction when he states that "No quería ser descubierto, por lo que le estoy conver-

sando yo, para que este hecho no se diera a conocer a la publici-
dad" ("I didn't want to be discovered, because of what I am talking
to you about, so that this fact isn't publicized"; 48). It is as if he
syntactically expressed the testimonial informant's dilemma: expose
and protect yourself. The problem is, we do not know what he is
saying; so much of the narration is the promise of what he knows.
He subverts what we expect of the testimonial negotiation by entic-
ing our desire to know without supplying the story. The story he
does tell, however, may ultimately be accurate: confusion, fear, loss,
and corruption.[4]

Without a coherent story el Padre Mío deprives the reader of a
unified identity to grasp and hold, and of "las ideologías culturales
de la identidad dominante que *sujetan* el *sujeto*, fundacionalmente,
a posiciones y roles invariables" ("the cultural ideologies of dominant identity that *subject* the *subject*, foundationally, to invariable
positions and roles"; Richard, "Tres" 49). The confusion of names
and pronouns lead to a continuous, illogical chain of deferments
and associations where his own identity can only be tied to that
series of displacements, or to links with the state and bureaucracy:
"él le trabaja a la usurpación permanente" ("he works toward permanent corruption"; 26). Later, "Las representa el señor Luengo
que es el señor Colvin y el Padre Mío tampoco" ("Mr. Luengo represents them, who is Mr. Colvin and neither the Father of Mine";
39). El Padre Mío's name was elected by a nameless government
figure (27) and he exists in documents and identification that he
has yet to recover (66). Identity consists of influences and insurance
policies, or names and positions gambled away like the social guarantees lost in a game of chance (25), and thus identity becomes
inseparable from one's value as object of exchange. The majority's
value dropped after the elite lost its game of chance with consumer
spending when interest rates soared. The absence of spending power or exchange value disintegrates el Padre Mío's existence within
the social body as defined under Pinochet. As in the formation of a
unified testimonial identity, identity is assigned from outside, like
the flashing advertisement in *Lumpérica*.

---

[4] This recalls the ending to another Borges story, "Emma Zunz." After a chain
of events creating circumstantial evidence that obscures how a crime really tran-
spired, the text concludes that the tone, shame, and hatred were authentic; only the
circumstances, time, and one or two names were false.

The sign that flashes names on the bodies of L. Iluminada and the *pálidos* merges commercial, discursive, and sexual identity imposed from without. The *luminoso* identifies them as objects with product names that do not distinguish among them, yet under those conditions grant them existence and self-recognition. "Están esperando su turno, para que el luminoso los confirme como existencia, es decir, los nombre de otra manera: renacen así en este transcurso purificante, ya menos empalidecidos, porque se borra su color verificando la pérdida voluntaria de sus anales ciudadanos" ("They await their turn, for the illuminated sign to confirm them as existence, that is, name them another way: they are reborn that way in this purifying passage, less impallored now, because it blots out their color, confirming the voluntary loss of their civil records"; 21, 26). Erasing their personal names and previous relationship with the social body, the light baptizes them. After smashing her head against a tree, a bleeding L. Iluminada waits for the light to fall on her wound, then cries out, bringing the *pálidos* close around her. "Ha adquerido otra identidad: por literatura fue. / Así se reconoce en su propia imagen, la que se reflecta sobre el piso cuando el luminoso deja caer un nuevo haz de luz" ("She has assumed another identity: did it through literature. / That way she recognizes herself in her own image, the one reflected on the ground when a new pencil of light falls from the luminous sign"; 20, 25). The ad provides her with a set image in which to recognize herself, to recognize her self-authored wound: it was through literature. Her wound writes her agency on her body, agency to testify using what she has left: her body in the light that urges us to buy, buy, buy. "De pedrerías es su cara, su piel como diamantes" . . . "Sí, cuerpos se venden en la plaza" . . . "¿Dónde fuera de la plaza se obtendría ese privilegio?" ("Her face of glass beads, her skin like diamonds" . . . "That's right, bodies are sold in the square" . . . "Where outside the square could they obtain that privilege?"; 20, 13, 21; 26, 18, 26).

Like feminized sexual objects the homeless receive the light's penetration and naming, combining the father and violent sex or rape (implicit in *Lumpérica*'s third chapter where L. Iluminada becomes a filly in heat who needs a colt or who has a rider digging his spurs into her loins). The dictatorship's patriarchal rhetoric of the father who keeps order is exposed as the violent father who carries out sexual torture on his daughters, as did the Pinochet regime. This perverted patriarchal order is thus implicated in repressive or objectifying identity formation through the name of the father and abandonment by the mother, an idea developed especially in the novel's section 4.5: "qué padres? Qué raza más bien posee el animal? / qué padre? / Qué nombre le inscribieron? / L'incesto actúa de indolora forma. Funda y precisa el continuo apellido, . . ." ("what sires? what breed rather is the animal? / what sire? / What name did they inscribe on her? / Thincest works painlessly. It founds and specifies the continous name, . . ."; 91, 91). The father cares for the race (92), and this name, with the light, inscribes the citizenship that she inherits through the male (91).[5]

El Padre Mío's title refers to this same order of distortions and violence. While "el Padre Mío" refers to Pinochet in the homeless man's speech, the title refers to the homeless man himself who takes on the role of father to Eltit and the country: this is what Chile inherits. Eltit writes in her presentation of *El Padre Mío*: "Es Chile, pensé. Chile entero y a pedazos en la enfermedad de este hombre: jirones de diarios, fragmentos de exterminio, sílabas de muerte, pausas de mentira, frases comerciales, nombres de difuntos. Es una honda crisis del lenguaje, una infección en la memoria, una desarticulación de todas las ideologías. Es una pena, pensé" ("It's Chile, I thought. Chile whole and in pieces in this man's illness: shreds of newspaper, fragments of extermination, syllables of death, pauses of lies, commercial phrases, names of the dead. It is a deep crisis of language, an infection of the memory, a disarticulation of every ideology. It's a shame, I thought"; 17). While previous testimonial writing tends to replace old national discourse with a new one, albeit inclusive of persecuted groups, the self-contradictory repetitions in Eltit's work do not allow the construction of a homogenizing discourse or coherent national identity. As Richard states, she does not suture the cuts and fragments, but leaves possibilities open (*La insubordinación* 62). Eltit does repeat official discourse, however, in order to deconstruct it through el Padre Mío and L. Iluminada's

---

[5] Tierney-Tello describes how in Eltit's novel *Por la patria* (1986) the character Juan serves as a symbolic father and authoritarian agent who tries to seduce Coya, the protagonist. As Tierney-Tello asserts, he also wishes to rob her of her memory and impose his own "signifying system." Juan suggests he take notes on his dialogue with Coya, notes that will put her language in order again (Tierney-Tello, *Allegories* 92). Juan's desire to maintain the status quo through his "notes" on his conversations with Coya provide an interesting overlap of manipulating transcription and patriarchal, authoritarian repression.

linguistic and corporal distortions. References to his mental condition and medication interweave with bureaucratic language, references to financial guarantees, and a narration of procedural disintegration and dysfunction (32). Instead of constructing a system, "la Administración" works with "la máquina desintegradora" 'the disintegrating machine,' whose objective is to eliminate. His discourse was produced by the nation (Tierney-Tello, "Testimony" 84), and the repression for which that discourse worked produced its disintegration in el Padre Mío. At the beginning of Chapter 2 I described Miguel Barnet's view of testimonial writing as a national, foundational literature and how in his articulation of that literature he seemed to discount genres of women's foundational writing. In *El Padre Mío* we encounter a testimonial discourse that is anti-foundational in gendered terms. "It's Chile" and it is Chile's father, a disintegrated father. *Lumpérica*'s title, in turn, suggests an alternative, gendered foundational literature: lumpen + America and a woman's name. Both el Padre Mío and L. Iluminada are those who have been eliminated, who have disappeared from recognition by the social body, but on whom the nation rests in its abused condition. Their bodies eventually disappear, as well (later, Eltit cannot find el Padre Mío, who left his usual area, and as daylight comes L. Iluminada ironically fades from others' sight while she watches the plaza's growing activity). In Eltit's transcription (and video that was made) of el Padre Mío and her novel, their bodies perform their status as invisible; their bodies are excessively visible and become the foundation of their testimonial and national discourse. [6]

PERFORMANCE

This chapter now turns principally to *Lumpérica*, beginning with the importance of the performative for undermining normative identities and binary distinctions. *Lumpérica*'s testimony to a historical moment of repression and violence in the form of corporeal spectacle, ritual, and performance mimics and purges the rigid

---

[6] I do not see this as a move that relegates the subaltern to the material, assuming he or she cannot speak, following Spivak. First of all, as a performance artist and activist Eltit values the body and performance as media for committed art. Second, the rest of these texts indicate Eltit signals what is left when language has been destroyed.

identities and boundaries imposed by military order, purposely destabilizing fixed identity, including gender, and exposing the artifice of social order. In contrast to the disappearances and sacrifices in the texts studied in previous chapters, the ritual mutilations L. Iluminada displays are self-imposed to repeat and expiate those disappearances and mutilations kept invisible.

Lumpérica is explicit in its specularity and performance: *pálidos*, plaza, *luminoso*, camera, spectacle. Eltit's texts clearly highlight their sense of performance, and in 1980 Eltit did carry out her own performance of self-mutilation in front of a house of prostitution, while reading from *Lumpérica*. The performance issued from layers of meaning, a performance by both Eltit's written words and the content of those words, enacts the exploration of identity arising from *testimonio*. It also acts out boundaries and their transgression. Eltit demonstrates the artificiality of *testimonio's* authenticity through her protagonist's own performance, the homeless woman's consciousness of her objectification, and her full exploitation of her observed status to act out her assigned role to its extreme. Like a violent parody Eltit reveals as gesture and artifice the discursive capture of truly subaltern experience and L. Iluminada asserts herself as agent of her story's physical telling. The focus here on performance does not mean questioning the brutal reality of testimonial informants' experiences. Rather, I assert that as a work of fiction framed by testimonial writing, *Lumpérica* boldly addresses the destruction caused by repression by not even representing solidarity in the form of a sympathetic transcriber nor presenting a coherent, more palatable text.

Upon comparing performance "in its emptying out, the nothing which comes of nothing" to ideology and the unconscious–in their relationship to the inconceivable void outside their existence–Herbert Blau suggests performance is "an existence without a history" (2) that at the same time can also be engaged in what memory wants to forget (1). Thus, performance connotes an emptiness and eternal present while it draws upon a past resisted by memory. Similarly, L. Iluminada signifies emptiness in her absence from public view and total lack of possessions and officially sanctioned identity. Captured in the moment of the flashing advertisement and the eternal present of the film take, she testifies with her body to a past, and present, in Chile that memory wants to forget. The show on display repeats the acts and effects of the past in the present.

Performance is a way of reappropriating the plaza robbed of its public condition (Lorenzano 194, Pratt 27), and of undoing exclusionary dichotomies of inner and outer, private and public, invisible and visible, decent virgin/mother and prostitute, object and subject, them and us, through repetitions of the violence committed by the dictatorship. Diana Taylor emphasizes how during the Argentinean "Dirty War" the military enforced strict separations and control (94), as does Richard in the case of Chile: "es la rigidez dictotómica [*sic*] de la separación entre lo superior y lo inferior, lo exterior y lo interior, lo claro y lo oscuro, lo puro y lo contaminado, etc., la que estructura categorialmente el simbolismo mítico-político que inspira los discursos fundacionales" ("it is the dichotomous rigidity of the separation between the superior and the inferior, the exterior and the interior, the light and the dark, the pure and the polluted, etc., that categorically structures the mytho-political symbolism that inspires foundational discourses"; *La insubordinación* 56). In addition, the dictatorship committed the double violence of establishing strict order and then violating the boundaries it enforced, violations exposed by the bodies in the plaza. Under dictatorship, inner and outer, us and them, desire and appearance, the body's interior and surface, must remain separate, but at the same time the body is cut open, exposing the inside to the outside: L. Iluminada cuts herself, transgressing the same boundaries as the torturers. This returns us to the border crossings discussed in Chapter 3, those that the privileged or powerful establish, and then cross to come to know the other that they have determined as such, or in this case to violate the other's integrity. L. Iluminada does not leave this incursion invisible, but rather ritualistically performs it and "rewrites" it as subject as well as object, albeit repeating her reification. The expiatory replication of violence and objectification, of boundary crossings, thus also becomes a new beginning, the "bautizo" that announces the subject as agent (Ortega, "Diamela Eltit" 58, Lorenzano 194, Tafra 34). She mimics the dictatorship's appropriation of the plaza through its own sinister rituals, such as the lighting ceremony that took place on the second anniversary of the coup, described by Pratt (29-30). In that ceremony, anonymous citizens representing women, youth and workers hand torches to cadets who add their fire to a central torch on a podium. The luminoso high above the plaza parodies this lighting ceremony, and L. Iluminada writes the pain inflicted by what the fire represents by burning herself, writing her presence in her flesh. The ritual becomes demonic, simultaneously purifying and blasphemous, simultaneously pleasurable and painful. The ritual is also simultaneously compensatory and not so, as it requires repetition of the same violences. L. Iluminada relates her own story as purification ritual where her blood releases the sins of the past in a communion "rhetorically organized through prosopopoeia," as Avelar asserts, yet undermined by "the cynical atheism of the eternal return" ("Overcodification" 177). The sacrificial border crossing in *Lumpérica* is excess, does not reestablish the status quo because it does not reinforce limits, and thus displays its own inadequacy to compensate the violence it reiterates.

In a perversion of those boundaries that do protect individual liberty, under the dictatorship public spaces are no longer safe or open under curfew, and that which was considered private is always watched: L. Iluminada performs intimate acts in the public square (Lorenzano 194). Under the dictatorship everyone and everything is under scrutiny, and yet those who were seen are disappeared, detentions in broad daylight are invisible, the agents of repression cannot be seen: L. Iluminada makes visible the invisible. Under dictatorship women's role is limited to the home; women in political, public life are transfigured into prostitutes. L. Iluminada performs that division by enacting libidinal desire in public, by offering her body as object of consumption, by becoming the subject of those acts in which people are made objects. Her scars thus become an act of her own will, her writing her own body against the acts imposed upon her: "Y así la quemada le dará nueva cicatriz que le forjará el cuerpo a voluntad" ("And so the burn will give her a new scar that will forge her body as she wills"; 35, 42 with my alteration).

Like the parodic repetitions Judith Butler's work describes as key subversions of "natural" gender identities, *Lumpérica* denaturalizes the order mystified as foundational by the State. The divisions under the regime are not prior to it, but an effect of it. Butler conceptualizes the definition of "woman" and gender not as an epistemological question, but as a problem of signification since notions of the body do not exist outside of the very discourses that seek to investigate the nature of the gendered body. Therefore, subversion of traditional binary divisions of gender, or other epistemological categories, should come from within discourse through repetitions that turn against that discourse. According to Butler, the parodic, or repetitions in different contexts (for example, heterosexual assumptions in a non-heterosexual frame) does not consolidate the law or fixed identity, but displaces it by underscoring its constructed, performative nature rather than foundational nature. In the context of the lumpen's assemblage in the plaza, *Lumpérica*'s self-repetitions and carnivalesque repetitions of official and consumerist practice function similarly to bring into relief the constructed, performative nature of the totalitarian order. Eltit's novel undermines foundational truths in the various film takes suggesting false starts or alternative perspectives, complicating any unified explanation of the identities displayed under the lit advertisement. L. Iluminada's enactment of her stigmatized status as homeless and female, exposing hidden exclusions and violence, parodies the strict divisions set up by the dictatorship and consumer society, including *testimonio* in its sense as consumer product, and performs the intersecting discourses of military dictatorship and patriarchy.

Diana Taylor links nation-ness in totalitarian Argentina to Butler's concept of gender, both inscribed on physical bodies: "National/gender identity is not so much a question of being as of doing, of being seen doing, of identifying with the appropriate performative model" (92). Doing creates the effect of being as long as the willing suspension of disbelief holds. Eltit's text articulates and reveals that moment with which Blau is concerned: when any practice becomes like ideology, like theatre "before it identified itself," before its appearance was distinguished from its reality. Acts, gestures, desires produce the effect of internal substance, but the essence expressed is a fabrication, a performance, through "corporeal signs" (Butler 136). The crucial importance of L. Iluminada's repetitions thus lies in their excesses that make visible not just the rigid roles the populace must represent, but also the military's own spectacle, that displace the military's own performance into a context that lets the mask fall from the "theatre of absenting and deterritorialization" (Taylor 95), allowing seeing and *recognition* of seeing.

The camera's presence in *Lumpérica* is not only significant in its possibilities of replication and production of an audience for the performance, but also in its accentuation of *seeing* and voyeurism. Diana Taylor describes the alteration of seeing under the dictatorship in Argentina where "Argentineans were assigned to spectatorship," under surveillance, watching others, internalizing surveillance (94). Yet seeing was selective as people were dragged off the streets in broad daylight, and as the reciprocity of the look became dangerous. Taylor terms this self-blinding "percepticide" as people were forced to collude with the violence visible in the streets by looking away (119-24). The detailed, baroque, textured, brutal images Eltit describes create the "luxury" of conscious voyeurism: "es el placer de extenderse jugando con el deleite de su propia imagen" ("it's the pleasure of spreading out playing, with the delight in her own image"; 99, 98). We are conscious of watching, as Avelar also notes (171-2), and that watching is multiplied by the camera and its repeated takes. Seeing, being seen and being seen seeing are central spectacles in this event, whereby the *pálidos* and L. Iluminada see and recognize each other and she poses to best be seen: "Ya no importa el frío, perdería el placer de la observación si se confundiera con uno de ellos y por eso mismo nadie testificaría la escena . . ." ("Now the cold doesn't matter, she would forfeit pleasure in the viewing if she merged with one of them and for that same reason nobody would bear witness to the scene . . ."; 33, 39). Observation is crucial to the government's methods of control, but also to testifying to the government's violence. In addition, the division that occurs in the novel between "yo" 'I' and "ella" 'she'–either a split within L. Iluminada or between her and the figure "diamela eltit"–accentuates reciprocal seeing: "Sus ojos son a mis ojos sufrientes de la mirada, por eso son el escaso nexo que priva del abandono" ("Her eyes are to my eyes sufferers from the gaze, that's why they are the slight nexus that staves off abandonment"; 88, 88). Only being seen, through that tenuous connection, is she protected from abandonment. One could also say, reflecting upon the vicarious identity studied throughout this book, that only through the overlapping of these eyes and of their twin gazes can L. Iluminada be seen, be recognized: "Sus ojos generan en mis ojos la misma mirada gemela contaminada de tanta ciudad de Santiago reducida al césped" ("Her eyes generate in my eyes the same twin gaze contaminated by so much of the city of Santiago reduced to grass"; 88, 88).

While its gaze lends L. Iluminada an identity, the camera is not visible. As a machine, at face value the ideally objective anthropologist/observer, the camera also becomes an instrument of interrogation as it records. For example, among the "errors" of the first take, "[l]os cuerpos tensados estaban rígidos, no por necesidad

interna, sino por efectos de cámera: como terror" ("The tense bodies were rigid, not from inner necessity, but from effects of the
camera: such as terror"; 17, 23). An ordinary experience of stage
fright clearly suggests another terror in Eltit's text. In addition,
Richard describes how photography's reproduction of the human
face was explored by critics and artists of the *avanzada* as a
metaphor through its

> procedimientos de *detención* y *captura* de la identidad fotográfi-
> ca: la prisión del encuadre, la camisa de fuerza de la pose, la sen-
> tencia del montaje, la condena del pie de foto, etc. Detención y
> captura de la imagen cuyas retóricas aprisionadoras subrayaban,
> por analogía de procedimientos, el control represivo que afecta-
> ba diariamente los cuerpos sometidos a los métodos de la violen-
> cia militar. (*La insubordinación* 20)
>
> procedures of *detention* and *capture* of photographic identity:
> the prision of the frame, the straight jacket of the pose, the ruling
> of the montage, the legal sentence of the caption, etc. The deten-
> tion and capture of the image whose imprisioning rhetoric high-
> lighted, by procedural analogy, the repressive control that daily
> affected the bodies subjugated to military violence's methods.

Eltit, however, reveals and subverts the vigilant camera's presence
by another route, a particularly gendered route. In her submission
to an imagined, attentive audience/torturer/lover L. Iluminada
flaunts the terror tactics of surveillance and transforms the framing
gaze of the lens into pleasure, although ambiguously. This implicates the military in the discourses of material consumption that
Eltit condemns as an artifice to obscure the economic conditions
worsened under the military. The watchful eye of social control,
ostensibly working to purify the polluted populace, ends up producing an object of sexual commodification. Eltit transfigures a
State instrument that empties people of personal identity, by denying them private space or economic means, into a reappropriated
instrument of intimate desire, in a public space by one defined by a
lack of economic means.

Through performance *Lumpérica* repeats, and, most importantly, makes visible the multiple levels of theatre and spectacle under
dictatorship. Using as metaphor Borges's "La busca de Averroes,"
which began my introduction, the insistence on singular, stable

identity in the repeated phrase from the Koran "No hay otro dios que el Dios" 'There is no other god but God' contrasts sharply with the layers of representation surrounding him. The binary distinctions on which totalitarian and patriarchal discourse found a natural, *a priori* order and the essentialized identities originating in the enforcement of that order as truth are acted out in a subversive deterritorialization that itself is a repetition of the deterritorializations carried out by repression. Military order displaced onto a performance in the plaza by the *pálidos* serves as a testimony of sorts to acts of terror, violence, and disappearing as well as to the resulting fragmentation of identity. As Robert Neustadt has well described, the discursive incisions in the text correspond to those in the body and identity, making a coherent, "truthful" narration from a stable speaking position impossible.

Lumpérica aestheticizes precisely that which points to lack: the scarred, marginalized body bereft of possessions, roof, name. That aestheticization, however, functions to undermine the "order" that defines center and margin, using performance to critique essentialist concepts of identity policed by the State and consumer culture. Performance makes visible the *pálidos'* superfluous status and discourse's implication in mechanisms of repression.

I by no means equate military violence and the inherent contradictions in testimonial discourse since the comparison would be absurd, but I wish to suggest how Eltit's textual response to the dictatorship constitutes a writing of subalternity and recuperated, collective memory that in some ways points to routes around the partial failures of *testimonio*. Performance in *Lumpérica* indirectly exteriorizes the apparatus of testimonial discourse, an apparatus that in what it hides may contribute to the essentialization of marginalized identity even as it seeks a space for that identity's agency. Since testimonial writing's authority comes to depend on its appearance of unaltered truth, the inconsistencies are often overlooked or signaled as a negative reflection on the narrator's intentions. Those inconsistencies form the basis for, to use Nelly Richard's word, "hiperestetización" 'hyperaesthetization' of unstable truths in Eltit's work, leaving the fragmentary quality of abjection for the eye to see, both in the images she describes, and in the words on the page. The scars on the body replace a written document, permitting "el reconocimiento y de allí la reconquista del cuerpo de la sujeto" ("the recognition and from there the reconquest of the subject's body"; Brito 128).

In addition, libidinal spectacle subverts the limitations created by expectations of the testimonial subject to conform to hegemonic concepts of truth. Blau asserts that an ideology of desire directs the discourse of the body, bringing the psyche to the surface, to the stage, confounding representation and bringing the inside outside (90). The performativity of L. Iluminada's "testimony," its bringing the tortured mind to the surface, resists the representationality of *testimonio*. Butler might say Eltit's work emphasizes identity's location in signification, while *testimonio* emphasizes the epistemological. Yet, in fact we have seen how the content of testimonies often contains reference to masks and disguises signifying the shifting appearances, poses and performances of which testimonial informants are well aware. The concomitant mobility of meanings corresponds to performance. *Lumpérica*, like performance, reveals in its repetition of "reality," in its own masks, what lies behind appearances, causing the mask to fall. Yet, L. Iluminada reveals the mask only by *dramatizing* her theatricality, for, as Taylor points out, theatre also allows us to deny what we see with our own eyes (125). In *Lumpérica* the connections created by reciprocal looking, and recognition of that looking, combat percepticide and recreate the collective that in testimonial discourse is captured in the representative subject, further encouraging a monolithic notion of the group represented.

While testimonial discourse more easily lends itself to the ventriloquizing by which the informant's authenticity lends authority to the political opinions of the intellectual, the metaphorical identifications seen in certain *testimonios* encounter no easy correspondence in Eltit's novel or *testimonio* other than the overlapping gazes. We cannot easily appropriate el Padre Mío's confusion or the abject state of L. Iluminada: the horror of her wounds resists our identification; her absolute lack cannot fulfill any lack we may perceive in ourselves; and despite a total absence in terms of officially sanctioned identity she does not allow herself to disappear. In fact, the final chapter of the novel emphasizes her act of seeing, rather than being seen as she observes the awakening neighborhood after the night. Her lack is an overwhelming presence. Richard writes of the "nueva escena": "no buscaron rellenar los huecos de identidad con palabras de consuelo. Prefirieron desnudar–en esos huecos–la falta de todo" ("they did not seek to fill the voids in one's identity with consoling words. They preferred to expose–in those voids–the lack of everything"; *La insubordinación* 28). *Testimonio* writers strive to compensate previous absences, yet do not expose the modes of testimonial production that complicate that compensatory gesture. After all, once the *testimonio* is completed and public interest wanes, absence may again describe the informant, as was the case with Carolina Maria de Jesus. Neustadt points out that mutilation of the (discursive) body in fact rearticulates the body in a critique of the mutilating order (155). Similarly, el Padre Mío and L. Iluminada perform their absent status, critiquing that absence. [7]

Blau calls "anti-bodies" the bodies whose absence is so profound they are not even statistics. When discussing the critical mass of desiring bodies in the festival (and revolutionary) crowd, and its relation to the staged reflection of reality, Blau describes the spectacle of the anti-bodies on view in the cities in terms relevant to performance in *Lumpérica*, despite the different context:

> What is real enough, to be sure, is that some desiring bodies are so disaffected, so (visibly) marginal or extruded, yet so raveled in the loop of the integrated circuit, that they are hardly even statistics, more like anti-bodies. . . . they are now in all the metropolises a burgeoning aspect of the spectacle, within the circuit to the extent that they are among the empty signifiers, both replicated and dematerialized on the TV screens. While they convey, no doubt, quite basic forms of desire, there is still the leveraged appearance of a postscarcity world, where poverty and victimization are overshadowed in the general excess of reality by the material energies of mass culture and consumer goods in abundance. (90)

The *pálidos* are invisible in their extreme marginality, excluding them from the statistics that reinforce one's position in recognized society. Nevertheless, their marginality is at the same time extremely visible in the absence of private space and in the consequent exteriority of which Eltit speaks in her introduction to *El Padre Mío* (12-13). They are officially unseen, yet a photographic "negative" integral to the "positive" of the rest of the city (11), appearing replicated "photographically" on the TV screen or the text's film takes. Their poverty and victimization fade with the abundance of

---

[7] Tierney-Tello also points out the testimonial subject's ultimate disappearance in *El Padre Mío* ("Testimony" 85).

consumer goods, in which they ironically participate as they absorb the luminoso's flashes and also become objects of visual consumption. The *pálidos'* performance, the "mask" they perform, causes the mask to fall and impels us to "see things as they are" (Blau, referring to Artaud, 101). *Lumpérica* emphasizes the spectacle for consumption, the subaltern as attraction for sale, while few critics have focused on the commercial consumption of the testimonial text. The bodies in the plaza are commercial objects that enact their commodification subversively. L. Iluminada overacts her object status and takes command of the performance.

Eltit's aestheticized bodies stand in contrast to the relatively unadorned *testimonio* posited as document (proof, truth). The shifting identities and fragmented language contrast with the testimonial memory that Richard associates with the images used to refer to Chile's political past: "La referencia [a la memoria como libro] retiene la metáfora del volumen de escritos en el que se depositan sentidos ordenados para consultas futuras" ("The reference [to memory as a book] retains the metaphor of a volume of writings where ordered meanings are deposited for future consultation"; *La insubordinación* 31). Yet, in fact *testimonio* itself ends up as performance: performance of stable truth, a performance rewritten in L. Iluminada's corporeal enactment of Chile's political past. In relation to performance art of the seventies, Blau describes the rhetoric of transgression as displacement of the volatilized (social) body (89). The rhetoric of transgression takes the place of the crowd and of the individual body, yet Eltit's text, as well as her performance of cutting her own body, describes a scene where the rhetoric of transgression is located once again in the body itself. Rhetorical mediation is momentarily absent as L. Iluminada writes her testimony with chalk, with blood, with movement. *Lumpérica* suggests that historically, in "literature" the *pálidos'* "aura" has been obscured and they have been denied the light that shows their scourge (106). "Estrujados e impresos les han negado esa luz para conformar estampas perfectamente falsas–sin riesgos–esa imagen que les permite intermitentes, la ilusa distancia del que ha creído en una clase de permanencia diferida" ("Wrung out and printed they have been denied that light so as to compose perfectly false illustrations–without risks–that image which allows them intermittencies, the deluded distance of the person who has believed in a kind of deferred permanence"; 107, 106).

The reality of life under Pinochet brings about the dissolution of the speaking subject who is the subject of *testimonio*: not the *testimonio* of those who survived intact, but of those who did not. Eltit's text "nació del desafío de tener que darles nombre a fracciones de experiencia que ya no eran verbalizables en el idioma que sobrevivió a la catástrofe de sentido" ("was born from the challenge of having to name fractions of experience that were no longer expressable in the language that survived the catastrophe of meaning"; Richard, *La insubordinación* 17). In this text we find those marked by the catastrophe of meaning. L. Iluminada's disappearance in discourse is performed and displaced by the excessive presence of the injured, fragmented, and eroticized body that baroquely displays its ornament and simultaneous pain and pleasure. The female body is not only the locus of past violence, but also an actor in testifying to that violence. The female body as traditionally an object of desire and a page onto which others' desires are projected emphasizes the permeation of gender throughout the power relationships Eltit's work explores. In other words, if this text that resists essentializing categories of identity and truth lacked that desiring, female body, also absent would be the agency to question those categories. In contrast, Menchú's, Jesusa's and Carolina Maria de Jesus's *testimonios*, the female body is oddly absent in this sense, even when the subject's gender fosters the transcriber's approximation.

Female Sexuality and Testimonial Purity

In *Hasta no verte* Jesusa Palancares's sexuality is purposely obscured behind textual absence, Jesusa's traditional morality, and her adoption of masculine roles. Rigoberta Menchú, despite her unusual independence and worldliness, carefully reaffirms women's traditional roles in Quiché society, as discussed in Chapter 1. After she describes the suspicion surrounding a young woman who has left the community like herself, Menchú adds this is not such a problem when the woman's parents are sure she is a virgin (86), the implication being Menchú is pure and of good moral character. I also repeat here Doris Sommer's observation that both Jesusa and Menchú privilege male models in their lives ("Not Just" 129), and add that the consequent freedom of that identification does not include sexual freedom, *in the text*. Carolina is the only woman with children of the three testimonial narrators. In *Quarto de Despejo*, any references to sexual vulgarity among the *favelados* and to her affairs with white men, the fathers of her children, are cushioned in her otherwise conventional morality, her general loneliness, and the low probability of finding a man who would understand her desire to write. They are also cushioned in Dantas's editing. In Carolina's unedited diaries that encompass material cut by Dantas, there appear more references to, for example, vulgarity (54), a supposed book about her many loves (140), and a female reporter's insistance that she talk about love and her sex life (112-5). In fact, even feminists did not defend Carolina because of her open sexuality, one of the characteristics that disenchanted intellectuals and diminished interest in her later books (*Unedited* 194, 196). Her lack of emotional compromise also emphasizes her scientific distance from the community and supports her pose of authoritative objectivity. For all of these women recognition as a sexual being outside of such an arrangement would undermine their authority. Carolina frames the absence of a partner within her general loneliness and the low probability of finding a man who would understand her desire to write.

Jesusa, Menchú, Carolina, and the fictional L. Iluminada's sexual representations, both in the sense of their self-representation and of the authors' devices, appropriately embody the many differences between these testimonial and fictional explorations of gendered subalternity. The distinct sexual representations in these texts synecdochically mark a broader distinction between texts arising from testimonial discourse's methodology and those that in many ways deconstruct the contradictions that plague testimonial discourse. Thus, theoretical questions of genre are framed in gender terms, establishing a place for female sexuality at the heart of the discussion of *testimonio*. Let me clarify that the absence of the sexual is not a characteristic of all women's *testimonios*, but the fact that its absence accompanies these particular *testimonios* (that also share strong self-reflection on their truth value and legitimation) further supports the link between the treatment of female sexuality and subaltern identity. The sexual purity of these three *testimonios* reflects the insistence on textual purity, on a chaste text unadorned and unaestheticized by suggestions of literature or a narrator who may stray from the truth. Within patriarchal, well-defined gender divisions, female sexuality runs counter to truth. Just as testimonial writing must defend its authority (honor?) by maintaining truthful appearances according to readers' concepts of the truth, the female testimonial narrator must defend her authority by maintaining morally decent appearances and sexual absence. While L. Ilumina-da's female desire to touch against the others and to touch herself lends her agency and aids her transgression of physical and discursive limits, sexuality in the testimonial project of these three books remains as controlled as their performance of truth. In this sense the testimonial text itself is femininized under the careful vigilance of what can threaten its moral value...and exchange value as commodity.

Interestingly, the works of fiction studied in Chapter 2, which reflect back on this mimetic violence through explicit disappearances and sacrifices, sexualize or sensualize the female other. G.H. admires the cockroach, metonymically the departed maid Janair, for her reproductive potential and she sensually communes with the roach when she tastes its substance. Rodrigo playfully desires his virgin Macabéa. Although Lispector's novels insert sexual desire into the discursive desires and disappearances present in testimonial writing, Eltit's work moves beyond their repetition of appropriative violence since the protagonists' sexualization in Lispector depends on others' desires imposed like ideological desires on testimonial texts.

Feminist concerns with sexuality, like tendencies toward the literary, have been suspect as counter-revolutionary, as bourgeois, as distraction from political crises. Guarding the truth value of testimonial writing, including testimonial novels, and overlooking its fundamental paradoxes becomes a strategy against discourses that attempt to erase not just the speaker's version of events, but indeed the body of the informant herself. The oppressions recounted involve violences that disappear, torture, or slowly starve the informant's body. The erotic and desire may seem inappropriately frivolous when confronted with the violence described in writing marginality, motivating the need for moral rectitude to support testimonial discourse's apparatus of authenticity as opposed to voyeuristic sensationalism. Nevertheless, sexuality's relevance in Eltit to the study of power, violence and authoritarianism underscores its relevance to *testimonio*. It is the connection between authoritarianism and female sexuality that Eltit's L. Iluminada performs in *Lumpérica* and that in part moves representation of marginality beyond the authentication that has dominated readings of testimonial literature. Female eroticism and desire reappropriate a social body scarred by dictatorship and rigid sexual control, and *Lumpérica* is anything but a frivolous text. Moreover, in her essay on *Lumpérica* Sara Castro-Klarén links mixing the erotic with the rhetorical to pain's resistance to description, creating the need to use "language of the imaginary" (47). Eltit's text aesthetically "documents" the corporeal, subjective experience of fragmented identity arising from the physical pain of torture or homelessness, from the constant surveillance represented by film takes, or from the commodification of the body and society represented by submission to the flashing advertisement.

Guarding testimonial veracity vaguely evokes the idea of guarding its virginity, erasing the sexuality of the informant's body. The text must appear pure and untouched, hiding certain manipulations and inconsistencies that in patriarchal discourse of rigid oppositions and boundaries taint the quality of the textual body. The inconsistencies in that story, however, point to a deeper truth–certainly a more interesting truth–that emphasizes female agency within repressive limitations, that emphasizes desire in the face of sexual denial or forced violation of bodily boundaries. Female sexuality is vulnerability. It reminds us we are speaking with someone whose body poses a threat to the status quo, and to her dedication to the cause. As object of desire, women's sexuality is precisely what can initiate mimetic violence, and this includes the testimonial subject in general as object of desire to reinforce one's own ideology, projected onto the page of her body like the flashing light naming L. Iluminada and the *pálidos*.

The flashing sign becomes the lover, the voyeuristic camera, and the surveillance apparatus that inscribe her apparent pleasure as that of a prostitute from an authoritarian perspective. As the *luminoso*'s light hits her, penetrates her, she wets her lips, and swings her open legs. "Podría ser–tal vez–el Amado por lo masculino de su grosor que al llamarla la asedia para poseerla, a esa vaga que yace tirada en la plaza, evocando con sus indecentes movimientos quizás qué sueños de entrega" ("It could be–perhaps–from the virility of its massiveness the Beloved who on summoning her lays siege in order to possess her, this vagrant who lies stretched out in the square, arousing with her indecent movements who knows what dreams of surrender"; 13, 19). L. Iluminada performs her sexuality and the reification of her nameless body, making public that which should remain unseen under authoritarian divisions. In this sense her gestures and her later screams and moans allow her to become subject of her self-representation without allowing her a stable identity from which to enact that self-representation, without erasing her role as object, to which she testifies.

In the process, L. Iluminada's sexualized body testifies to a series of acts of repression and violence. The voyeuristic nature of the camera's and the reader's watching her movements turn the dictatorship's surveillance apparatus in the name of enforcing decent society into a participant in the selling of bodies. Surveillance by the personified advertisement, imagined audience, and hidden camera also mixes the constant control over bodies by the authoritarian regime with the sensuous pleasure of explicitly, collectively seeing. The pain of her self-inflicted burn does not diminish the "placer de la mirada" ("gaze's pleasure"; 9): "Porque alguno podría decir que nadie quemaría su propia mano por una simple mirada/ ah si tú dices eso es que no sabes nada de la vida" ("Because someone might say that nobody would burn her own hand for a mere look/ oh if you say that it's because you know nothing about life"; 38, 45). The exorcizing effect of hidden wounds exposed to observation partly explains the confusion of ecstasy and pain in *Lumpérica*. After she smashes her head against a tree L. Iluminada "se muestra en el goce de su propia herida, la indaga con sus uñas y si el dolor existe es obvio que su estado conduce al éxtasis" ("she parades her pleasure in her own wound, she probes it with her fingernails and if there is pain it is obvious that her state leads to ecstasy"; 19, 24). Her condition changes her to "otra especie y a otro estado animal" ("another species and another animal state"; 60, 63), her loins "ancas" in order to "soportar bien esa montada" ("to really support this mounted pack"; 61, 64), a mounting that suggests a violent act of sexual torture: "¿bajo qué condición se enterrarían las espuelas en sus ijares? montarla/ cabalgarla/ cansarla o tal vez apurarla suavemente con las puntas de metal a su cadera" ("In what circumstance would spurs dig into her flanks? Mounting her/ riding her/ exhausting her or maybe hurrying her gently on with the metal points to her hip"; 62, 64).

The norms of experience that guide testimonial narrative's construction of a stable identity are confronted with dehumanization of the body and the unmediated sounds of the *pálidos*: "Con sonidos guturales llenan el espacio en una alfabetización virgen que altera las normas de la experiencia" ("With gutteral sounds they fill the space in a virginal alphabetization that alters the norms of experience"; 13, 18). Here virginity does not denote sexual/textual purity, but rather the crossing of normative boundaries protected to construct fixed identity. Contradictions repressed by readings of *testimonio*, the sexuality repressed by *testimonio*, take center stage in *Lumpérica* to produce discomfort. The sexuality performed rewrites fictions of absent desire or of an intact sexual border simultaneously enforced by authoritarian divisions and violated by authoritarian violence. As Castro Klarén states, the "fiction of the female body unfolds as we read" (45). This fiction is the truth, unfolding both in the sense of displaying itself and unraveling. Castro-Klarén has noted Eltit does not signal the difference between pain and pleasure, thus eliminating another boundary "crucial to a moral and religious view of the body" (44). L. Iluminada's subversion of the commercial and authoritarian structures causing her lack underscores those structures' mechanisms. Through her body gender becomes a frame for examining materialist exploitation, social class, and torture under dictatorship. L. Iluminada's "testimony" is her body and her sexuality. Eltit's representation of subalternity beyond access to the printed word, in a place where bodies receive the multiple degradations of torture, poverty, and commodification, turns mediation from a homogenizing process into a transcription that resists an easy reading or an easily packaged subalternity. In the end, while testimonial strategies erase female sexuality in the production of authenticity and persuasion, L. Iluminada's performed sexuality, as subject and object, becomes integral to the denunciation of nationalist rhetoric and violence.

Yet, does Eltit's text go beyond *testimonio* if it cannot escape its written, published medium of elite consumption? Tierney-Tello raises the similar question of if *El Padre Mío* "serves Eltit's ends alone," considering it embodies her political and aesthetic concerns ("Testimony" 81-2). Does it not also reproduce testimonial paradoxes? *Lumpérica* as an act instead of transcribed speech suggests a "truer," more democratic, collective testimony without the mediation of publication to make it more digestible. Yet, while the camera's presence and Eltit's fragmented language resist a comfortable reading and highlight our voyeurism, interrogation, and commodification of L. Iluminada's body, the film takes remind us of our appropriating gaze and the fact that we hold a written, commercial object. In this sense Tierney-Tello correctly perceives a productive questioning of ourselves as readers of the testimonial process (82). Eltit returns economic value to el Padre Mío and L. Iluminada as texts. Neustadt highlights the bodies for sale not only in the plaza, but also in the bookstore: "Publishing *Lumpérica*, Eltit both sells a narrative body, L. Iluminada, and her own textual/sexual body" (quoted in Lorenzano 193). Furthermore, Brito sees the principal "significante" that moves *Lumpérica* as the search for being subject—the same that moves testimonial discourse—and the novel fails in its attempts: "son remanentes, caídas, fallas" ("they are remnants, falls or spills, failures"; 113). Avelar asserts Eltit turns the figure of the marginal into one of epic proportions, yet "an epic of marginality can only be a fallacious one, for all epic is by definition an epic of the center. To marginals the possibility of speaking epically is not given." *Lumpérica* is simultaneously a "compensatory epic" and a "reflection on the impossibility of such an epic" ("Overcodification" 177). After all, at daybreak the *luminoso* turns off and the show is over. Nevertheless, Eltit's work offers a provocative response to the paradoxes encountered in testimonial discourse, moving outside the rhetorical, ethnographic structure to, with all its own "spills" and "failures" suggest new ways of remembering and democratizing constructions of history and identity. When Eltit writes, "No hay literatura que los haya retratado en toda su inconmesurabilidad" ("No literature has portrayed them in all their immeasurability"; *Lumpérica* 107, 106), we cannot help but see *Lumpérica* and *El Padre Mío* as the writing that attempts that task of portraying the enormity of violence and marginality under authoritarianism.

CHANGING THE SUBJECT

F: *What was your childhood like, what happened to you before you came here?*
DOÑA MARTINA: *I don't remember.*
F: *You don't remember anything?*
ELVIRA: *Come on, mom, just tell her.*
DOÑA MARTINA: *Well, yes; it seems my mother left me when I was around six years old.*
....

But perhaps most important is the story of persistence in pursuit of your goal, in this case making sure that the Mapuche people maintain their own culture. And in relation to this last point I think it's important to emphasize the right of all peoples to autonomy. This is what I'd like readers to see in my book, but if I want to boil it down even further, I'd say that I hope they see how difficult it is to be a social and political leader in the kind of world we're living in at the turn of the century.
F: *With this last comment you also cross other boundaries, because even if the Mapuche people and their leaders face difficulties with political organization in today's world, so do the rest of us.*
I think that's right. I think all leaders who go public and step outside their house and their family face the scrutiny of the larger society, the positive and negative comments about what they did and didn't do. You lose your privacy and that of your family, and what you say is no longer simply your opinion but represents others. Other people start seeing you as a role model.

Rosa Isolde Reuque Paillalef,
When a Flower Is Reborn

C HANGING the subject, evading the issue, keeping secrets, avoiding an uncomfortable topic. Changing the direction of conversation, negotiating the terms of dialogue, resisting. Using a point of
contact to shift between subjects. Changing roles. Changing the
other's subjectivity or identity, changing one for another, representing others with one.

"Don't keep changing the subject: I want to talk to you."
"You're not listening."

At what junctures in testimonial texts, fiction, and theory does
the subject (object of attention) become subject (autonomous
agent) or the other way around? Who legitimates the change of
subject? Who changes the subject's terms of self-representation?
How do circumstances change rhetorical strategies?

These questions exhibit overlapping relevance to testimonial
discourse and women's self-representation, one reason for my focus
on women's texts. As I asserted at the beginning of this book, to
ignore gender is to incompletely investigate the hierarchies testimonial writing strives to undermine and the conditions under which
the speaker can narrate her story. Testimonial discourse's more
democratic mode of production and obvious concern for writing
about difference, despite the contradictions and complications to
which this book is dedicated, mean the body of work by and about
women is large and begs specific attention to gender. Resistance to
a feminist reading of *testimonio* arises in part from the same notions
that have resisted its intertextual reading with fiction or a discussion of aesthetics, resistances that limit our understanding of *testimonio*'s lessons about self-expression from outside centers of
privilege. *Testimonio*'s irrefutable collective significance, whether a
collective identity stressed by the speaker or by the framing texts,
establishes a particularly critical link between testimonial and feminist discourses, and a common point where both discourses run the
risk of repeating hegemonic essentializations of identity. As they
construct a new, alternative articulation of identity that is politically
empowering, they can write new borders and limits to that articulation. Thus, testimonial discourse belies naive notions of female
identification across differences, and at the same time feminist perspectives highlight *testimonio*'s purity: of sexual identity for female
narrators that reflects the broader desire for pure truth.

The intersection of gender and national identities forms another
important point of contact in *testimonio*. Testifying to personal

experience in alternative narrative forms "bears similarity to women's foundational writing, and Miguel Barnet defined testimonial writing as a foundational writing for the nation. Testimonial discourse posits an alternative national identity from the bottom up (when embraced by enabling intellectuals): a Guatemala that recognizes its Indian population; a Brazil that recognizes its racism and economic underclass; and a Mexico that recognizes the working-class, independent women who fought in the Revolution that is the quintessential origin of Mexican patriotic rhetoric. Scholars in literature have explored women as metaphors of nascent Latin American nations in the region's nineteenth-century "foundational fictions" and ethnographic studies have provided examples of women's role to maintain traditional culture. [1] Therefore, women become logical narrators of a testimonial discourse invested in establishing new national foundations. Another dimension of this overlap of nation and gender appears in authoritarian adoption of patriarchal rhetoric to legitimate its regime, as in the case of Pinochet. Eltit's work "performs" this overlap in her subversive embodiments of a broken Chile. Eltit reveals the paradox of a propaganda that glorifies women and workers, then plunges them into an economic distress that leaves them living in the plaza under a sign that advertises their exclusion from the economic miracle.

That paradoxical truth performs both the repressive political structure to which the texts testify, and the paradoxes of the testimonial process. I began my discussion with legitimation's and authority's links to paradoxical truth. As postmodern theory has made familiar, possession of the truth lends authority, and in these texts legitimation of authority depends on testimony that affirms a document's veracity and authenticity. Testimonial discourse strives to contain meaning at the same time it opens meaning, illustrated by simultaneous desires to maintain laws or borders and to break

[1] Regarding literature, here I am thinking specifically of Doris Sommer, *Foundational Fictions: The National Romances of Latin America* (Berkeley and Oxford: U of California P, 1991) and Mary Louis Pratt, "Women, Literature, and National Brotherhood," *Women, Culture, and Politics in Latin America*, Seminar on Feminism and Culture in Latin America (Berkeley and Oxford: U of California P, 1990) 48-73. Regarding ethnographic studies, I am thinking of the essays in Marit Melhuus and Kristi Anne Stølen, eds., *Machos, Mistresses, Madonnas: Contesting the Power of Latin American Gender Imagery* (London, New York: Verso, 1996) and Rosario Montoya, Lessie Jo Frazier, and Janise Hurtig, eds., *Gender's Place: Feminist Anthropologies of Latin America* (New York: Palgrave, 2002).

law's limitations. In order to legitimate itself under the very rules it challenges, *testimonio*'s content must exhibit a contained meaning, a story that does not deviate from truth. Although contradictions actually reinforce the oral origin, and thus authenticity, of the text, the concept of truth in oral narrative opposes that of the written document. Furthermore, the texts contain silences utilized by informants as strategies toward authority and also impose silences and disappearances. The testimonial subject's reticence creates power through knowledge of a truth withheld since she possesses what the transcriber desires and she can undermine the transcriber's authority by leaving the testimony incomplete, by frustrating the power of "hacer hablar." The transcriber's knowledge of the subject's revealed truth initiates a process of self-legitimation that potentially culminates in the subject's silence. The "authentic" life story requires the informant remain on the margins as the embodiment of what is acceptably authentic. This initiates the paradoxical approximation and distancing of transcriber and testimonial subject, the paradoxical desire to reconcile disparate discourses, "disappearing" some of the more challenging differences that reinforce the testimonial narrator's autonomous subjectivity.

The most publicized case of these paradoxes is of course the Menchú/Stoll controversy, where the limits to self-constructed identity from the margin become clear. That is, a translatable identity requires reconciling disappearances in the service of persuasive verisimilitude, so that the subaltern *can* speak (on certain terms), so that we *will* listen (Sommer, *Proceed* 20). To play on Elaine Scarry's words from the epigraph to Chapter 4: on the particular morning when the artifactuality of that translatable identity becomes suddenly and insistently visible (if we accept the factual doubts raised by Stoll), what should be striking is not the fact that the identity is constructed, or the sense that its reality was a fraud, or that there is no difference between the real and the artifactual, but rather that the testimonial process requires artifice like any discursive self-representation, and that the artifice of a more easily consumable identity of "otherness" entailed at its center, up until last night, the appearance and force and responsibilities of "the real." In recent years testimonial readers have woken up the next day. The Menchú/Stoll controversy has made more visible the dynamics of testimonial discourse as negotiation, dynamics not limited to Menchú's situation. Testimonial discourse ultimately constitutes a writing that highlights its artifactuality through precisely its fundamental, extra-literary aspect: another speaking subject. The testimonial narrator's presence and demands require particular attention to the text's crafting through dialogue with her presence. With respect to readers' presence in *testimonio*'s process, Lispector's novels serve to display the artifactuality of those readers' desires that ignore the subject's complicated speaking position: here is the fiction we desire–with a wink of complicity–embodied in the prehistoric and essentialized roach/Janair and Macabéa. Eltit's work, in contrast, critiques our (authoritarian) reading by *denying* us that fiction of a reconcilable, easily translatable speaking subject.

In a sense, the contrast between Lispector's and Eltit's translations of difference illustrate yet another articulation of the paradoxes inherent to the testimonial project as translation. Like *testimonio*, translation strives for a certain neutral invisibility while it also opens and changes meaning: the desert of multiple interpretations that Averroes fears in Borges's story and that G.H. encounters in the maid's room, where it threatens the tidy question marks containing G.H.'s world. Deleuze and Guattari's nomads inhabit this non-hierarchical space as well, but never quite appear. Alternative interpretations must be controlled at the same time that the testimony lays bare official discourse's disguises and thus subjects all truths to the aperture of multiple interpretations. Thus Rodrigo S.M.'s concern to control meaning within limits, to maintain law and order while also violating boundaries, reflects the testimonial conflict. Ultimately the law results in violent sacrifice because just when Macabéa begins to test her limits and threatens to encroach on the narrator's territory, she is cut short, protecting singular, authoritative interpretation of the text. She changed the subject.

Changing the subject in testimonial texts is permeated by violence: the violence they denounce, the violence experienced by the speaker, the discursive violences they threaten against official history and hierarchy, and the discursive sacrifices in their translations. There must be violence for there to be *testimonio* and violence becomes inextricably implicated in the questions of subjectivity that motivate testimonial writing. *Testimonio*'s explicit accusations and its linkage between text and action reinforce, beyond the self-evident etymology of its name, the kinship between testimonial and legal acts of interpretation and vengeance. This relationship reminds us of that aspect of *testimonio* that preserves the status quo through sacrifices and controlled violence on which legal authority rests. Legal authority and scholarly authority, through acts of interpretation, can keep the testimonial subject (agent) subject to (object of) their definitions of truth and identity. This is not new with testimonial discourse's arrival, but the extraliterary charges the question with greater ethical weight. Again, while Menchú's *testimonio* is the most well-known example, Jesusa continually addresses misinterpretations of her truths from figures of authority. Also, Carolina Maria de Jesus's later books do not sell as well once the public gets to know her following *Quarto de Despejo*'s success, when she asserts the autonomy won through translating the *favela* into terms appetizing for readers. Once the testimonial subject's differences reach their most powerful by really threatening an ideological or structural change to that which facilitated the publication of her story in the first place, that is when we begin to hear dishes smash.[2]

Lispector's texts illustrate through ritual the sacralization of an essentialized otherness (the "aura" of *testimonio* in Moreira's words) that accompanies that otherness's danger for the self, a danger that leads to G.H.'s and Rodrigo's appropriation of the mystified other's identity and of the other's entitlement to rectification. In G.H.'s and Rodrigo's supposedly redemptive readings vengeance is reversed and the other's subjectivity changes: from agent of violence to object of violence. The "anti-*testimonio*" *El Padre Mío* evades that reversal as it disturbingly violates readers' expectations of textual purity or transparency, yet the speaker ultimately disappears. Eltit's novel *Lumpérica* emphasizes performance in such a way that denounces political, gendered, and economic violence through L. Iluminada's acts as agent of violence and of female sexuality, rather than object, yet her ritual repetition of the regime's crimes are ultimately directed against her own body, the only surface at her disposal. What is especially compelling about the exhibitionist violence in *Lumpérica* when read with testimonial texts is its implication in practices of desiring and material consumption. L. Iluminada's enactment of her status as consumer object, as object of

---

[2] I am referring back to a quotation from *A Hora da Estrela* that I discussed in the section "Vengeance and Sacrifice" in Chapter 3: "Estou com raiva. Uma cólera de derrubar copos e pratos e quebrar vidraças. Como me vingar? Ou melhor, como me compensar?" ("I am enraged. The kind of anger that makes you smash cups and plates and break windows. How am I going to avenge myself? Or, better yet, how am I going to be compensated?"; 33).

possession, creates not just an apt metaphor for the discursive cannibalism of reading *testimonio*, but also a reminder of *testimonio*'s commodification: packaged identity is for sale in the plaza.

While this book posits bidirectional readings between and among testimonial texts, feminist approaches, works of fiction, and critical theories, its subtitle places priority on the lessons of Latin American women's *testimonio* for the other discourses. This order of priority aims, with a different perspective, to continue the trend that Nelly Richard already articulated in the early 1990s: *testimonio*'s absorption into the academic center and its consequent loss of outsider status. That trend meant absorption of testimonial writing in terms of: grasping truths that present an alternative to official history in crisis periods; questioning historical and literary canons; and empowering not only the testimonial subject's narrative through empathy abroad, but also sympathetic intellectuals' ideologies. Now, at the beginning of the twenty-first century, after attacks on *testimonio*'s legitimacy based on its most valued characteristic (truth), and after economic globalization has motivated closer attention to international divisions of intellectual labor in the academic center and its appropriative readings, my subtitle encourages, with other recent scholarship, another approach to testimonial discourse's academic absorption. In the academic center mediated testimonial discourse's complex negotiations of narrative agency do not simply provide raw material, raw data, for US and European theories. Testimonial discourse's own subjectivity has changed; it has lessons to teach. The reiteration above of the book's most salient points addresses those lessons. One of them is understanding the negotiation of self-representation on borders where different subjects meet, more ethically complex than the heteroglossia Bakhtin taught us. Another is the truth of definitions' construction across boundaries, rather than the usefulness of those definitions separately: the truth of relationships and dialogues between genders, between genres, between truth and fiction, and between testimonial transparency and theoretical or aesthetic abstraction. These lessons come down to diminishing attention to our moves from locations of privilege to democratize discourse and increasing attention to how others are structuring that democratization. In the introduction to her book focused on the encounters between readers and "particularist" texts in the Americas, both of fiction and testimony, Doris Sommer writes: "The messiness of asymmetrical histories and the responsibilities they imply are the lessons here, . . ." (*Proceed* 14). It is the responsibilities to which Sommer refers, the ethics of the face-to-face encounter with the interlocutor, that lead to the desire for rhetorical transparency and that therefore overlook the consequences of its written medium. *Testimonio* obviously constitutes a bridge between social reality and discourse in a more profound way than the fictions and theories that engage with that social reality, textually, without coming face-to-face with someone who can talk back. As the title to Debra Castillo's insightful book *Talking Back* suggests for Latin American women's writing, what occurs when the outsider talks back? That which in fiction and theory remains rhetorical, though emerging from socio-political circumstances, in testimonial writing requires translations, displacements, negotiations, and a struggle with what empowerment for the subject really means for the transcriber's subjectivity. As Sommer puts it: messiness.

Displacements occur not only in the appropriation of another voice in testimonial texts, in works of fiction, and in poststructuralist theory, but also in our own approaches to Latin American literature. In the conclusion to Debra Castillo's same book, the Mexican woman from the *azotea* replaces the Madwoman in the Attic and actually occupies the center of the house in a move to undo hierarchies. Castillo writes:

> I add now that the practice undertaken in this book is like the housework done by that woman from the *azotea*; . . . And this housework/bookwork is undertaken in the knowledge that once it is done, everything is still to be done, that in the doing I undermine the possibility of its ever being, once and forever, done. There is still and always the cleaning of the house of fiction to be done, the polishing of the prose, the finding of the lost object. And other tasks. And while the subject and object of this task might be continuous, the practice and the instrumentality are always in process. (305)

Castillo's consideration of the woman of the *azotea* is appropriate for its relevance to the literature she examines, to Castillo's awareness of class as one of the defining features of Latin American women's experience, and hence to the Latin American feminist literary criticism that she intelligently develops, and on which the present book partly relies. Nevertheless, this seems to carry out a legitimating displacement like those seen throughout my preceding chapters. Academics receive personal recognition and prestige for their intellectual work and publications. It is not physical labor. The polished prose and found objects belong to them. The identification between bookwork and the woman of the *azotea*'s housework serves a legitimating function through its displacement of women academics' privilege and its justification of their solidarity with less privileged women. Does women academics' work allow us a privileged understanding of the economic marginalization so basic to comprehension of the Latin American context? I do not question the sincerity or value of academics' solidarity, and of course include myself, but wish to point out how displacements become easy in the linguistic medium with which we work.

This leads me to conclude with the epigraphs from *When a Flower Is Reborn*, a *testimonio* published too recently for extensive inclusion in this study. As one can see from the two passages, Florencia E. Mallon's transcription of her conversations with the Mapuche feminist activist Rosa Isolde Reuque Paillalef include Mallon's questions. This format asserts *testimonio* as dialogue with its pushing, prodding, deviations, subject changes, and–critically– the testimonial subject's participation in the process. If we imagine the first dialogue I quote without the leading question, denial, and intervention by Elvira, we have lost doña Martina's role in the creation of the final information, as well as telling nuances about that information's emotional resonance. Mallon's preface addresses the dilemmas of subjectivity in testimonial discourse and the text itself responds to legitimating displacements and disappearances. Mallon's presence in fact brings into relief the other subject's complexity, whereby Mallon's increased visibility and role beyond simply transcription enhances Reuque Paillalef's and the other interviewees' agency. In addition, the book concludes with a dialogue between Mallon and Reuque Paillalef about the project itself; the testimonial subject participates in the framing text and circumvents a certain division of labor. In the second epigraph, from this concluding dialogue, Reuque Paillalef describes a collective identity that creates tension, that comes from within and without, and that evades mystification of a speaking position located in the past. She reiterates the importance of the Mapuche's autonomy in maintaining their own culture, but the speaker places herself as an actor at the present turn of the century. In this *testimonio* the simultaneity of her links to Mapuche traditions and her participation in twenty-first century activism does not have to be explained and does not create deauthorizing contradictions, but rather a demystified, truthful representation of the testimonial subject's evolving agency. Testimonial subjects evolve as they shift strategies and negotiate their identity in context. Therefore, those who listen will also have to allow their theories and ideologies to be subject to change.

WORKS CITED

Achugar, Hugo. "Historias paralelas/historias ejemplares: La historia y la voz del otro." Beverley and Achugar 49-71.

Archer, Deborah J. "Receiving the Other: The Femenine Economy of Clarice Lispector's *The Hour of the Star.*" *Anxious Power: Reading, Writing and Ambivalence in Narratives by Women.* Albany: SUNY Press, 1993.

Arias, Arturo, ed. *The Rigoberta Menchú Controversy.* With a response by David Stoll. Minneapolis: U of Minnesota P, 2001.

———. "Rigoberta Menchú's History within the Guatemalan Context." Arias, *Rigoberta Menchú Controversy* 3-28.

Avalos, David, with John C. Welchman. "Response to the Philosophical Brothel." *Rethinking Borders.* Ed. John C. Welchman. Minneapolis: U of Minnesota P, 1996.

Avelar, Idelber. "An Anatomy of Marginality: Figures of the Eternal Return and the Apocalypse in Chilean Post-Dictatorial Fiction." *Studies in Twentieth Century Literature* 23.2 (Summer 1999): 211-37.

———. "Overcodification of the Margins: Figures of the Eternal Return and the Apocalypse." *The Untimely Present: Postdictatorial Latin American Fiction and the Task of Mourning.* Durham and London: Duke UP, 1999. 164-85.

Barnet, Miguel. *Biografía de un cimarrón.* La Habana: Academia de ciencias de Cuba, Instituto de Etnología y Folklore, 1966.

———. "La novela testimonio. Socio-literatura." Jara and Vidal 280-302.

———. "Testimonio y comunicación: una vía hacia la identidad." Jara and Vidal 303-14.

Barthes, Roland. *A Lover's Discourse.* Trans. Richard Howard. New York: Hill and Wang, 1993.

Behar, Ruth. "Out of Exile." Introduction. Behar and Gordon 1-29.

———. *Translated Woman. Crossing the Border with Esperanza's Story.* Boston: Beacon, 1993.

Behar, Ruth and Deborah A. Gordon. *Women Writing Culture.* Berkeley and Los Angeles: U of California P, 1995.

"Benita. Una escritora que todavía no ha aprendido a escribir con su propia mano." *Fem* 2.6 (March 1978): 64-6.

Benjamin, Walter. "The Task of the Translator: An Introduction to the Translation of Baudelaire's Tableaux Parisiens." *Illuminations.* Ed. and intro. Hannah Arendt. Trans. Harry Zohn. New York: Harcourt, Brace and World, 1968. 69-82.

Beverley, John. Introducción. Beverley and Achugar 7-18.

———. "The Margins at the Center: On *Testimonio*." Smith and Watson 91-114.

———. "The Real Thing." Gugelberger 266-86.

———. "Second Thoughts on Testimonio." *Against Literature*. Minneapolis: U of Minnesota P, 1993. 69-99.

———. "What Happens When the Subaltern Speaks: Rigoberta Menchú, Multiculturalism, and the Presumption of Equal Worth." Arias, *Rigoberta Menchú Controversy* 219-36.

Beverley, John and Hugo Achugar, eds. *La voz del otro: testimonio, subalternidad y verdad narrativa*. Lima, Pittsburgh: Latinoamericana Editores, 1992.

Blau, Herbert. *To All Appearances: Ideology and Performance*. New York and London: Routledge, 1992.

Borges, Jorge Luis. "Averroës' Search." Trans. Anthony Kerrigan. *A Personal Anthology*. New York: Grove Press, 1967. 101-10.

———. "La busca de Averroes." *El Aleph*. Buenos Aires: Alianza/Emecé, 1985. 93-104.

Borland, Katherine. "'That's Not What I Said': Interpretive Conflict in Oral Narrative Research." Gluck and Patai 63-75.

Braidotti, Rosi. *Nomadic Subjects: Embodiment and Sexual Difference in Contemporary Feminist Theory*. New York: Columbia UP, 1994.

Brink, Andre. "An Act of Violence: Thoughts on the Functioning of Literature." *Pretexts: Studies in Writing and Culture* 3.1-2 (1991): 32-47.

Brito, Eugenia. "La narrativa de Diamela Eltit: un nuevo paradigma socio-literario de lectura." *Campos minados (Literatura post-golpe en Chile)*. 2nd ed. Santiago: Cuarto Propio, 1994.

Brooksbank Jones, Anny and Catherine Davies, eds. *Latin American Women's Writing: Feminist Readings in Theory and Crisis*. Oxford and New York: Oxford UP, 1996.

Burgos, Elizabeth. *Me llamo Rigoberta Menchú y así me nació la conciencia*. 8th edition. Mexico: Siglo XXI, 1993.

Burgos-Debray, Elisabeth, ed. and intro. *I...Rigoberta Menchú: An Indian Woman in Guatemala*. Trans. Ann Wright. London: Verso, 1984.

Butler, Judith. *Gender Trouble*. New York: Routledge, 1990.

Camacho de Schmidt, Aurora. "¡Únete a la lucha!: receptores del texto testimonial latinoamericano." *La seducción de la escritura: Los discursos de la cultura hoy, 1996*. Rosaura Hernández Monroy and Manuel F. Medina, eds. Mexico: Universidad Autónoma Metropolitana-Azcapotzalco, 1997. 34-42.

Castillo, Debra A. *Talking Back: Toward a Latin American Feminist Criticism*. Ithaca; London: Cornell UP, 1992.

Castro-Klaren, Sara. "The Lit Body or the Politics of Eros in *Lumpérica*." *Indiana Journal of Hispanic Literatures* 1.2 (Spring 1993): 41-52.

Cavallari, Héctor Mario. "Ficción, Testimonio, Representación." Jara and Vidal 73-84.

Chamberlain, Daniel F. "Revealing Belief, and Discovering Ethics in the Worlds of Latin American Narrative." *Revista Canadiense de Estudios Hispánicos* 16.1 (Fall 1991): 29-44.

Chevigny, Bell Gale. "The Transformation of Privilege in the Work of Elena Poniatowska." *Faith of a (Woman) Writer*. Eds. Alice Kessler-Harris and William McBrien. Westport, CT: Greenwood, 1988. 209-20.

Cixous, Hélène. "Extreme Fidelity." *Writing Difference, Readings from the Seminar of Hélène Cixous*. Ed. Susan Sellers. Milton Keynes, England: Open UP, 1988. 9-36.

Cixous, Hélène. *Reading with Clarice Lispector*. Ed., trans., and intro. Verena Amdermatt Conley. Theory and History of Literature 73. Minneapolis, MN: U Minnesota P, 1990.

———. *Vivre l'orange. To live the Orange.* Paris: des femmes, 1979.

Clayton, Ellen Wright and Jay Clayton. "Afterword: Voices and Violence - A Dialogue." *Vanderbilt Law Review* 43.6 (Nov. 1990): 1807-18.

Clifford, James. "Introduction: Partial Truths." *Writing Culture: The Poetics and Politics of Ethnography.* Eds. James Clifford and George E. Marcus. Berkeley and Los Angeles: U of California Press, 1986. 1-26.

———. "Traveling Cultures." *Routes: Travel and Translation in the Late Twentieth Century.* Cambridge and London: Harvard UP, 1997.

Colás, Santiago. "What's Wrong with Representation?: *Testimonio* and Democratic Culture." Gugelberger 161-71.

Cornejo-Parriego, Rosalía. "*Racialización* colonial y diferencia femenina en 'Love story' de Poniatowska y 'Cuando las mujeres quieren a los hombres' de Ferré." *Afro-Hispanic Review.* 16.2 (Fall 1997): 10-8.

Cover, Robert M. "Violence and the Word." *The Yale Law Journal* 95 (1986): 1601-29.

De Certeau, Michel. *Heterologies–Discourse on the Other.* Trans. Brian Massumi. Minneapolis: U of Minnesota P, 1986.

De Lauretis, Teresa. "The Violence of Rhetoric: Considerations on Representation and Gender." *Semiotica* 54.1/2: 11-31.

Deleuze, Gilles and Félix Guattari. *A Thousand Plateaus: Capitalism and Schizophrenia.* Trans. and for. Brian Massumi. Minneapolis: U of Minnesota P, 1987.

———. "What is a Minor Literature?" *Out There: Marginalization and Contemporary Cultures.* Eds. Russell Ferguson, Martha Gever, Trinh T. Minh-ha, and Cornel West. Foreward, Marcia Tucker. New York: The New Museum of Contemporary Art; Cambridge, MA: MIT, 1990. 59-69.

Derrida, Jacques. *Spurs: Nietzsche's Styles/Éperons: Les Styles de Nietzsche.* Trans. Barbara Harlow. Intro. Stefano Agosti. Chicago and London: U of Chicago P, 1979.

———. "The Violence of the Letter: From Lévi-Strauss to Rousseau." *Of Grammatology.* Trans. Gayatri Chakravorty Spivak. Baltimore: Johns Hopkins UP, 1974. 101-40.

Docherty, Thomas. *On Modern Authority: The Theory and Condition of Writing 1500 to the Present Day.* Sussex: Harvester; New York: St. Martin's, 1987.

Dorfman, Ariel. *Imaginación y violencia en América.* Letras de América 26. Santiago de Chile: Editorial Universitaria, 1970.

Eltit, Diamela. *E. Luminata.* Trans. Ronald Christ. Santa Fe, NM: Lumen, 1997.

———. *Lumpérica.* 1983. Santiago: Planeta, 1991.

———. *El padre mío.* Santiago: Francisco Zegers, 1989.

Etter-Lewis, Gwendolyn. "Black Women's Life Stories: Reclaiming Self in Narrative Texts." Gluck and Patai 43-58.

Feder, Ellen K. and Emily Zakin. "Flirting with the Truth: Derrida's Discourse with 'Woman' and Wenches." Feder, Rawlinson and Zakin 21-51.

Feder, Ellen K., Mary C. Rawlinson and Emily Zakin, eds. *Derrida and Feminism: Recasting the Question of Woman.* London and New York: Routledge, 1997.

Felman, Shoshana. "In an Era of Testimony: Claude Lanzmann's *Shoah*." *Yale French Studies* 79 (1991): 39-81.

Ferman, Claudia. "Textual Truth, Historical Truth, and Media Truth: Everybody Speaks about the Menchús." Arias, *Rigoberta Menchú Controversy* 156-70.

Ferré, Rosario. "Cuando las mujeres quieren a los hombres." *Papeles de Pandora.* México: Joaquín Mortiz, 1979. 26-44.

Finn, Janet L. "Ella Cara Deloria and Mourning Dove: Writing for Cultures, Writing against the Grain." Behar and Gordon. 131-47.

Franco, Jean. "Afterword: From Romance to Refractory Aesthetic." Brooksbank Jones and Davies 226-37.

———. "Beyond Ethnocentrism: Gender, Power and the Third World Intelligentsia." *Marxism and the Interpretation of Culture.* Cary Nelson and Lawrence Grossberg, eds. Chicago: U of Illinois P, 1988. 503-15.

———. "Marcar diferencias. Cruzar fronteras." Ludmer, *Las culturas de fin de siglo* 34-43.

———. "*Si me permiten hablar:* la lucha por el poder interpretativo." Beverley and Achugar 109-16.

Galeana, Benita. *Benita.* México, D.F.: Extemporáneos, 1974.

Gallop, Jane. "'Women' in *Spurs* and Nineties Feminism." Feder, Rawlinson and Zakin 7-19.

Galvez-Breton, Mara. "Post-feminist Discourse in Clarice Lispector's *The Hour of the Star.*" Guerra Cunningham 63-78.

Garabano, Sandra, and Guillermo García-Corales. "Diamela Eltit." Interview. *Hispamerica* 21.62 (Aug 1992): 65-75.

Garber, Marjorie, Rebecca L. Walkowitz and Paul B. Franklin, eds. *Field Work: Sites in Literary and Cultural Studies.* London and New York: Routledge, 1996.

Giardinelli, Mempo. "Novel, testimonio y *non-fiction-novel:* una opinión." *Puro Cuento* 16 (May/June 1989): 28-31.

Gilmore, Leigh. *Autobiographics: a Feminist Theory of Women's Self-Representation.* Reading Women Writing. Ithaca and London: Cornell UP, 1994.

Girard, René. *Violence and the Sacred.* Trans. Patrick Gregory. Baltimore: Johns Hopkins UP, 1977.

Gluck, Sherna Berger and Daphne Patai, eds. *Women's Words: The Feminist Practice of Oral History.* NY: Routledge, 1991.

González, Patricia Elena and Eliana Ortega, eds. *La sartén por el mango: encuentro de escritoras latinoamericanas.* Río Piedras, PR: Huracán, 1984.

González Echevarría, Roberto. *The Voice of the Masters: Writing and Authority in Modern Latin American Literature.* Austin: U Texas P, 1985.

Guerra Cunningham, Lucía, ed. and intro. *Splintering Darkness: Latin American Women Writers in Search of Themselves.* Pittsburgh, PA: Latin American Literary Review P, 1990.

Gugelberger, Georg M. *The Real Thing: Testimonial Discourse and Latin America.* Durham and London: Duke UP, 1996.

Gutiérrez, Mariela. "Rosario Ferré y el itinerario del deseo: un estudio lacaniano de 'Cuando las mujeres quieren a los hombres.'" *Revista Canadiense de Estudios Hispánicos* 16.2 (Winter 1992): 203-17.

Handley, George B. "'It's an Unbelievable Story': Testimony and Truth in the Work of Rosario Ferré and Rigoberta Menchú." *Violence, Silence and Anger: Women's Writing as Transgression.* Deirdre Lashgari, ed. Charlottesville and London: U of Virginia P, 1995. 62-79.

Jara, René and Hernán Vidal, eds. *Testimonio y literatura.* Minneapolis, MN: Institute for the Study of Ideologies and Literature, 1986.

Jardine, Alice. "Woman in Limbo: Deleuze and His Br(others)." *Sub-stance* 13.3-4 (1984): 46-60.

Jesus, Carolina Maria de. *Diário de Bitita.* Rio de Janeiro: Nova Fronteira, 1986.

———. *Quarto de Despejo: Diário de uma Favelada.* Ed. Audálio Dantas. Rio de Janeiro: Paulo de Azevedo, 1963.

———. *The Unedited Diaries of Carolina Maria de Jesus.* Eds. Robert M. Levine and José Carlos Sebe Bom Meihy. Trans. Nancy P. S. Naro and Cristina Mehrtens. New Brunswick, NJ: Rutgers UP, 1999.

Jörgensen, Beth E. *The Writing of Elena Poniatowska: Engaging Dialogues.* Austin: U of Texas P, 1994.

Sor Juana Inés de la Cruz (Juana de Asbaje). *Respuesta a Sor Filotea de la Cruz.* 1691. *Obras completas.* Mexico: Porrúa, 1985.

Kaminsky, Amy Katz. "Women Writing about Prostitutes: Amalia Jamilis and Luisa Valenzuela." *The Image of the Prostitute in Modern Literature.* Ed. and intro. Pierre L. Horn and Mary Beth Pringle. NY: Ungar, 1984. 119-39.

Kaplan, Caren. "Deterritorializations: The Rewriting of Home and Exile in Western Feminist Discourse." *Cultural Critique* (Spring 1987): 187-98.

―――. *Questions of Travel: Postmodern Discourses of Displacement.* Durham and London: Duke UP, 1996.

―――. "Resisting Autobiography: Outlaw Genres and Transnational Feminist Subjects." Smith and Watson 115-38.

Kerr, Lucille. "Gestures of Authorship: Lying to Tell the Truth in Elena Poniatowska's *Hasta no verte, Jesús mío.*" *MLN* 106 (1991): 370-94.

Kristeva, Julia. *Powers of Horror: An Essay on Abjection.* New York: Columbia UP, 1982.

Krupnick, Mark, ed. and intro. *Displacement: Derrida and After.* Theories of Contemporary Culture 5. Bloomington: Indiana UP, 1983.

Labanyi, Jo. "Topologies of Catastrophe: Horror and Abjection in Diamela Eltit's *Vaca sagrada.*" Brooksbank Jones and Davies 85-103.

Lancaster, Roger. Letter. *New York Times* 20 Dec. 1998, early ed., Week in Review: 12.

Lértora, Juan Carlos. "Diamela Eltit: hacia una poética de literatura menor." Lértora, *Una poética* 27-35.

―――, ed. *Una poética de literatura menor: la narrativa de Diamela Eltit.* Santiago de Chile: Cuarto Propio, 1993.

Levine, Robert M., and José Carlos Sebe Bom Meihy. *The Life and Death of Carolina Maria de Jesus.* Albuquerque: U of New Mexico P, 1995.

Levinson, Brett. "The Death of the Critique of Eurocentrism: Latinamericanism as a Global Praxis/Poiesis." *Revista de Estudios Hispánicos* 31 (1997): 169-201.

Lispector, Clarice. *A Hora da Estrela.* Rio de Janeiro: José Olympio, 1977.

―――. *The Hour of the Star.* Trans. and afterword Giovanni Ponteiro. New York: Carcanet, 1986.

―――. *A Legião Estrangeira.* Rio de Janeiro: Editôra do Autor, 1964.

―――. *A Paixão Segundo G.H..* 1964. Ed. Benedito Nunes. São Paulo: Unesco, Coleção Arquivos, 1988.

Lorenzano, Sandra. "Escritura y acciones de arte: una búsqueda transgresora." *La seducción de la escritura: los discursos de la cultura hoy.* Mexico, D.F.: UAM-Azcapotzalco, 1996. 189-95.

Ludmer, Josefina. *Las culturas de fin de siglo en América Latina.* Rosario, Argentina: Beatriz Viterbo, 1994.

―――. "Tretas del débil." González 47-54.

Magnarelli, Sharon. "The Discourse of the Body in the Body of Discourse: *Hay que sonreír.*" *Reflections/Refractions: Reading Luisa Valenzuela.* NY; Bern; Frankfurt am Main; Paris: P. Lang, 1988. 15-28.

Malverde Disselkoen, Ivette. "Esquizofrenia y literatura: la obsesión discursiva en *El Padre Mío*, de Diamela Eltit." Lértora, *Una poética* 155-66.

McKenna, Andrew J. *Violence and Difference: Girard, Derrida and Deconstruction.* Urbana and Chicago: U of Illinois P, 1992.

Menchú, Rigoberta. *Rigoberta: la nieta de los mayas.* In colaboration with Dante Liano and Gianni Minà. Mexico: Aguilar, 1998.

Merewether, Charles. "Zones of Marked Instability: Woman and the Space of

Emergence." *Rethinking Borders*. Ed. John C. Welchman. Minneapolis: U of Minnesota P, 1996. 101-24.

Miller, Christopher L. "The postidentitarian Predicament in the Footnotes of *A Thousand Plateaus*: Nomadology, Anthropology, and Authority." *Diacritics* 23.3 (Fall 1993): 6-35.

Molloy, Sylvia. "At Face Value: Autobiographical Writing in Spanish America." *Dispositio* 9.24-26 (1984): 1-18.

———. *At Face Value: Autobiographical Writing in Spanish America*. Cambridge: Cambridge UP, 1991.

———. "From Serf to Self: The Autobiography of Juan Francisco Manzano." *MLN* 104.2 (March 1989): 393-417.

———. "La política de la pose". *Las culturas de fin de siglo en América Latina*. Ed. Josefina Ludmer. Rosario, Argentina: Beatriz Viterbo, 1994. 128-38.

Moreiras, Alberto. "The Aura of Testimonio." 1996. *The Exhaustion of Difference: The Politics of Latin American Cultural Studies*. Durham and London: Duke UP, 2001. 208-38.

Nance, Kimberly. "Disarming Testimony: Speakers' Resistance to Readers' Defenses in Latin American *Testimonio*." *Biography* 24.3 (Summer 2001): 570-88.

Neuhouser, Kevin. "Transitions to Democracy: Unpredictable Elite Negotiation or Predictable Failure to Achieve Class Compromise?" *Sociological Perspectives* 41.1 (1998): 67-93. Wilson Web. 23 January 2001.

Neustadt, Robert. "Incisive Incisions: (Re)articulating the Discursive Body in Diamela Eltit's *Lumpérica*." *Cincinnati Romance Review* 14 (1995): 151-6.

Olsen, Tillie. *Silences*. NY: Delacorte, 1978.

Ong, Walter. *Orality and Literacy*. NY: Methuen, 1982.

Ortega, Julio. "Diamela Eltit y el imaginario de la virtualidad." Lértora, *Una poética* 53-81.

———. "Resistencia y sujeto femenino: entrevista con Diamela Eltit." *La Torre* 4.14 (1990): 229-41.

Patai, Daphne. *Brazilian Women Speak: Contemporary Life Stories*. New Brunswick; London: Rutgers UP, 1988.

———. "U.S. Academics and Third World Women: Is Ethical Research Possible?" Gluck and Patai 137-53.

———. "Whose Truth? Iconicity and Accuracy in the World of Testimonial Literature." Arias, *Rigoberta Menchú Controversy* 270-87.

Paulson, William. "Closing the Circle: Science, Literature and the Passion of Matter." *New England Review and Bread Loaf Quarterly* 12 (Summer 1990): 512-26.

Peixoto, Marta. *Passionate Fictions: Gender, Narrative, and Violence in Clarice Lispector*. Minneapolis: U of Minnesota P, 1994.

Poniatowska, Elena. *La "Flor de Lis"*. México, D.F.: Era, 1988.

———. *Hasta no verte, Jesús mío*. 24th ed. México, D.F.: Era, 1969.

———. *Here's To You, Jesusa!*. Trans. Deanna Heikkinen. New York: Farrar, Straus and Giroux, 2001.

———. "Hasta no verte, Jesús mío." *Vuelta* 24 (Nov 1978): 5-11.

———. "El limbo." *De noche vienes*. México, D.F.: Era, 1985. 31-45.

———. "La literatura de las mujeres es parte de la literatura de los oprimidos." *Fem* 6.21 (February-March 1982): 23-7.

———. "Love Story." *De noche vienes*. México, D.F.: Era, 1985. 83-92.

———. "La muerte de Jesusa Palancares." *La historia en la literatura iberoamericana. Memorias del XXVI Congreso del Instituto Internacional de Literatura Iberoamericana*. Raquel Chang-Rodríguez and Gabriela de Beer, eds. Hanover, NH: Ediciones del Norte, 1989. 9-22.

———. Personal interview. June 5, 1993.

Poniatowska, Elena. "Presentación al lector mexicano." *Se necesita muchacha*. Ed. Ana Gutiérrez. México: FCE, 1983, 7-86.

———. "Prólogo." *Benita*. Benita Galeana. 4th ed. México: Lince Editores, 1990. vii-xvii.

———. "Rosario Castellanos: ¡Vida, nada te debo!" *¡Ay vida, no me mereces!* México: Joaquín Mortiz, 1985. 93-132.

———. "Testimonios de una escritora: Elena Poniatowska en Micrófono." González 155-162.

Pratt, Mary Louise. "*I, Rigoberta Menchú* and the 'Culture Wars.'" Arias, *Rigoberta Menchú Controversy* 29-48.

———. "Overwriting Pinochet: Undoing the Culture of Fear in Chile." *The Places of History: Regionalism Revisited in Latin America*. Ed. Doris Sommer. Durham and London: Duke UP, 1999. 21-33.

Reuque Paillalef, Rosa Isolde. *When a Flower Is Reborn: The Life and Times of a Mapuche Feminist*. Ed., trans., intro. by Florencia E. Mallon. Durham and London: Duke UP, 2002.

Rich, Adrienne. "Notes Toward a Politics of Location." *Blood, Bread and Poetry*. NY: W.W. Norton, 1986. 210-31.

Richard, Nelly. "Bordes, diseminación y postmodernismo: una metáfora latinoamericana de fin de siglo." *Las culturas de fin de siglo en América Latina*. Ed. Josefina Ludmer. Rosario, Argentina: Beatriz Viterbo, 1994. 240-8.

———. *La insubordinación de los signos (Cambio político, transformaciones culturales y poéticas de la crisis)*. Santiago: Cuarto Propio, 1994.

———. "Tres funciones de escritura: desconstrucción, simulación, hibridación." Lértora, *Una poética* 37-51.

Ricoeur, Paul. *History and Truth*. Trans. and intro. Charles A. Kelbley. Evanston, Illinois: Northwestern UP, 1965.

Rogachevsky, Jorge R. "David Stoll vs. Rigoberta Menchú: Indigenous Victims or Protagonists?" *Delaware Review of Latin American Studies* 2.2 (July 15, 2001). 21 May 2002 <http://www.udel.edu/LASP/>.

———. "Rejoinder." *Delaware Review of Latin American Studies* 2.2 (July 15, 2001). 21 May 2002 <http://www.udel.edu/LASP/>.

Rohter, Larry. "Nobel Winner Finds Her Story Challenged." *New York Times* 15 Dec. 1998, early ed.: A1+.

Sá, Olga de. *A Escritura de Clarice Lispector*. Petrópolis: Ed. Vozes Ltda., 1979.

Scarry, Elaine. "The Made-Up and the Made-Real." Garber, Walkowitz and Franklin 214-24.

Schur, Edwin M. "Commoditization of Female Sexuality: Prostitution." *Labeling Women Deviant: Gender, Stigma and Social Control*. Philadelphia: Temple UP, 1983. 164-72.

Schwarz, Roberto. *Os Pobres na Literatura Brasileira*. São Paulo: Brasiliense, 1983.

Shaw, Deborah. "Jesusa Palancares as Individual Subect in Elena Poniatowska's *Hasta no verte, Jesús mío*." *Bulletin of Hispanic Studies* 73 (1996): 191-204.

Sklodowska, Elzbieta. "The Poetics of Remembering, the Politics of Forgetting: Rereading *I, Rigoberta Menchú*." Arias, *Rigoberta Menchú Controversy* 251-69.

———. *Testimonio hispanoamericano: historia, teoría, práctica*. New York: Peter Lang, 1992.

Smith, Sidonie and Julia Watson, eds. *De/Colonizing the Subject: The Politics of Gender in Women's Autobiography*. Minneapolis: U of Minnesota P, 1992.

Sommer, Doris. "Conocimiento interruptus: una ética de lectura." Ludmer, *Las culturas de fin de siglo* 232-9.

———. "'Not Just a Personal Story': Women's *Testimonios* and the Plural Self." *Life/Lines: Theorizing Women's Autobiography*. Bella Brodzki and Celeste Schenck, eds. Ithaca, NY: Cornell UP, 1988, 107-30.

Sommer, Doris. *Proceed with Caution, When Engaged by Minority Writing in the Americas*. Cambridge, Mass. and London: Harvard UP, 1999.

———. "OUR AmeRíca." Garber, Walkowitz and Franklin 77-86.

———. "Sin secretos." Beverley and Achugar 135-53.

———. "Taking a Life: Hot Pursuit and Cold Rewards in a Mexican Testimonial Novel." *Signs* 20.4 (1995): 913-40.

Spivak, Gayatri Chakravorty. "Can the Subaltern Speak? Speculations on Widow-Sacrifice." *Marxism and the Interpretation of Culture*. Eds. Cary Nelson and Lawrence Grossberg. Chicago: U of Illinois P, 1988. 271-313.

———. "Displacement and the Discourse of Woman." *Displacement: Derrida and After*. Ed. and intro. Mark Krupnick. Theories of Contemporary Culture 5. Bloomington: Indiana UP, 1983. 169-95.

———. *The Post-Colonial Critic: Interviews, Strategies, Dialogues*. Ed. Sarah Harasym. New York: Routledge, 1990.

Stacey, Judith. "Can There Be a Feminist Ethnography?" Gluck and Patai 111-9.

Steele, Cynthia. "The Other Within: Class and Ethnicity as Difference in Mexican Women's Literature." *Cultural and Historical Grounding for Hispanic and Luso-Brazilian Feminist Literary Criticism*. Ed. Vidal, Hernán. Literature and Human Rights 4. Minneapolis, MN: Institute for the Study of Ideologies and Literature, 1989. 297-328.

———. *Politics and Gender in the Mexican Novel 1968-1988: Beyond the Pyramid*. Austin, TX: U Texas P, 1992.

Stoll, David. "Conundrums or Non Sequiturs? The Case of Vicente Menchú." *Delaware Review of Latin American Studies* 2.2 (July 15, 2001). 21 May 2002 <http://www.udel.edu/LASP/>.

———. *Rigoberta Menchú and the Story of All Poor Guatemalans*. New York: Westview Press, 1999.

Tabuenca Córdoba, María Socorro. "La Obra Espiritual como obra escritural en *Hasta no verte, Jesús mío* de Elena Poniatowska." Narradoras mexicanas contemporáneas y crítica literaria. Colegio de México. Mexico City, 21 January, 1993.

Taracena, Arturo. "Arturo Taracena Breaks His Silence." Interview by Luis Aceituno. Arias, *Rigoberta Menchú Controversy* 82-94.

Tafra, Sylvia. *Diamela Eltit: el rito de pasaje como estrategia textual*. Santiago, Chile: RiL Editores, 1998.

Taylor, Diana. *Disappearing Acts: Spectacles of Gender and Nationalism in Argentina's "Dirty War."* Durham and London: Duke UP, 1997.

Tierney-Tello, Mary Beth. *Allegories of Transgression and Transformation: Experimental Fiction by Women Writing Under Dictatorship*. Albany: SUNY Press, 1996.

———. "Testimony, Ethics, and the Aesthetic in Diamela Eltit." *PMLA* 114.1 (January 1999): 78-96.

Valenzuela, Luisa. Interview. *Women's Voices from Latin America*. Ed. Evelyn Picon Garfield. Wayne State UP, 1985. 142-65, 170-1.

———. "Entrevista con Luisa Valenzuela." *Historias íntimas*. Ed. Magdalena García Pinto. Hanover, NH: Ediciones del Norte, 1988. 215-49.

———. "The Five Days That Changed My Paper." Presidential Forum. *Profession* (1991): 6-9.

———. *Hay que sonreír*. Buenos Aires: Américalee, 1966.

———. "La mala palabra." *Revista Iberoamericana* 132-133 (1985): 489-91.

———. "Máscaras de espejos, un juego especular: entrevista-asociaciones con la escritora argentina Luisa Valenzuela." *Revista Iberoamericana* 132-133 (1985): 511-9.

Valenzuela, Luisa. "Mis brujas favoritas." *Theory and Practice of Feminist Literary Criticism*. Eds. Gabriela Mora and Karen S. Van Hooft. Ypsilanti, MI: Bilingual, 1982. 88-95.

————. "The Other Face of the Phallus." *Reinventing the Americas: Comparative Studies of Literature of the United States and Spanish America*. Eds. Bell Gale Chevigny and Gari Laguardia. Cambridge: Cambridge UP, 1986. 242-8.

Vega, Patricia. "Elena habla de sus libros." *La Jornada* (México, D.F.) (February 19, 1993): 25-6.

————. "Novelas testimoniales son las que deben hacerse; no tenemos historia novelada." *La Jornada* (México, D.F.) (February 19, 1993): 25-6.

Vera-León, Antonio. "Hacer hablar: la transcripción testimonial." Beverley and Achugar 181-99.

Vieira, Else Ribeiro Pires. "Can Another Subaltern Speak/Write?" *Renaissance and Modern Studies* 38 (1995): 95-125.

Visweswaran, Kamala. *Fictions of Feminist Ethnography*. Minneapolis and London: U of Minnesota P, 1994.

Vogt, Carlos. "Trabalho, pobreza e trabalho intelectual (*O Quarto de Despejo*, de Carolina Maria de Jesus)." Schwarz 204-13.

Watson, Julia and Sidonie Smith. "De/Colonization and the Politics of Discourse in Women's Autobiographical Practices." Introduction. Smith and Watson xiii-xxxi.

Welchman, John C. "The Philosophical Brothel." *Rethinking Borders*. Minneapolis: U of Minnesota P, 1996. 160-86.

White, Hayden. "The Fiction of Factual Representation." *The Literature of Fact*. Angus Fletcher, ed. New York: Columbia UP, 1976.

Williams, Gareth. "The Fantasies of Cultural Exchange in Latin American Subaltern Studies." Gugelberger 225-53.

Yúdice, George. "Testimonio y concientización." Beverley and Achugar 207-27.

Zimmerman, Marc. "El *otro* de Rigoberta: los testimonios de Ignacio Bizarro Ujpan y la resistencia indígena en Guatemala." Beverley and Achugar 229-43.

INDEX

Auratic and postauratic of testimony, 51 (n. 14), 154, 234

Authenticity of representation, 15-16, 35, 41, 55-56, 102, 106, 119, 139-40, 231-32; and oral culture, 49, 50, 51

Autobiographics, 76. *See also* Feminist theory: of self-representation

Becoming-woman, 192-93. *See also* Identity as absence: and theories of Deleuze and Guattari

Benita (Galeana), 12, 18

Body as testimony, 200, 205, 209-21, 226-27, 234. *See also* Performance

Borders. *See* Boundaries

Borges, Jorge Luis: "Averroës' Search," 13-15; relevance to testimony, 14-16, 28; "Emma Zunz," 208 (n. 4)

Boundaries: of meaning, 15, 114-15, 135-37, 163, 174, 178-80, 192, 207, 210, 233; transgressed, 26, 97-98, 146, 148, 163, 165, 174-76, 213, 221; constructed to be transgressed, 71, 146, 167-69, 171-73, 182-83, 213; between binary opposites, 135-36, 160, 162, 172-73, 180, 183, 186, 192, 194, 203, 213, 215, 218; displacement across, 146-47, 178-83, 236; and enforced hierarchies, 159-60, 163, 171-76, 203, 204, 214, 218, 227, 233; one-way that reinforce limits, 164, 165, 170-72, 182-83, 192-94; between self and other, 167-72, 175-77, 187, 194; and Lispector's experimental writing, 174-75; and deterritorialization, 189-

92; overflowing of in identity, 205-7, 214. *See also* Transcriber: identification with testimonial narrator; Violence

Braidotti, Rosi. *See* Nomadology: feminist readings of

Burgos Debray, Elisabeth: metaphoric identification with Menchú, 38, 78, 80-81, 87; role as transcriber, 64, 65. See also *Me llamo Rigoberta Menchú*

Cixous, Hélène. *See* Lispector, Clarice

Collective identity, 19, 36, 48, 73-74, 103, 104, 109, 190-91, 219, 237; in *Me llamo Rigoberta Menchú*, 62-66, 68, 80; vs. individual in *Me llamo Rigoberta Menchú*, 66-70, 72-73; and women's self-representation, 74-79; and women's testimony, 75-79; metaphor and metonymy to describe, 77-79; vs. individual in *Quarto de Despejo*, 88-89, 93-95, 97. *See also* Legitimation; Self-representation

Commodification of identity, 71-72, 138, 140-41, 198-99, 200, 202, 208-9, 214, 217, 218, 221, 224-28 passim, 232, 234-35

Deleuze, Gilles, and Félix Guattari. *See* Identity as absence: and theories of Deleuze and Guattari; Minor literature; Nomadology

De-orientalism and Latinamericanist orientalism, 146, 165, 171, 172-73. *See also* Boundaries: constructed to

249

be transgressed; Boundaries: one-way that reinforce limits

Derrida, Jacques. *See* Identity as absence: and Derrida's theory of "woman"; Violence: Derrida on Deterritorialization, 189. *See also* Boundaries: displacement across; Identity as absence

Disappearance. *See* Silence: as disappearance; Violence: and discursive disappearance

Displacement. *See* Boundaries

Eltit, Diamela: father figure in works by, 209-11. See also *Lumpérica; Padre mío, El*

Essentialized identity, 51, 79, 81, 84, 88, 106-9, 120-21, 140-41, 148, 156-57, 169, 171-95 passim, 232-33; of Rigoberta Menchú, 61, 64, 65, 67, 69-70, 71-72; of Carolina Maria de Jesus, 95-96, in Eltit's work, 202-3, 205, 208, 218, 223-25, 227. *See also* Boundaries: one-way that reinforce limits; Rodrigo S. M.: search for essential truth by; Violence: and discursive disappearance

Female sexuality: and legitimation, 61-62, 222-23; and suggestion of rape, 141-42, 158, 169-70, 209-10, 225-26; and prostitution in authoritarian rhetoric, 214, 217, 225-26; in relation to narrative transparency, 223-25, 227. *See also* Body as testimony; Violence

Feminist ethnography, 37-38

Feminist theory: used to read texts by Latin American women, 13, 184-88; relevance to testimonial texts, 16-20, 36-38, 74-79, 109-10, 145-46, 177, 223-27, 230-31; of self-representation, 74-79, 109-10; of female identity, 74-75; of autobiography, 75-79. *See also* Female sexuality; Identity as absence: and Derrida's theory of "woman"

Gilmore, Leigh. *See* Autobiographics

Girard, René. *See* Violence: sacrificial

Hasta no verte, Jesús mío (*Here's To You, Jesusa!*), 12, 25, 39-56 passim, 150, 181; silence in, 39-44, 48; shifting self-representation in, 43, 44, 46, 75, 81-82; distrust of appearances, 51-56. *See also* Poniatowska, Elena

Hora da Estrela, A (*The Hour of the Star*), 25-26, 110-11, 118-37, 137-42 passim, 151-52, 156-59, 169-70, 180, 186-88; religious allusions, 118, 124-25, 134-35, 156-59; Macabéa's self-knowledge, 125-27; contradictory truth, 129-32; and violence, 151-52, 156-59; and Cixous's reading of Lispector, 186-88. *See also* Lispector, Clarice; Rodrigo S. M.

Identity. *See* Collective identity; Commodification of identity; Essentialized identity; Identity as absence

Identity as absence, 80-81, 85-86, 112-19 passim, 125-29 passim, 133, 135, 139, 142-43, 158-65, 169-70, 173, 177, 185; and Derrida's theory of "woman," 26, 188-89; and theories of Deleuze and Guattari, 189-93; in *El padre mío*, 202; in *Lumpérica*, 212, 218, 219-20

Jesus, Carolina Maria de: and writing, 50, 90-93; and relationship with *favelados*, 88-89, 90, 91-95; shifting self-representation of, 88-89, 93-95, 96-97; relationship to Audálio Dantas, 96-97. See also *Quarto de Despejo*

Juana Inés de la Cruz, Sor, 39-40, 41

Legal discourse. *See* Testimonial texts: and legal discourse; Violence: legal

Legitimation: of testimony, 21, 23, 24-25, 33-38, 41, 44, 45, 49, 61, 98-99, 231-32; and written vs. oral culture, 49-51; and collective identity, 64-65, 67, 68-70, 74; of intellectual discourse through testimony, 67-68, 71-72, 90, 94, 106-7, 185, 234, 235; of transcriber through testimony, 80, 83-88, 154, 166, 232; through insistence on truth in *Quarto de Despejo*, 90-92; through position of moral superiority, 92-95, 155, 222-24. *See also* Authenticity; Sexuality; Truth; Violence

Levinson, Brett. *See* De-orientalism and Latinamericanist orientalism

Lispector, Clarice: Hélène Cixous's reading of, 26, 184-88; behind narrator Rodrigo S.M., 118, 121, 141, 170; narrative act in works by, 159, 180. See also *A Hora da Estrela*; *A Paixão Segundo G.H.*; Rodrigo S.M.
Lumpérica (E. Luminata), 27, 200-1, 204-6, 209-10, 211-22; shifting self-representation in, 206, 218

Me llamo Rigoberta Menchú (I...Rigoberta Menchú), 25, 57-72 passim, 181-82; distrust of dominant discourses in, 52, 60-61; silence in, 57-60, 63; shifting self-representation in, 69-70, 75, 80-81. See also Burgos-Debray, Elisabeth; Menchú, Rigoberta
Menchú, Rigoberta: controversy, 25, 67-72, 232; and gender roles, 61-62. See also *Me llamo Rigoberta Menchú*
Minor literature, 190-92
Moreiras, Alberto. See Auratic and postauratic of testimony

Nahual (*nagual*): in *Hasta no verte, Jesús mío*, 51-52, 79-80, 83; in *Me llamo Rigoberta Menchú*, 59, 79-80, 181-82
Nomadology, 26, 192-94; feminist readings of, 193-94

Orality: relation to truth, 47-51, 63, 232

Padre mío, El (*Father of Mine*), 27, 199-200, 202-3, 206-8, 210-11; shifting self-representation in, 202, 206-8
Paixão Segundo G.H, A (*The Passion According to G.H.*), 25-26, 110, 111-18, 159-65, 178, 179; maid's absence in, 111-13, 115; search for essential truth through others in, 112-17; G.H. as reflection of testimonial transcriber, 114-15, 162; language's inadequacy in, 115-17; ritual violence in, 159-64. See also Lispector, Clarice
Performance, 212-21, 224-25, 234. See also Body as testimony
Poniatowska, Elena: and metaphoric identification with Jesusa, 38, 81, 83-88; Jesusa's resistance to authority of, 43-44, 53-56; and Josefina Bórquez, 53-54; and distancing from Jesusa, 86-87. See also *Hasta no verte, Jesús mío*

Quarto de Despejo (*Child of the Dark*), 12, 23-24, 25, 88-97 passim, 150-51, 180-81; Audálio Dantas's editing of, 88, 95-97; shifting self-representation in, 88-89, 93-95, 96-97; silence in, 92-93; reflection on role of transcriber in, 94; and violence, 150-51. See also Jesus, Carolina Maria de

Reuque Paillalef, Rosa Isolde, 229, 237-38
Rodrigo S.M.: as ironic reflection of testimonial transcriber, 118-20, 121, 122, 128, 131-33, 136, 141; shifting approximation to and distancing from Macabéa, 118, 125, 128, 129-30, 131-32, 135, 138, 157; legitimation of through Macabéa, 119, 131, 133, 134; usurps and silences voice of Macabéa, 119, 120, 122-23, 134-35; search for truth through Macabéa, 119-20, 123-28, 135, 136

Sacrifice. See Violence
Seeing: act of, 213-18, 220-21, 225-26. See also Body as testimony; Performance
Self-representation: autonomy of, 21, 46, 61, 70-72, 95, 109, 121, 165, 167, 171, 175, 214, 219, 232, 235-36, 238; as negotiation of instability, 21, 43, 46, 52, 56, 64-66 passim, 69-71 passim, 80, 93-98 passim, 142, 150, 171-72, 182-83, 197-98, 204-6; and textual disguises, 43, 51-66, 84, 92, 142, 161-62; shifting, 76, 219. See also Collective identity; Feminist Theory: of self-representation; *Hasta no verte, Jesús mío*; *Me llamo Rigoberta Menchú*; *Padre mío, El*; *Quarto de Despejo*; Rodrigo S.M.; Silence
Sexuality. See Female sexuality
Silence: as resistance strategy, 38, 39, 40-41, 47, 232; as disappearance, 115, 118, 165, 171, 232. See also *Hasta no verte, Jesús mío*; *Me llamo Rigoberta Menchú*; *Quarto de Despejo*; Violence
Sklodowska, Elzbieta: on testimonial texts, 22, 23, 47
Sommer, Doris, 235-36. See also Feminist theory: relevance to testimonial texts; Transcriber: metonymic vs.

metaphoric relationship with testimonial narrator
Stoll, David, 57, 67-73. *See also* Menchú, Rigoberta: controversy

Testimonial novel: definition of, 24, 103-4; and truth, 46-47, 103-4. See also *Hasta no verte, Jesús mío*; Testimonial texts
Testimonial texts: vs. autobiography, 12, 35, 64-65, 67, 73, 75-79; and national identity, 12, 56, 71, 80-81, 85-86, 103-4, 109, 210-11, 214-15, 230-31; read with fiction or literature, 13, 25-26, 27, 100-3, 108-9, 137-43, 197, 201, 203-5, 218-20, 222-28 passim, 233; vs. fiction or literature, 20-24, 25-26, 103-8; parallels with theory, 13, 16, 26-27, 183-96; readers of, 33, 67-68, 69-72, 74, 78-79, 90, 94, 105-7, 139; and legal discourse, 34-36, 39. *See also* Testimonial novel; Testimony
Testimonio. See Testimonial texts; Testimony
Testimony: definition and purpose, 11-13, 22-24, 77, 105-9. *See also* Body as testimony; Testimonial texts
Transcriber: role of, 12, 17, 19, 23, 25, 33, 64; identification of with testimonial narrator, 25, 50, 79-88, 138-39, 175; role of vs. narrator, 33-34, 55, 56, 139, 237; problematic identification of with narrator as woman, 37-38, 141-42; questioned by testimonial narrator, 43-44, 53-54, 55, 175, 232; from oral testimony to written word, 48-50; metonymic vs. metaphoric relationship of with testimonial narra-

tor, 78-79, 83. *See also* Burgos-Debray, Elisabeth; Poniatowska, Elena
Translation, 179-82, 233. *See also* Boundaries: displacement across
Truth: and authenticity, 21, 35, 45-51, 69, 71-72, 76-77, 105, 139-40, 231-32, 234; as unreliable criterion to define testimony, 25, 45-46, 56, 59, 61, 105, 107-9, 139-41; and orality, 47-51; and appearances, 50, 51-56, 91; and women's self-representation, 76-77; in Eltit's texts, 198-208, 221-22, 225, 227. *See also* Authenticity; Legitimation; Orality; Self-representation

Vengeance, 152-55, 158-65, 169, 233, 234. *See also* Violence: sacrificial
Violence: resulting in discursive disappearance, 26, 81, 83, 147, 148, 152-65 passim, 171, 175, 207, 211, 233, 234; sacrificial, 26, 147, 154-65, 167-73, 186, 213-14, 233, 234; discursive, 145-49, 151-52, 166-76, 180; Derrida on, 146, 148, 156, 195; physical 148-51; legal 152-55, 233-34; testimony as statement against, 148, 149-52, 154, 155, 162-63, 167, 174, 203; testimony implicated in, 146-47, 149, 151-53, 174, 233; under Pinochet, 204-5, 209, 213, 224-25, 226. *See also* Essentialized identity; *Hora da Estrela, A*: violence in; *Paixão Segundo G.H., A*: ritual violence in; Silence: as disappearance

Women: rhetorical construction of in theory, 26, 188-89, 192-95, rhetorical construction of under Pinochet, 199, 214

NORTH CAROLINA STUDIES IN THE ROMANCE LANGUAGES AND LITERATURES

I.S.B.N. Prefix 0-8078-

Recent Titles

'PUEBLOS ENFERMOS': THE DISCOURSE OF ILLNESS IN THE TURN-OF-THE-CENTURY SPANISH AND LATIN AMERICAN ESSAY, by Michael Aronna. 1999. (No. 262). -9266-1.

RESONANT THEMES. LITERATURE, HISTORY, AND THE ARTS IN NINETEENTH- AND TWENTIETH-CENTURY EUROPE. ESSAYS IN HONOR OF VICTOR BROMBERT, by Stirling Haig. 1999. (No. 263). -9267-X.

RAZA, GÉNERO E HIBRIDEZ EN EL LAZARILLO DE CIEGOS CAMINANTES, por Mariselle Meléndez. 1999. (No. 264). -9268-8.

DEL ESCENARIO A LA PANTALLA: LA ADAPTACIÓN CINEMATOGRÁFICA DEL TEATRO ESPAÑOL, por María Asunción Gómez. 2000. (No. 265). -9269-6.

THE LEPER IN BLUE: COERCIVE PERFORMANCE AND THE CONTEMPORARY LATIN AMERICAN THEATER, by Amalia Gladhart. 2000. (No. 266). -9270-X.

THE CHARM OF CATASTROPHE: A STUDY OF RABELAIS'S QUART LIVRE, by Alice Fiola Berry. 2000. (No. 267). -9271-8.

PUERTO RICAN CULTURAL IDENTITY AND THE WORK OF LUIS RAFAEL SÁNCHEZ, by John Dimitri Perivolaris. 2000. (No. 268). -9272-6.

MANNERISM AND BAROQUE IN SEVENTEENTH-CENTURY FRENCH POETRY: THE EXAMPLE OF TRISTAN L'HERMITE, by James Crenshaw Shepard. 2001. (No. 269). -9273-4.

RECLAIMING THE BODY: MARÍA DE ZAYA'S EARLY MODERN FEMINISM, by Lisa Vollendorf. 2001. (No. 270). -9274-2.

FORGED GENEALOGIES: SAINT-JOHN PERSE'S CONVERSATIONS WITH CULTURE, by Carol Rigolot. 2001. (No. 271). -9275-0.

VISIONES DE ESTEREOSCOPIO (PARADIGMA DE HIBRIDACIÓN EN EL ARTE Y LA NARRATIVA DE LA VANGUARDIA ESPAÑOLA), por María Soledad Fernández Utrera. 2001. (No. 272). -9276-9.

TRANSPOSING ART INTO TEXTS IN FRENCH ROMANTIC LITERATURE, by Henry F. Majewski. 2002. (No. 273). -9277-7.

IMAGES IN MIND: LOVESICKNESS, SPANISH SENTIMENTAL FICTION AND DON QUIJOTE, by Robert Folger. 2002. (No. 274). -9278-5.

INDISCERNIBLE COUNTERPARTS: THE INVENTION OF THE TEXT IN FRENCH CLASSICAL DRAMA, by Christopher Braider. 2002. (No. 275). -9279-3.

SAVAGE SIGHT/CONSTRUCTED NOISE. POETIC ADAPTATIONS OF PAINTERLY TECHNIQUES IN THE FRENCH AND AMERICAN AVANT-GARDES, by David LeHardy Sweet. 2003. (No. 276). -9281-5.

AN EARLY BOURGEOIS LITERATURE IN GOLDEN AGE SPAIN. LAZARILLO DE TORMES, GUZMÁN DE ALFARACHE AND BALTASAR GRACIÁN, by Francisco J. Sánchez. 2003. (No. 277). -9280-7.

METAFACT: ESSAYISTIC SCIENCE IN EIGHTEENTH-CENTURY FRANCE, by Lars O. Erickson. 2004. (No. 278). -.

THE INVENTION OF THE EYEWITNESS. A HISTORY OF TESTIMONY IN FRANCE, by Andrea Frisch. 2004. (No. 279). -9283-1.

SUBJECT TO CHANGE: THE LESSONS OF LATIN AMERICAN WOMEN'S TESTIMONIO FOR TRUTH, FICTION, AND THEORY, by Joanna R. Bartow. 2005. (No. 280). -9284-X.

QUESTIONING RACINIAN TRAGEDY, by John Campbell. 2005. (No. 281). -9285-8.

When ordering please cite the ISBN Prefix plus the last four digits for each title.

Send orders to: University of North Carolina Press
P.O. Box 2288
Chapel Hill, NC 27515-2288
U.S.A.
www.uncpress.unc.edu
FAX: 919 966-3829